ACCA

PAPER F7
FINANCIAL REPORTING

BPP Learning Media is an **ACCA Approved Content Provider** for the ACCA qualification. This means we work closely with ACCA to ensure our products fully prepare you for your ACCA exams.

In this Practice & Revision Kit, which has been reviewed by the **ACCA examination team**, we:

- Discuss the **best strategies** for revising and taking your ACCA exams

- Ensure you are well **prepared** for your exam

- Provide you with **lots of great guidance** on tackling questions

- Provide you with **three** mock exams

- Provide ACCA **exam answers** as well as our own for selected questions

Our **Passcards** also support this paper.

FOR EXAMS IN SEPTEMBER 2016, DECEMBER 2016, MARCH 2017 AND JUNE 2017

PRACTICE & REVISION KIT

First edition 2008

Tenth edition February 2016
ISBN 9781 4727 4439 5
(previous ISBN 9781 4727 2689 6)
e-ISBN 9781 4727 4654 2

British Library Cataloguing-in-Publication Data

A catalogue record for this book
is available from the British Library

Published by

BPP Learning Media Ltd
BPP House, Aldine Place
London W12 8AA

www.bpp.com/learningmedia

Printed in the United Kingdom by
Polestar Wheatons
Hennock Road
Marsh Barton
Exeter
EX2 8RP

Your learning materials, published by BPP Learning Media Ltd, are
printed on paper obtained from traceable sustainable sources.

We are grateful to the Association of Chartered Certified
Accountants for permission to reproduce past examination
questions. The suggested solutions in the Practice & Revision Kit
have been prepared by BPP Learning Media Ltd, except where
otherwise stated.

BPP Learning Media is grateful to the IASB for permission to
reproduce extracts from the International Financial Reporting
Standards including all International Accounting Standards, SIC and
IFRIC Interpretations (the Standards). The Standards together with
their accompanying documents are issued by:

The International Accounting Standards Board (IASB) 30 Cannon
Street, London, EC4M 6XH, United Kingdom. Email: info@ifrs.org
Web: www.ifrs.org

Disclaimer: The IASB, the International Financial Reporting
Standards (IFRS) Foundation, the authors and the publishers do not
accept responsibility for any loss caused by acting or refraining
from acting in reliance on the material in this publication, whether
such loss is caused by negligence or otherwise to the maximum
extent permitted by law.

About this Practice & Revision Kit

ACCA will start to transition F5–F9 to computer-based examination (CBE), beginning with a pilot in limited markets in September 2016. Students will initially have the choice of CBE or paper exams and as a result, changes will be made to BPP's learning materials to ensure that we fully support students through this transition.

This Practice & Revision Kit is valid for exams from the September 2016 sitting through to the June 2017 sitting and in this Practice & Revision Kit you will find questions in both multiple choice question (MCQ) and objective testing question (OTQ) format. OTQs include a wider variety of questions types including MCQ as well as number entry, multiple response and drag and drop. More information on these question types will be available on the ACCA website.

OTQs will only appear in computer-based exams but these questions will still provide valuable practice for all students whichever version of the exam is taken. These are clearly marked on the contents page as either CBE style OTQ bank or CBE style OT case.

In addition please note that the specimen paper-based exam paper has been included as Mock Exam 3 in this Practice & Revision Kit. The questions in Sections A and B are MCQ only whereas in the computer-based exam these sections will contain OTQs.

More information on the exam formats can be found on page xv-xvii

At the time of going to print, ACCA had not yet announced the proposed duration of the computer-based exam and so all timings given throughout this Practice & Revision Kit are based on the paper-based exam which is 3 hours and 15 minutes long. Time management is a key skill for success in this exam and so we recommend you use these indicative timings when attempting questions.

ACCA are recommending that all students consult the ACCA website on a regular basis for updates on the launch of the new CBEs.

Contents

BPP
LEARNING MEDIA

Question index

The headings in this checklist/index indicate the main topics of questions, but many questions cover several different topics.

Each topic area begins with Section A questions on the topic. Your exam will have 15 section A questions.

Part 6: Revenue

Part 7: Introduction to groups

Part 8: Consolidated statement of financial position

Part 9: Consolidated statement of profit or loss and other comprehensive income

Part 10: Accounting for associates

Part 11: Financial instruments

Part 12: Leasing

Part 13: Provisions and events after the reporting period

Part 14: Inventories and biological assets

Part 15: Taxation

Part 21: Statement of cash flows

Section A questions				
246-248 MCQ bank – statement of cash flows	6	12	83	152
249-250 CBE style OTQ bank – statement of cash flows	4	8	84	153
Section C questions				
251 Dickson	20	39	85	154
252 Mocha (12/11)	20	39	86	156

Part 22: Accounting for inflation

Section A questions				
253-255 MCQ bank – accounting for inflation	6	12	88	158
256-258 CBE style OTQ bank – accounting for inflation	6	12	88	158

Part 23: Specialised not-for-profit and public sector entities

Section A questions				
259-262 MCQ bank – specialised, not-for-profit and public sector entities	8	16	89	159
263-265 CBE style OTQ bank – specialised, not-for-profit and public sector entities	6	12	90	159

Mock exam 1

Mock exam 2 (CBE style)

Mock exam 3 (Specimen paper)

Helping you with your revision

Tackling revision and the exam

Using feedback obtained from ACCA examination team review:

- We look at the dos and don'ts of revising for, and taking, ACCA exams

- We focus on Paper F7; we discuss revising the syllabus, what to do (and what not to do) in the exam, how to approach different types of question and ways of obtaining easy marks

Selecting questions

We provide a full **question index** to help you plan your revision.

Making the most of question practice

At BPP Learning Media we realise that you need more than just questions and model answers to get the most from your question practice.

- Our **top tips** included for certain questions provide essential advice on tackling questions, presenting answers and the key points that answers need to include.

- We show you how you can pick up **easy marks** on some questions, as we know that picking up all readily available marks often can make the difference between passing and failing.

- We include **marking guides** to show you what the examination team rewards.

- We include **comments from the examination team** to show you where students struggled or performed well in the actual exam.

- We refer to the **2016 BPP Study Text** (for exams in September 2016, December 2016, March 2017 and June 2017) for detailed coverage of the topics covered in questions.

Attempting mock exams

There are three mock exams that provide practice at coping with the pressures of the exam day. We strongly recommend that you attempt them under exam conditions. **Mock exams 1 and 2** reflect the question styles and syllabus coverage of the paper-based and computer-based exams respectively; **Mock exam 3** is the Specimen exam paper.

Revising F7

From September 2016 the F7 paper has a Section A with 15 2-mark OTQs and a Section B with a further 15 2-mark OTQs based on three scenarios. This gives the examination team greater scope to examine the whole of the syllabus and bring in topics that do not feature in the longer questions. Section C will have two 20-mark questions. Sections A and B account for 60% of the marks on the paper. So it is really not possible to pass this paper by only revising certain topics.

A consolidation question could feature in Section C and can be a statement of financial position or statement of profit or loss or both, and it may include an associate, so be prepared for all of this. Therefore you must revise all the consolidation workings, and you must know how to account for an associate. All questions are compulsory.

A single company accounts preparation question allows the examining team to bring in more complex issues that they would not test in the consolidation question. Make sure you can deal with finance leases, deferred tax, calculating finance costs using the effective interest rate, prior period adjustments and discontinued operations

Other possibilities for Section C are statements of cash flow or interpretation of accounts. You have studied both of these at F3/FFA, so make sure you can do them well.

Issues that could appear anywhere are non-current assets and impairment, intangible assets, EPS, provisions and regulatory issues.

This is the most important thing to do if you want to get through. Many of the most up-to-date exam questions are in this Kit, amended to reflect the new exam format. Practise doing them under timed conditions, then go through the answers and go back to the Study Text for any topic you are really having trouble with. Come back to a question a week later and try it again – you will be surprised at how much better you are getting. Be very ruthless with yourself at this stage – you have to do the question in the time, without looking at the answer. This will really sharpen your wits and make the exam experience less worrying. Just keep doing this and you will get better at doing questions and you will really find out what you know and what you don't know.

Passing the F7 exam

If you have honestly done your revision then you can pass this exam. What you must do is remain calm and tackle it in a professional manner. There are a number of points which you should bear in mind. These apply particularly to the long questions.

- You must read the question properly. Students often fail to read the question properly and miss some of the information. Time spent reading the question a second time would be time well spent. Make yourself do this, don't just rush into it in a panic.

- Workings must be clear and cross-referenced. If the marker can read and understand your workings they can give you credit for using the right method, even if your answer is wrong. If your answer is wrong and there are no workings, or they are illegible and incomprehensible, you will get no marks for that part of the question.

- Stick to the timings and answer all questions. Do not spend too long on one question at the expense of others. The number of extra marks you will gain on that question will be minimal, and you could have at least obtained the easy marks on the next question.

- Do not neglect the short parts of the question. If you get a consolidation with a five-mark discussion topic at the end, leave time for that last part. You can't afford to throw away five marks.

- Make sure you get the easy marks. If an accounts preparation question contains something that you are unable to do, just ignore it and do the rest. You will probably only lose a few marks and if you start trying to puzzle it out you might waste a lot of minutes.

- Answer the question. In a discussion-type question, such as an interpretation question, you may be tempted to just write down everything you know about the topic. This will do you no good. The marking parameters for these questions are quite precise. You will only get marks for making points that answer the question exactly as it has been set. So don't waste your time waffling – you could be scoring marks somewhere else.

Avoiding weaknesses

- There is no choice in this paper, all questions have to be answered. You must therefore study the entire syllabus, there are no short-cuts.

- Ability to answer multiple choice questions and cases improves with practice. Try to get as much practice with these questions as you can.

- The longer questions will be based on simple scenarios and answers must be focused and specific to the organisation.

Gaining the easy marks

Easy marks in this paper tend to fall into three categories.

Multiple choice questions

Some MCQs are easier than others. Answer those that you feel fairly confident about as quickly as you can. Come back later to those you find more difficult. This could be a way of making use of the time in the examination most efficiently and effectively.

Many MCQs will not involve calculations. Make sure that you understand the wording of 'written' MCQs before selecting your answer.

Calculations in Section C questions

There will be some relatively straightforward calculations at the start of the question and they will then probably get progressively more difficult. If you get stuck, make an assumption, state it and move on.

Discussions in Section C questions

A Section C question may separate discussion requirements from calculations, so that you do not need to do the calculations first in order to answer the discussion part. This means that you should be able to gain marks from making sensible, practical comments without having to complete the calculations.

Discussions that are focused on the specific organisation in the question will gain more marks than regurgitation of knowledge. Read the question carefully and more than once, to ensure you are actually answering the specific requirements.

Pick out key words such as 'describe', 'evaluate' and 'discuss'. These all mean something specific.

- 'Describe' means to communicate the key features of
- 'Evaluate' means to assess the value of
- 'Discuss' means to examine in detail by argument

Clearly label the points you make in discussions so that the marker can identify them all rather than getting lost in the detail.

Provide answers in the form requested. Use a report format if asked for and give recommendations if required.

Tackling Objective Test Case Questions

First, read the whole case scenario. Make a note of any specific instructions or assumptions.

Then skim through the requirements of the five questions. The questions are independent of each other and can be answered in any order.

Some of the OTs will be easier than others. Answer these OTs quickly.

Other OTs will be more difficult and/or complex. There are two types of OT that may take you longer to answer.

The first more time-consuming OT will involve doing a computation. You will probably need to jot down a quick proforma to answer a computational question. If the OT is a multiple choice question, remember that the wrong answers will usually involve common errors so don't assume that because you have the same answer as one of the options that your answer is necessarily correct! Double check to make sure you haven't made any silly mistakes, If you haven't got the same answer as any of the options, rework your computation, thinking carefully about what errors you could have made. If you still haven't got one of the options, choose the one which is nearest to your answer.

The second more time-consuming OT is one where you are asked to consider a number of statements and identify which one (or more) of them is correct. Make sure that you read each statement at least twice before making your selection. Be careful to follow the requirements of the OT exactly, for example if you are asked to identify **two** correct statements.

Exam information

Computer based Exams

ACCA have announced that they intend to commence the launch of computer based exams (CBE's) for F5-F9. They will be piloting computer based exams in limited markets in September 2016 with the aim of rolling out into all markets internationally over a 5 year period. Paper based examinations will be run in parallel while the CBE's are phased in and BPP materials have been designed to support you, whichever exam option you choose.

Format of the exam

All questions are compulsory.

	Number of marks
Section A – 15 MCQs/OTQs	30
Section B – 15 MCQs/OTQs	30
Section C – 2 long-form questions	40
	100

Time allowed: 3 hours and 15 minutes

Section B has three case questions. These consist of a scenario followed by five MCQs/OTQs based on the scenario. OTQs can be MCQs or other types of OT question and each is worth 2 marks. Each 2-mark question is independent of the others. You do not need to use the answer from one question in order to arrive at the answer to another question. Make sure you take the time to read the scenario carefully.

In the paper-based exam Sections A and B will consist of MCQs only. In the computer-based exam Sections A and B will consist of OTQs, some of which can be MCQs,

The exam format is the same irrespective of the mode of delivery and will comprise 3 exam sections

Section	Style of question type	Description	Proportion of exam, %
A	Objective test (OT)	15 questions x 2 marks	30
B	Objective test (OT) case	3 questions x 10 marks Each question will contain 5 subparts each worth 2 marks	30
C	Constructed Response (Long questions)	2 questions x 20 marks	40
Total			100

Section A and B questions will be selected from the entire syllabus. The paper version of these objective test questions contain multiple choice only and the computer based versions will contain a variety. The responses to each question or subpart in the case of OT cases are marked automatically as either correct or incorrect by computer.

Section C questions will mainly focus on the following syllabus areas but a minority of marks can be drawn from any other area of the syllabus

- Interpretation of financial statements (syllabus area C)
- Preparation of financial statements (syllabus area D)

The responses to these questions are human marked.

Additional information

The Study Guide provides more detailed guidance on the syllabus.

Useful websites

The websites below provide additional sources of information of relevance to your studies for *Financial Reporting*.

- www.accaglobal.com

  ACCA's website. The students' section of the website is invaluable for detailed information about the qualification, past issues of Student Accountant (including technical articles) and a free downloadable Student Planner App.

- www.bpp.com

  Our website provides information about BPP products and services, with a link to the ACCA website.

Questions

MCQ bank – conceptual framework

1   How does the *Conceptual Framework* define an asset?

   A   A resource owned by an entity as a result of past events and from which future economic benefits are expected to flow to the entity

   B   A resource over which an entity has legal rights as a result of past events and from which economic benefits are expected to flow to the entity

   C   A resource controlled by an entity as a result of past events and from which future economic benefits are expected to flow to the entity

   D   A resource to which an entity has a future commitment as a result of past events and from which future economic benefits are expected to flow from the entity   **(2 marks)**

2   Which one of the following would be classified as a liability?

   A   Dexter's business manufactures a product under licence. In 12 months' time the licence expires and Dexter will have to pay $50,000 for it to be renewed.

   B   Reckless purchased an investment 9 months ago for $120,000. The market for these investments has now fallen and Reckless's investment is valued at $90,000.

   C   Carter has estimated the tax charge on its profits for the year just ended as $165,000.

   D   Expansion is planning to invest in new machinery and has been quoted a price of $570,000. **(2 marks)**

3   Which one of the following would correctly describe the net realisable value of a two year old asset?

   A   The original cost of the asset less two years' depreciation
   B   The amount that could be obtained from selling the asset, less any costs of disposal
   C   The cost of an equivalent new asset less two years' depreciation
   D   The present value of the future cash flows obtainable from continuing to use the asset   **(2 marks)**

4   The *Conceptual Framework* identifies an **underlying assumption** in preparing financial statements. This is:

   A   Going concern
   B   Materiality
   C   Substance over form
   D   Accruals   **(2 marks)**

   (8 marks)

CBE style OTQ bank – conceptual framework

5   The *Conceptual Framework* identifies four enhancing qualitative characteristics of financial information. For which of these characteristics is **disclosure of accounting policies** particularly important?

   ☐   Verifiability
   ☐   Timeliness
   ☐   Comparability
   ☐   Understandability   **(2 marks)**

6   Which of the following is **not** a purpose of the IASB's *Conceptual Framework*?

   ☐   To assist the IASB in the preparation and review of IFRS
   ☐   To assist auditors in forming an opinion on whether financial statements comply with IFRS
   ☐   To assist in determining the treatment of items not covered by an existing IFRS
   ☐   To be authoritative where a specific IFRS conflicts with the Conceptual Framework   **(2 marks)**

7   Recognition is the process of including within the financial statements items which meet the definition of an element according to the IASB's *Conceptual Framework for Financial Reporting*.

Which of the following items should be recognised as an asset in the statement of financial position of a company?

☐   A skilled and efficient workforce which has been very expensive to train. Some of these staff are still in the employment of the company.

☐   A highly lucrative contract signed during the year which is due to commence shortly after the year end

☐   A government grant relating to the purchase of an item of plant several years ago, which has a remaining life of four years

☐   A receivable from a customer which has been sold (factored) to a finance company. The finance company has full recourse to the company for any losses.   **(2 marks)**

8   Comparability is identified as an enhancing qualitative characteristic in the IASB's *Conceptual Framework for Financial Reporting*.

Which of the following does NOT improve comparability?

☐   Restating the financial statements of previous years when there has been a change of accounting policy

☐   Prohibiting changes of accounting policy unless required by an IFRS or to give more relevant and reliable information

☐   Disclosing discontinued operations in financial statements

☐   Applying an entity's current accounting policy to a transaction which an entity has not engaged in before   **(2 marks)**

(8 marks)

Lisbon – MCQ case question

19 mins

Information relevant to Questions 9-13

The accountant of Lisbon is considering a number of transactions and events and how they should be treated in accordance with the concepts and qualitative characteristics of financial information as set out in the *Conceptual Framework*.

During the year ended 31 March 20X6, Lisbon experienced the following transactions or events.

(i)   Sold an asset to a finance company and leased it back for the remainder of its useful life. The accountant has decided that this should be treated as a secured loan.

(ii)   The company's statement of profit or loss prepared using historical costs showed a loss from operating its shops, but the company is aware that the increase in the value of its properties during the period far outweighed the operating loss.

(iii)   Inventory has up to this year been valued using FIFO but the accountant is considering changing to the weighted average method for the year to 31 March 20X6.

9   The accountant is aware that some members of the Board of Lisbon have little understanding of accounting and he is worried about his presentation of the financial statements at the Board meeting.

      How should he deal with this situation?

      A   In doing his presentation he should omit any complex issues, so that everybody can understand what he is saying.

      B   He should open his presentation with the advice that some of them may not understand all of it.

      C   He should classify, characterise and present the information clearly and precisely.

      D   He should deliver his presentation just to those who are financially qualified.

10   Which concept or qualitative characteristic has influenced the decision in (i) above?

      A   Faithful representation
      B   Verifiability
      C   Accruals
      D   Comparability

11   In looking at issue (ii) above, the accountant decides that the properties should be revalued.

      Which concept or qualitative characteristic has been applied in making this decision?

      A   Materiality
      B   Going concern
      C   Relevance
      D   Timeliness

12   Because loss on operating the shops, the accountant is considering the issue of going concern. If it were decided that Lisbon was no longer a going concern at 31 March 20X6, which of the following would apply in accordance with the *Conceptual Framework?*

      A   Financial statements do not need to be prepared.

      B   All the assets should be liquidated.

      C   The financial statements should be prepared on a different basis.

      D   The financial statements should be prepared as normal and the going concern status disclosed in the notes.

13   In applying the principle of comparability, how should the change of inventory valuation basis be accounted for?

   A   The change should just be disclosed.

   B   The financial statements for 31 March 20X6 should show both methods.

   C   The notes should show what the profit would have been if the change had not taken place.

   D   The financial statements for the prior period as shown at 31 March 20X6 should be restated using the weighted average basis.

(10 marks)

MCQ bank – regulatory framework

14   The process for developing an International Financial Reporting Standard involves a number of stages. Following receipt and review of comments on a Discussion Paper, what will be the next step undertaken by the IASB?

   A   Publication of an Exposure Draft
   B   Establishment of an Advisory Committee
   C   Consultation with the Advisory Committee
   D   Issue of a final IFRS   (2 marks)

15   Which one of the following would **not** be an advantage of adopting IFRS?

   A   It would be easier for investors to compare the financial statements of companies with those of foreign competitors.

   B   Cross-border listing would be facilitated.

   C   Accountants and auditors would have more defence in case of litigation.

   D   Multinational companies could more easily transfer accounting staff across national borders.

(2 marks)

(4 marks)

CBE style OTQ – regulatory framework

16   Which **TWO** of the following statements regarding systems of regulation of accounting are true?

   ☐   A rules-based system will require more detailed regulations than a principles-based system.

   ☐   A principles-based system will tend to give rise to a larger number of accounting standards than a rules-based system.

   ☐   A rules-based system seeks to cover every eventuality.

   ☐   A rules-based system requires the exercise of more judgement in application than a principles – based system.

(2 marks)

MCQ bank – tangible non-current assets

17 Foster has built a new factory incurring the following costs:

	$'000
Land	1,200
Materials	2,400
Labour	3,000
Architect's fees	25
Surveyor's fees	15
Site overheads	300
Apportioned administrative overheads	150
Testing of fire alarms	10
Business rates for first year	12
	7,112

What will be the total amount capitalised in respect of the factory?

- A $6,112,000
- B $6,950,000
- C $7,112,000
- D $7,100,000

(2 marks)

18 Capita had the following bank loans outstanding during the whole of 20X8:

	$m
9% loan repayable 20X9	15
11% loan repayable 20Y2	24

Capita began construction of a qualifying asset on 1 April 20X8 and withdrew funds of $6 million on that date to fund construction. On 1 August 20X8 an additional $2 million was withdrawn for the same purpose.

Calculate the borrowing costs which can be capitalised in respect of this project for the year ended 31 December 20X8.

- A $560,000
- B $472,500
- C $750,000
- D $350,000

(2 marks)

19 Leclerc has borrowed $2.4 million to finance the building of a factory. Construction is expected to take two years. The loan was drawn down and incurred on 1 January 20X9 and work began on 1 March 20X9. $1 million of the loan was not utilised until 1 July 20X9 so Leclerc was able to invest it until needed.

Leclerc is paying 8% on the loan and can invest surplus funds at 6%.

Calculate the borrowing costs to be capitalised for the year ended 31 December 20X9 in respect of this project.

- A $130,000
- B $192,000
- C $100,000
- D $162,000

(2 marks)

20 Which one of the following would be recognised as an investment property under IAS 40 in the consolidated financial statements of Buildco?

- A A property intended for sale in the ordinary course of business
- B A property being constructed for a customer
- C A property held by Buildco under a finance lease and leased out under an operating lease
- D A property owned by Buildco and leased out to a subsidiary

(2 marks)

21 Which one of the following is **not true** concerning the treatment of investment properties under IAS 40?

A Following initial recognition, investment property can be held at either cost or fair value.

B If an investment property is held at fair value, this must be applied to all of the entity's investment property.

C An investment property is initially measured at cost, including transaction costs.

D A gain or loss arising from a change in the fair value of an investment property should be recognised in other comprehensive income.

(2 marks)

22 A company has the following loans in place throughout the year ended 31 December 20X8.

	$m
10% bank loan	140
8% bank loan	200

On 1 July 20X8 $50 million was drawn down for construction of a qualifying asset which was completed during 20X9.

What amount should be capitalised as borrowing costs at 31 December 20X8 in respect of this asset?

A $5.6 million
B $2.8 million
C $4.4 million
D $2.2 million

(2 marks)

(12 marks)

CBE style OTQ bank – tangible non-current assets

23 Wetherby purchased a machine on 1 July 20X7 for $500,000. It is being depreciated on a straight line basis over its expected life of ten years. Residual value is estimated at $20,000. On 1 January 20X8, following a change in legislation, Wetherby fitted a safety guard to the machine. The safety guard cost $25,000 and has a useful life of five years with no residual value.

What amount will be charged to profit or loss for the year ended 31 March 20X8 in respect of depreciation on this machine?

$ [   ]

(2 marks)

24 An aircraft requires a planned overhaul each year at a cost of $5,000. This is a condition of being allowed to fly.

How should the cost of the overhaul be treated in the financial statements?

☐ Accrued for over the year and charged to maintenance expenses

☐ Provided for in advance and charged to maintenance expenses

☐ Capitalised and depreciated over the period to the next overhaul

☐ Charged to profit or loss when the expenditure takes place

(2 marks)

25 Kaplow purchased a machine for $30,000 on 1 January 20X5 and assigned it a useful life of 12 years. On 31 March 20X7 it was revalued to $32,000 with no change in useful life.

What will be depreciation charge in relation to this machine in the financial statements of Kaplow for the year ending 31 December 20X7?

$ [   ]

(2 marks)

26   Carter vacated an office building and let it out to a third party on 30 June 20X8. The building had an original cost of $900,000 on 1 January 20X0 and was being depreciated over 50 years. It was judged to have a fair value on 30 June 20X8 of $950,000. At the year end date of 31 December 20X8 the fair value of the building was estimated at $1.2 million.

Carter uses the fair value model for investment property.

What amount will be shown in revaluation surplus at 31 December 20X8 in respect of this building?

$ ☐   **(2 marks)**

(8 marks)

Section B

Plethora plc – MCQ case

Information relevant to questions 27-31

The draft financial statements of Plethora plc for the year to 31 December 20X9 are being prepared and the accountant has requested your advice on dealing with the following issues.

(i) Plethora plc has an administration building which it no longer needs. On 1 July 20X9 Plethora plc entered into an agreement to lease the building out to another company. The building cost $600,000 on 1 January 20X0 and is being depreciated over 50 years, based on the IAS 16 cost model. Plethora plc applies the fair value model under IAS 40 *Investment property* and the fair value of the building was judged to be $800,000 on 1 July 20X9. This valuation had not changed at 31 December 20X9.

(ii) Plethora plc owns another building which has been leased out for a number of years. It had a fair value of $550,000 at 31 December 20X8 and $740,000 at 31 December 20X9.

(iii) Plethora plc owns a retail business which has suffered badly during the recession. Plethora plc treats this business as a separate cash generating unit.

The carrying amounts of the assets comprising the retail business are:

	$'000
Building	900
Plant and equipment	300
Inventory	70
Other current assets	130
Goodwill	40

An impairment review has been carried out as at 31 December 20X9 and the recoverable amount of the cash generating unit is estimated at $1.3m.

27 What is the amount of the revaluation surplus that will be recognised in respect of the building in (i)?

- A $200,000
- B $314,000
- C $308,000
- D Nil

---

28 In respect of the building in (ii), how will the increase in value from $550,000 to $740,000 be accounted for?

- A Credited to profit or loss
- B Credited to the revaluation surplus
- C Credited to retained earnings
- D Credited to an investment property reserve

---

29 When an impairment review is carried out, a potentially impaired asset is measured at what amount?

- A Fair value
- B Value in use
- C Recoverable amount
- D Carrying amount

---

30 What will be the carrying amount of the inventory after the impairment loss in (iii) has been accounted for?

- A $64,000
- B $70,000
- C Nil
- D $65,000

---

31   What will be the carrying amount of the building after the impairment loss has been accounted for?

    A $900,000
    B $836,000
    C $795,000
    D $825,000

(10 marks)

Dearing MCQ case

19 mins

Information relevant to questions 32-36

(a)   On 1 October 20X5 Dearing acquired a machine under the following terms.

	Hours	$
Manufacturer's base price		1,050,000
Trade discount (applying to base price only)		20%
Early settlement discount taken (on the payable amount of the base cost only)		5%
Freight charges		30,000
Electrical installation cost		28,000
Staff training in use of machine		40,000
Pre-production testing		22,000
Purchase of a three-year maintenance contract		60,000

On 1 October 20X7 Dearing decided to upgrade the machine by adding new components at a cost of $200,000. This upgrade led to a reduction in the production time per unit of the goods being manufactured using the machine.

32   What amount should be recognised under non-current assets as the cost of the machine?

    A $840,000
    B $920,000
    C $898,000
    D $870,000

33   How should the $200,000 worth of new components be accounted for?

    A   Added to the carrying amount of the machine
    B   Charged to profit or loss
    C   Capitalised as a separate asset
    D   Debited to accumulated depreciation

34   Every five years the machine will need a major overhaul in order to keep running. How should this be accounted for?

    A   Set up a provision at year 1
    B   Build up the provision over years 1-5
    C   Capitalise the cost when it arises and amortise over five years
    D   Write the overhaul off to maintenance costs

35   By 27 September 20X7 internal evidence had emerged suggesting that Dearing's machine was impaired. Which one of the following would be internal evidence of impairment?

    A   The economic performance of the machine had declined.
    B   There were legal and regulatory changes affecting the operating of the machine.
    C   There was an unexpected fall in the market value of the machine.
    D   New technological innovations were producing better machines.

36 On 30 September 20X7 the impairment review was carried out. The following amounts were established in respect of the machine:

	$
Carrying amount	850,000
Value in use	760,000
Fair value	850,000
Costs of disposal	30,000

What should be the carrying amount of the machine following the impairment review?

A $760,000
B $820,000
C $850,000
D $790,000

(10 marks)

MCQ bank – intangible assets

37 Geek is developing a new product and expects to be able to capitalise the costs. Which one of the following would preclude capitalisation of the costs?

A   Development of the product is not yet complete.
B   No patent has yet been registered in respect of the product.
C   No sales contracts have yet been signed in relation to the product.
D   It has not been possible to reliably allocate costs to development of the product.   (2 marks)

38 A company had $20 million of capitalised development expenditure at cost brought forward at 1 October 20X7 in respect of products currently in production and a new project began on the same date.

The research stage of the new project lasted until 31 December 20X7 and incurred $1.4 million of costs. From that date the project incurred development costs of $800,000 per month. On 1 April 20X8 the directors became confident that the project would be successful and yield a profit well in excess of costs. The project was still in development at 30 September 20X8. Capitalised development expenditure is amortised at 20% per annum using the straight line method.

What amount will be charged to profit or loss for the year ended 30 September 20X8 in respect of research and development costs?

A $8,280,000
B $6,880,000
C $7,800,000
D $3,800,000   (2 marks)

39 Which one of the following internally-generated items may be eligible for capitalisation as intangible assets in accordance with IAS 38 *Intangible Assets?* (Ignore business combinations.)

A   A customer list
B   A pre-production prototype
C   Goodwill
D   The cost of researching new material   (2 marks)

(6 marks)

CBE style OTQ bank – intangible assets

40 At 30 September 20X9 Sandown's trial balance showed a brand at cost of $30 million, less accumulated amortisation brought forward at 1 October 20X8 of $9 million. Amortisation is based on a ten-year useful life. An impairment review on 1 April 20X9 concluded that the brand had a value in use of $12 million and a remaining useful life of three years. However, on the same date Sandown received an offer to purchase the brand for $15 million.

What should be the carrying amount of the brand in the statement of financial position of Sandown as at 30 September 20X9?

- [ ] $12,500,000
- [ ] $14,250,000
- [ ] $15,000,000
- [ ] $10,000,000   (2 marks)

41 Dempsey's year end is 30 September 20X4. Dempsey commenced the development stage of a project to produce a new pharmaceutical drug on 1 January 20X4. Expenditure of $40,000 per month was incurred until the project was completed on 30 June 20X4 when the drug went into immediate production. The directors became confident of the project's success on 1 March 20X4. The drug has an estimated life span of five years; time apportionment is used by Dempsey where applicable.

What amount will Dempsey charge to profit or loss for development costs, including any amortisation, for the year ended 30 September 20X4?

$ [   ]   (2 marks)

                                                                   (4 marks)

Section B

Dexterity MCQ case

19 mins

Information relevant to questions 42-46

Dexterity is a public listed company. It has been considering the accounting treatment of its intangible assets and how the matters below should be treated in its financial statements for the year to 31 March 20X4.

1   On 1 October 20X3 Dexterity acquired Temerity, a small company that specialises in pharmaceutical drug research and development. The purchase consideration was by way of a share exchange and valued at $35 million. The fair value of Temerity's net assets was $15 million (excluding any items referred to below). Temerity owns a patent for an established successful drug that has a remaining life of eight years. A firm of specialist advisors, Leadbrand, has estimated the current value of this patent to be $10 million, however the company is awaiting the outcome of clinical trials where the drug has been tested to treat a different illness. If the trials are successful, the value of the drug is then estimated to be $15 million. Also included in the company's statement of financial position is $2 million for medical research that has been conducted on behalf of a client.

2   Dexterity has developed and patented a new drug which has been approved for clinical use. The costs of developing the drug were $12 million. Based on early assessments of its sales success, Leadbrand have estimated its market value at $20 million, which can be taken as a reliable measurement.

3   Dexterity's manufacturing facilities have recently received a favourable inspection by government medical scientists. As a result of this the company has been granted an exclusive five-year licence to manufacture and distribute a new vaccine. Although the licence had no direct cost to Dexterity, its directors feel its granting is a reflection of the company's standing and have asked Leadbrand to value the licence. Accordingly they have placed a value of $10 million on it.

4   In the current accounting period, Dexterity has spent $3 million sending its staff on specialist training courses. Whilst these courses have been expensive, they have led to a marked improvement in production quality and staff now need less supervision. This in turn has led to an increase in revenue and cost reductions. The directors of Dexterity believe these benefits will continue for at least three years and wish to treat the training costs as an asset.

42   Which of the following items should be recognised as intangible assets?

(i)   Patent for new drug
(ii)   Licence for new vaccine
(iii)   Specialist training courses

A   (i) and (ii)
B   (ii) and(iii)
C   (i) and (iii)
D   (i) only

43   Which of the following is one of the criteria for the recognition of development costs as an intangible asset?

A   The asset has been completed and is available for sale or use
B   It is possible that the asset can be sold or used
C   The proceeds from sale or use of the asset can be reliably measured
D   The asset will generate probable future economic benefits

44 IAS 38 gives examples of activities that would be regarded as research and therefore not eligible for recognition as an intangible asset.

Which one of the following would be an example of research costs?

A   The design and construction of chosen alternative products or processes
B   The design of pre-production prototypes and models
C   The design of possible new or improved product or process alternatives
D   The design, construction and operation of a pilot plant

45 At what amount should the patent acquired from Temerity be valued at 31 March 20X4?

A $10,000,000
B $9,375,000
C $15,000,000
D   Nil

46 How should Dexterity treat the goodwill arising on its acquisition of Temerity?

A   It should be capitalised and amortised over 20 years.
B   It should be capitalised and reviewed for impairment every year.
C   It should be capitalised and reviewed for impairment every five years.
D   It should be written off to retained earnings.

(10 marks)

CBE style OTQ bank – impairment of assets

47 A cash-generating unit comprises the following assets:

	$'000
Building	700
Plant and equipment	200
Goodwill	90
Current assets	20
	1,010

One of the machines, carried at $40,000, is damaged and will have to be scrapped. The recoverable amount of the cash-generating unit is estimated at $750,000.

What will be the carrying amount of the building when the impairment loss has been recognised? (to the nearest $'000)

☐ $597,000
☐ $577,000
☐ $594,000
☐ $548,000

(2 marks)

48 What is the **recoverable amount** of an asset?

☐   Its current market value less costs of disposal
☐   The lower of carrying amount and value in use
☐   The higher of fair value less costs of disposal and value in use
☐   The higher of carrying amount and market value

(2 marks)

49 A machine has a carrying amount of $85,000 at the year end of 31 March 20X9. Its market value is $78,000 and costs of disposal are estimated at $2,500. A new machine would cost $150,000. The company which owns the machine expects it to produce net cash flows of $30,000 per annum for the next three years. The company has a cost of capital of 8%.

What is the impairment loss on the machine to be recognised in the financial statements at 31 March 20X9?

☐ $7,687

☐ $9,500

☐ $1,667

☐ $2,200   (2 marks)

---

50 IAS 36 *Impairment of Assets* suggests how indications of impairment might be recognised.

Which **TWO** of the following would be **external** indicators that one or more of an entity's assets may be impaired?

☐ An unusually significant fall in the market value of one or more assets

☐ Evidence of obsolescence of one or more assets

☐ A decline in the economic performance of one or more assets

☐ An increase in market interest rates used to calculate value in use of the assets   (2 marks)

---

51 The following information relates to an item of plant.

- Its carrying amount in the statement of the financial position is $3 million.

- The company has received an offer of $2.7 million from a company in Japan interested in buying the plant.

- The present value of the estimated cash flows from continued use of the plant is $2.6 million.

- The estimated cost of shipping the plant to Japan is $50,000.

What is the amount of the impairment loss that should be recognised on the plant?

$ [   ]   (2 marks)

(10 marks)

MCQ bank – impairment of assets

52 A business which comprises a single cash-generating unit has the following assets.

	$m
Goodwill	3
Patent	5
Property	10
Plant and equipment	15
Net current assets	2
	35

Following an impairment review it is estimated that the value of the patent is $2 million and the recoverable amount of the business is $24 million.
At what amount should the property be measured following the impairment review?

A $8 million
B $10 million
C $7 million
D $5 million   (2 marks)

53   Riley acquired a non-current asset on 1 October 20W9 (ie 10 years before 20X9) at a cost of $100,000 which had a useful life of ten years and a nil residual value. The asset had been correctly depreciated up to 30 September 20X4. At that date the asset was damaged and an impairment review was performed. On 30 September 20X4, the fair value of the asset less costs of disposal was $30,000 and the expected future cash flows were $8,500 per annum for the next five years. The current cost of capital is 10% and a five-year annuity of $1 per annum at 10% would have a present value of $3.79.

What amount would be charged to profit or loss for the impairment of this asset for the year ended 30 September 20X4?

A $17,785
B $20,000
C $30,000
D $32,215   (2 marks)

54   The net assets of Fyngle, a cash generating unit (CGU) are:

	$
Property, plant and equipment	200,000
Allocated goodwill	50,000
Product patent	20,000
Net current assets (at net realisable value)	30,000
	300,000

As a result of adverse publicity, Fyngle has a recoverable amount of only $200,000.

What would be the value of Fyngle's property, plant and equipment after the allocation of the impairment loss?

A $154,545
B $170,000
C $160,000
D $133,333   (2 marks)

55   Which of the following is NOT an indicator of impairment under IAS 36 *Impairment of Assets*?

A   Advances in the technological environment in which an asset is employed have an adverse impact on its future use

B   An increase in interest rates which increases the discount rate an entity uses

C   The carrying amount of an entity's net assets is lower than the entity's number of shares in issue multiplied by its share price

D   The estimated net realisable value of inventory has been reduced due to fire damage although this value is greater than its carrying amount   (2 marks)

(8 marks)

Systria CBE style OT case

The following information is relevant to questions 56-60

Systria is preparing its financial statements for the year ended 31 December 20X7 and has a number of issues to deal with regarding non-current assets.

(i)   Systria has suffered an impairment loss of $90,000 to one of its cash generating units. The carrying amounts of the assets in the cash-generating unit prior to adjusting for impairment are:

	$'000
Goodwill	50
Patent	10
Land and buildings	100
Plant and machinery	50
Net current assets	10

The patent is now estimated to have no value.

(ii)   During the year to 31 December 20X7 Systria acquired Dominica for $10 million, its tangible assets being valued at $7 million and goodwill on acquisition being $3 million. Assets with a carrying amount of $2.5 million were subsequently destroyed. Systria has carried out an impairment review and has established that Dominica could be sold for $6 million, while its value in use is $5.5 million.

(iii) A freehold property originally costing $100,000 with a 50-year life has accumulated depreciation to date of $20,000. The asset is to be revalued to $130,000 at 31 December 20X7.

56   What is the post-impairment carrying amount of plant and machinery in (i) above?

$ [   ]

---

57   The Finance Director has been asked to report to the Board on the reasons for the impairment review on the cash-generating unit. Which TWO of the following would be an internal indicator of impairment of an asset under IAS 36 *Impairment of assets*?

[ ]   The market value of the asset has fallen significantly.

[ ]   There are adverse changes to the use to which the asset is put.

[ ]   The asset is fully depreciated.

[ ]   The operating performance of the asset has declined.

---

58   What is the carrying amount of the goodwill in (ii) following the impairment review?

$ [   ]

---

59   Which set of double entries is required to record the revaluation in (iii)?

[ ]   DR Accumulated depreciation $20,000 / CR Revaluation surplus $20,000

[ ]   DR Property at cost $50,000 / CR Revaluation surplus $50,000

[ ]   DR Accumulated depreciation $20,000
       DR Property at cost $30,000 / CR Revaluation surplus $50,000

[ ]   DR Revaluation surplus $50,000 / CR Accumulated depreciation $20,000
                                       CR Property at cost $30,000

---

60 What will be the depreciation charge on the asset in (iii) for the year ended 31.12.X8?

- ☐ $2,000
- ☐ $2,600
- ☐ $3,250
- ☐ $2,750

(10 marks)

MCQ bank – revenue

61 A company entered into a contract on 1 January 20X5 to build a factory. The total contract revenue was $2.8 million. At 31 December 20X5 the contract was certified as 35% complete. Costs incurred during the year were $740,000 and costs to complete are estimated at $1.4 million. $700,000 has been billed to the customer but not yet paid.

What amount will be recognised as a contract asset or liability in respect of this contract in the statement of financial position as at 31 December 20X5?

A $271,000 contract asset
B $509,000 contract asset
C $271,000 contract liability
D $509,000 contract liability

(2 marks)

62 Which of the following are acceptable methods of accounting for a government grant relating to an asset in accordance with IAS 20 *Accounting for Government Grants and Disclosure of Government Assistance*?

(i)   Set up the grant as deferred income
(ii)   Credit the amount received to profit or loss
(iii)   Deduct the grant from the carrying amount of the asset
(iv)   Add the grant to the carrying amount of the asset

A (i) and (ii)
B (ii) and (iv)
C (i) and (iii)
D (iii) and (iv)

(2 marks)

63 On 1 October 20X2 Pricewell entered into a contract to construct a bridge over a river. The total contract revenue was $50 million and construction is expected to be completed on 30 September 20X4. Costs to date are:

	$m
Materials, labour and overheads	12
Specialist plant acquired 1 October 20X2	8

The sales value of the work done at 31 March 20X3 has been agreed at $22 million and the estimated cost to complete (excluding plant depreciation) is $10 million. The specialist plant will have no residual value at the end of the contract and should be depreciated on a monthly basis. Pricewell recognises satisfaction of performance obligations on the percentage of completion basis as determined by the agreed work to date compared to the total contract price.

What is the profit to date on the contract at 31 March 20X3?

A $8,800,000
B $13,200,000
C $11,440,000
D $10,000,000

(2 marks)

64 The following details apply to a contract where performance obligations are satisfied over time at 31 December 20X5.

	$
Total contract revenue	120,000
Costs to date	48,000
Estimated costs to completion	48,000
Amounts invoiced	50,400

The contract is agreed to be 45% complete at 31 December 20X5.
What amount should appear in the statement of financial as at 31 December 20X5 as a contract asset?

A $8,400
B $48,000
C $6,000
D $50,400 **(2 marks)**

---

65 Sale and leaseback or sale and repurchase arrangements can be used to disguise the substance of loan transactions by taking them 'off balance sheet'. In this case the legal position is that the asset has been sold but the substance is that the seller still retains the benefits of ownership.

Which one of the following is **not** a feature which suggests that the substance of a transaction differs from its legal form?

A The seller of an asset retains the ability to use the asset.
B The seller has no further exposure to the risks of ownership
C The asset has been transferred at a price substantially above or below its fair value.
D The 'sold' asset remains on the sellers premises. **(2 marks)**

---

66 Springthorpe entered into a three-year contract on 1 January 20X2 to build a factory. This is a contract where performance obligations are satisfied over time. The percentage of performance obligations satisfied is measured according to certificates issued by a surveyor. The contract price was $12 million. At 31 December 20X2 details of the contract were as follows.

	$m
Costs to date	6
Estimated costs to complete	9
Amounts invoiced	4
Certified complete	40%

What amount should appear in the statement of financial position of Springthorpe as at 31 December 20X2 as contract assets/liabilities in respect of this contract?

A $1 million contract liability
B $2 million contract liability
C $1 million contract asset
D $2 million contract asset **(2 marks)**

67 On 25 June 20X9 Cambridge received an order from a new customer, Circus, for products with a sales value of $900,000. Circus enclosed a deposit with the order of $90,000.

On 30 June Cambridge had not completed credit checks on Circus and had not despatched any goods. Cambridge is considering the following possible entries for this transaction in its financial statements for the year ended 30 June 20X9.

(i)   Include $900,000 in revenue for the year
(ii)   Include $90,000 in revenue for the year
(iii) Do not include anything in revenue for the year
(iv)   Create a trade receivable for $810,000
(v)   Show $90,000 as a current liability

According to IFRS 15 *Revenue from contracts with customers*, how should Cambridge record this transaction in its financial statements for the year ended 30 June 20X9?

A   (i) and (iv)
B   (ii) and (v)
C   (ii) and (iv)
D   (iii) and (v)   **(2 marks)**

---

68 Repro, a company which sells photocopying equipment, has prepared its draft financial statements for the year ended 30 September 20X4. It has included the following transactions in revenue at the stated amounts below.

Which of these has been correctly included in revenue according to IFRS 15 *Revenue from contracts with customers*?

A   Agency sales of $250,000 on which Repro is entitled to a commission

B   Sale proceeds of $20,000 for motor vehicles which were no longer required by Repro

C   Sales of $150,000 on 30 September 20X4. The amount invoiced to and received from the customer was $180,000, which included $30,000 for ongoing servicing work to be done by Repro over the next two years

D   Sales of $200,000 on 1 October 20X3 to an established customer which, (with the agreement of Repro), will be paid in full on 30 September 20X5. Repro has a cost of capital of 10%.   **(2 marks)**

                                                                                                            (16 marks)

CBE style OTQ bank – revenue

69 Yling entered into a contract in respect of which performance obligations are satisfied over time on 1 January 20X4. The contract is expected to last 24 months. The price which has been agreed for the contract is $5 million. At 30 September 20X4 the costs incurred on the contract were $1.6 million and the estimated remaining costs to complete were $2.4 million. On 20 September 20X4 Yling received a payment from the customer of $1.8 million which was equal to the total of the amounts invoiced. Yling calculates the stage of completion of its performance obligations on contracts on the basis of amounts invoiced to the contract price.

What amount would be reported in Yling's statement of financial position as at 30 September 20X4 as the contract asset arising from the above contract?

☐   Nil
☐ $160,000
☐ $800,000
☐ $200,000   **(2 marks)**

70 Consignment inventory is an arrangement whereby inventory is held by one party but owned by another party. It is common in the motor trade.

Which **TWO** of the following indicate that the inventory in question is consignment inventory?

☐ Manufacturer can require dealer to return the inventory
☐ Dealer has no right of return of the inventory
☐ Manufacturer bears obsolescence risk
☐ Dealer bears slow movement risk

(2 marks)

71 A company receives a government grant of $500,000 on 1 April 20X7 to facilitate purchase on the same day of an asset which costs $750,000. The asset has a five year useful life and is depreciated on a 30% reducing balance basis. Company policy is to account for all grants received as deferred income.

What amount of income will be recognised in respect of the grant in the year to 31 March 20X9?

$ ▢

(2 marks)

72 Newmarket's revenue as shown in its draft statement of profit or loss for the year ended 31 December 20X9 is $27 million. This includes $8 million for a consignment of goods sold on 31 December 20X9 on which Newmarket will incur ongoing service and support costs for two years after the sale.

The supply of the goods and the provision of service and support are separate performance obligations under the terms of IFRS 15 *Revenue from contracts with customers*.

The cost of providing service and support is estimated at $800,000 per annum. Newmarket applies a 30% mark-up to all service costs.

At what amount should revenue be shown in the statement of profit or loss of Newmarket for the year ended 31 December 20X9? (Ignore the time value of money.)

$ ▢

(2 marks)

(8 marks)

Section B

Derringdo MCQ case

19 mins

Information relevant to questions 73-77

Derringdo is a broadband provider which receives government assistance to provide broadband to remote areas. Derringdo invested in a new server at a gross cost of $800,000 on 1 October 20X2. The server has an estimated life of ten years with a residual value equal to 15% of its gross cost. Derringdo uses straight-line depreciation on a time apportioned basis.

The company received a government grant of 30% of its cost price of the server at the time of purchase. The terms of the grant are that if the company retains the asset for four years or more, then no repayment liability will be incurred. Derringdo has no intention of disposing of the server within the first four years. Derringdo's accounting policy for capital-based government grants is to treat them as deferred credits and release them to income over the life of the asset to which they relate.

73   What is the net amount that will be charged to operating expenses in respect of the server for the year ended 31 March 20X3?

    A $10,000
    B $28,000
    C $22,000
    D $34.000

74   What amount will be presented under non-current liabilities at 31 March 20X3 in respect of the grant?
    A $228,000
    B $216,000
    C $240,000
    D $204,000

75   Derringdo also sells a package which gives customers a free laptop when they sign a two-year contract for provision of broadband services. The laptop has a stand-alone price of $200 and the broadband contract is for $30 per month.

In accordance with IFRS 15 *Revenue from contracts with customers*, what amount will be recognised as revenue on each package in the first year?

    A $439
    B $281
    C $461
    D $158

76   Determining the amount to be recognised in the first year is an example of which step in the IFRS 15 5-step model?

    A   Determining the transaction price
    B   Recognising revenue when a performance obligation is satisfied
    C   Identifying the separate performance obligations
    D   Allocating the transaction price to the performance obligations

77   Derringdo is carrying out a transaction on behalf of another entity and the finance director is unsure whether Derringdo should be regarded as an agent or a principal in respect of this transaction.

Which one of the following would indicate that Derringdo is acting as an agent?

A   Derringdo is primarily responsible for fulfilling the contract.
B   Derringdo is not exposed to credit risk for the amount due from the customer.
C   Derringdo is responsible for negotiating the price for the contract.
D   Derringdo will not be paid in the form of commission.

(10 marks)

Bridgenorth CBE style OTQ case   19 mins

Information relevant to questions 78-82

Bridgenorth has undertaken a $5 million contract to repair a railway tunnel. The contract was signed on 1 April 20X8 and the work is expected to take two years. This is a contract where performance obligations are satisfied over time and progress in satisfying performance obligations is to be measured according to % of work completed as certified by a surveyor. Bridgenorth has an enforceable right to payment for performance completed to date.

At 31 December 20X9 the details of the contract were as follows:

	20X9	20X8
	$	$
Total contract value	5,000,000	5,000,000
Costs to date	3,600,000	2,300,000
Estimated costs to completion	700,000	2,100,000
Work invoiced to date	3,000,000	2,000,000
Cash received to date	2,400,000	1,500,000
% certified complete	75%	40%

78   What is the profit recognised for the year ended 31 December 20X8?

$ [   ]

79   What amount would have been included in trade receivables at 31 December 20X8?

$ [   ]

80   What is the contract asset to be recognised at 31 December 20X9?

$ [   ]

81   Bridgenorth measures performance obligations completed by reference to percentage of completion.

Which one of these would also be an acceptable method of measuring the performance obligations completed?

☐ Work invoiced to date as a % of total contract price

☐ Cash received to date as a % of total contract price

☐ Costs incurred as a % of total expected costs

☐ Time spent as a % of total expected contract time

82   If at 31 December 20X8 Bridgenorth had completed only 10% of the contract for costs of $400,000 and felt that it was too early to predict whether or not the contract would be profitable, what amount, if any, could Bridgenorth have recognised as revenue?

$ ☐

(10 marks)

CBE style OTQ bank – introduction to groups

83   On what basis may a subsidiary be excluded from consolidation?

☐   The activities of the subsidiary are dissimilar to the activities of the rest of the group.

☐   The subsidiary was acquired with the intention of reselling it after a short period of time.

☐   The subsidiary is based in a country with strict exchange controls which make it difficult for it to transfer funds to the parent.

☐   There is no basis on which a subsidiary may be excluded from consolidation.   **(2 marks)**

84   When negative goodwill arises IFRS 3 *Business combinations* requires that the amounts involved in computing goodwill should first be reassessed. When the amount of the negative goodwill has been confirmed, how should it be accounted for?

☐   Charged as an expense in profit or loss

☐   Capitalised and presented under non-current assets

☐   Credited to profit or loss

☐   Shown as a deduction from non-current assets   **(2 marks)**

85   Which of the following is the criterion for treatment of an investment as an associate?

☐   Ownership of a majority of the equity shares

☐   Ability to exercise control

☐   Existence of significant influence

☐   Exposure to variable returns from involvement with the investee   **(2 marks)**

86   Which **TWO** of the following statements are correct when preparing consolidated financial statements?

☐   A subsidiary cannot be consolidated unless it prepares financial statements to the same reporting date as the parent.

☐   A subsidiary with a different reporting date may prepare additional statements up to the group reporting date for consolidation purposes.

☐   A subsidiary's financial statements can be included in the consolidation if the gap between the parent and subsidiary reporting dates is five months or less.

☐   Where a subsidiary's financial statements are drawn up to a different reporting date from those of the parent, adjustments should be made for significant transactions or events occurring between the two reporting dates.

(2 marks)

(8 marks)

MCQ bank – introduction to groups

87   IFRS 3 *Business combinations* requires an acquirer to measure the assets and liabilities of the acquiree at the date of consolidation at fair value. IFRS 13 *Fair value measurement* provides guidance on how fair value should be established.

Which of the following is **not** one of the issues to be considered according to IFRS 13 when arriving at the fair value of a non-financial asset?

A   The characteristics of the asset

B   The present value of the future cash flows that the asset is expected to generate during its remaining life

C   The principal or most advantageous market for the asset

D   The highest and best use of the asset   **(2 marks)**

88   IFRS 10 *Consolidated financial statements* provides a definition of control and identifies three separate elements of control. Which one of the following is **not** one of these elements of control?

A   Power over the investee
B   The power to participate in the financial and operating policies of the investee
C   Exposure to, or rights to, variable returns from its involvement with the investee
D   The ability to use its power over the investee to affect the amount of the investor's returns   **(2 marks)**

89   Petre owns 100% of the share capital of the following companies. The directors are unsure of whether the investments should be consolidated.

In which of the following circumstances would the investment NOT be consolidated?

A   Petre has decided to sell its investment in Alpha as it is loss-making; the directors believe its exclusion from consolidation would assist users in predicting the group's future profits

B   Beta is a bank and its activity is so different from the engineering activities of the rest of the group that it would be meaningless to consolidate it

C   Delta is located in a country where local accounting standards are compulsory and these are not compatible with IFRS used by the rest of the group

D   Gamma is located in a country where a military coup has taken place and Petre has lost control of the investment for the foreseeable future   **(2 marks)**

(6 marks)

90 Preparation question: Group financial statements

(a)   Set out the exemptions from the requirement to present consolidated financial statements which are available to a parent company.

(b)   Explain why intra-group transactions and balances are eliminated on consolidation.

Section C

91 Boo and Goose

39 mins

Boo acquired 80% of Goose's equity shares for $300,000 on 1 January 20X8. At the date of acquisition Goose had retained earnings of $190,000. On 31 December 20X8 Boo despatched goods which cost $80,000 to Goose, at an invoiced cost of $100,000. Goose received the goods on 2 January 20X9 and recorded the transaction then. The two companies' draft financial statements as at 31 December 20X8 are shown below.

STATEMENTS OF PROFIT OR LOSS AND OTHER COMPREHENSIVE INCOME
FOR THE YEAR ENDED 31 DECEMBER 20X8

	Boo	Goose
	$'000	$'000
Revenue	5,000	1,000
Cost of sales	2,900	600
Gross profit	2,100	400
Other expenses	1,700	320
Profit before tax	400	80
Income tax expense	130	25
Profit for the year	270	55
Other comprehensive income:		
Gain on revaluation of property	20	–
Total comprehensive income for the year	290	55

STATEMENTS OF FINANCIAL POSITION AT 31 DECEMBER 20X8

	$'000	$'000
Assets		
Non-current assets		
Property, plant and equipment	1,940	200
Investment in Goose	300	–
	2,240	200
Current assets		
Inventories	500	120
Trade receivables	650	40
Bank and cash	170	35
	1,320	195
Total assets	3,560	395
Equity and liabilities		
Equity		
Share capital	2,000	100
Retained earnings	500	240
Revaluation surplus	20	–
	2,520	340
Current liabilities		
Trade payables	910	30
Tax	130	25
	1,040	55
Total equity and liabilities	3,560	395

Required

Prepare a draft consolidated statement of profit or loss and other comprehensive income and statement of financial position. It is the group policy to value the non-controlling interest at acquisition at fair value. The fair value of the non-controlling interest in Goose at the date of acquisition was $60,000. **(20 marks)**

CBE style OTQ bank – consolidated statement of financial position

92   Witch acquired 70% of the 200,000 equity shares of Wizard, its only subsidiary, on 1 April 20X8 when the retained earnings of Wizard were $450,000. The carrying amounts of Wizard's net assets at the date of acquisition were equal to their fair values apart from a building which had a carrying amount of $600,000 and a fair value of $850,000. The remaining useful life of the building at the acquisition date was 40 years.

Witch measures non-controlling interest at fair value, based on share price. The market value of Wizard shares at the date of acquisition was $1.75.

At 31 March 20X9 the retained earnings of Wizard were $750,000. At what amount should the non-controlling interest appear in the consolidated statement of financial position of Witch at 31 March 20X9?

$ [   ]   **(2 marks)**

---

93   Cloud obtained a 60% holding in the 100,000 $1 shares of Mist on 1 January 20X8, when the retained earnings of Mist were $850,000. Consideration comprised $250,000 cash, $400,000 payable on 1 January 20X9 and one share in Cloud for each two shares acquired. Cloud has a cost of capital of 8% and the market value of its shares on 1 January 20X8 was $2.30.

Cloud measures non-controlling interest at fair value. The fair value of the non-controlling interest at 1 January 20X8 was estimated to be $400,000.

What was the goodwill arising on acquisition?

☐ $139,370

☐ $169,000

☐ $119,370

☐ $130,370   **(2 marks)**

---

94   On 1 June 20X1 Premier acquired 80% of the equity share capital of Sandford. At the date of acquisition the fair values of Sandford's net assets were equal to their carrying amounts with the exception of its property. This had a fair value of $1.2 million **below** its carrying amount. The property had a remaining useful life of eight years.

What effect will any adjustment required in respect of the property have on group retained earnings at 30 September 20X1?

$ [   ] Increase / decrease   **(2 marks)**

---

95   On 1 August 20X7 Patronic purchased 18 million of the 24 million $1 equity shares of Sardonic. The acquisition was through a share exchange of two shares in Patronic for every three shares in Sardonic. The market price of a share in Patronic at 1 August 20X7 was $5.75. Patronic will also pay in cash on 31 July 20X9 (two years after acquisition) $2.42 per acquired share of Sardonic. Patronic's cost of capital is 10% per annum.

What is the amount of the consideration attributable to Patronic for the acquisition of Sardonic?

☐ $105 million

☐ $139.5 million

☐ $108.2 million

☐ $103.8 million   **(2 marks)**

(8 marks)

MCQ bank – consolidated statement of financial position

96   On 1 April 20X0 Picant acquired 75% of Sander's equity shares by means of a share exchange and an additional amount payable on 1 April 20X1 that was contingent upon the post-acquisition performance of Sander. At the date of acquisition Picant assessed the fair value of this contingent consideration at $4.2 million but by 31 March 20X1 it was clear that the amount to be paid would be only $2.7 million.

How should Picant account for this $1.5 million adjustment in its financial statements as at 31 March 20X1?

A   Debit current liabilities/Credit goodwill
B   Debit retained earnings/Credit current liabilities
C   Debit goodwill/Credit current liabilities
D   Debit current liabilities/Credit retained earnings   (2 marks)

97   Crash acquired 70% of Bang's 100,000 $1 ordinary shares for $800,000 when the retained earnings of Bang were $570,000 and the balance in its revaluation surplus was $150,000. Bang also has an internally-developed customer list which has been independently valued at $90,000. The non-controlling interest in Bang was judged to have a fair value of $220,000 at the date of acquisition.

What was the goodwill arising on acquisition?

A $200,000
B $163,000
C $226,000
D $110,000   (2 marks)

98   Phantom acquired 70% of the $100,000 equity share capital of Ghost, its only subsidiary, for $200,000 on 1 January 20X9 when the retained earnings of Ghost were $156,000.

At 31 December 20X9 retained earnings are as follows.

	$
Phantom	275,000
Ghost	177,000

Phantom considers that goodwill on acquisition is impaired by 50%. Non-controlling interest is measured at fair value, estimated at $82,800.

What are group retained earnings at 31 December 20X9?

A $276,300
B $289,700
C $280,320
D $269,200   (2 marks)

99   Tazer, a parent company, acquired Lowdown, an unincorporated entity, for $2.8 million. A fair value exercise performed on Lowdown's net assets at the date of purchase showed:

	$'000
Property, plant and equipment	3,000
Identifiable intangible asset	500
Inventory	300
Trade receivables less payables	200
	4,000

How should the purchase of Lowdown be reflected in Tazer's consolidated statement of financial position?

A   Record the net assets at their values shown above and credit profit or loss with $1.2 million
B   Record the net assets at their values shown above and credit Tazer's consolidated goodwill with $1.2 million
C   Write off the intangible asset ($500,000), record the remaining net assets at their values shown above and credit profit or loss with $700,000
D   Record the purchase as a financial asset investment at $2.8 million   (2 marks)

(8 marks)

Section B

Root and Branch CBE style OTQ case

19 mins

Information relevant to questions 100-104

On 1 April 20X7 Root acquired 116 million of Branch's 145 million ordinary shares for an immediate cash payment of $210 million and issued at par one 10% $100 loan note for every 200 shares acquired.

At the date of acquisition Branch owned a recently built property that was carried at its depreciated construction cost of $62 million. The fair value of this property at the date of acquisition was $82 million and it had an estimated remaining life of 20 years.

Branch also had an internally-developed brand which was valued at the acquisition date at $25 million with a remaining life of 10 years.

The inventory of Branch at 31 March 20X9 includes goods supplied by Root for a sale price of $56 million. Root adds a mark-up of 40% on cost to all sales.

100   What is the total amount of the consideration transferred by Root to acquire the investment in Branch?

$ ☐ million

101   What will be the amount of the adjustment to group retained earnings at 31 March 20X9 in respect of the movement on the fair value adjustments?

☐ $7 million

☐ $3.5 million

☐ $5.6 million

☐ $2.8 million

102   What is the amount of the unrealised profit arising from intragroup trading?

$ ☐ million

103   How should the unrealised profit be posted?

☐ DR Cost of sales / CR Inventories

☐ DR Cost of sales / DR Non-controlling interest / CR Inventories

☐ DR Inventories / CR Cost of sales

☐ DR Inventories / CR Non-controlling interest / CR Cost of sales

104   Branch has recently lost some large contracts and the directors of Root are wondering if Branch can be excluded from consolidation next year.

Which one of the following situations would allow a subsidiary to be excluded from consolidation?

☐ The activities of the subsidiary are significantly different to the activities of the rest of the group.

☐ Control of the subsidiary has been lost.

☐ Control of the subsidiary is only intended to be temporary.

☐ The subsidiary operates under long-term restrictions which prevent it from transferring funds to the parent.

(10 marks)

Section C

105 Pedantic (12/08 amended)   39 mins

On 1 April 20X8, Pedantic acquired 60% of the equity share capital of Sophistic in a share exchange of two shares in Pedantic for three shares in Sophistic. At that date the retained earnings of Sophistic were $5 million. The issue of shares has not yet been recorded by Pedantic. At the date of acquisition shares in Pedantic had a market value of $6 each. Below are the summarised draft statements of financial position of both companies.

STATEMENTS OF FINANCIAL POSITION AS AT 30 SEPTEMBER 20X8

	Pedantic $'000	Sophistic $'000
Assets		
Non-current assets		
Property, plant and equipment	40,600	12,600
Current assets	16,000	6,600
Total assets	56,600	19,200
Equity and liabilities		
Equity shares of $1 each	10,000	4,000
Retained earnings	35,400	6,500
	45,400	10,500
Non-current liabilities		
10% loan notes	3,000	4,000
Current liabilities	8,200	4,700
Total equity and liabilities	56,600	19,200

The following information is relevant.

(i)   At the date of acquisition, the fair values of Sophistic's assets were equal to their carrying amounts with the exception of an item of plant, which had a fair value of $2 million in excess of its carrying amount. It had a remaining life of five years at that date (straight-line depreciation is used). Sophistic has not adjusted the carrying amount of its plant as a result of the fair value exercise.

(ii)   Sales from Sophistic to Pedantic in the post acquisition period were $8 million. Sophistic made a mark up on cost of 40% on these sales. Pedantic had sold $5.2 million (at cost to Pedantic) of these goods by 30 September 20X8.

(iii)   Sophistic's trade receivables at 30 September 20X8 include $600,000 due from Pedantic which did not agree with Pedantic's corresponding trade payable. This was due to cash in transit of $200,000 from Pedantic to Sophistic. Both companies have positive bank balances.

(iv)   Pedantic has a policy of accounting for any non-controlling interest at full fair value. The fair value of the non-controlling interest in Sophistic at the date of acquisition was estimated to be $5.9 million. Consolidated goodwill was not impaired at 30 September 20X8.

Required

(a)   Prepare the consolidated statement of financial position for Pedantic as at 30 September 20X8.   **(16 marks)**

(b)   Pedantic has been approached by a potential new customer, Trilby, to supply it with a substantial quantity of goods on three months credit terms. Pedantic is concerned at the risk that such a large order represents in the current difficult economic climate, especially as Pedantic's normal credit terms are only one month's credit. To support its application for credit, Trilby has sent Pedantic a copy of Tradhat's most recent audited consolidated financial statements. Trilby is a wholly-owned subsidiary within the Tradhat group. Tradhat's consolidated financial statements show a strong statement of financial position including healthy liquidity ratios.

Comment on the importance that Pedantic should attach to Tradhat's consolidated financial statements when deciding on whether to grant credit terms to Trilby.   **(4 marks)**

(20 marks)

106 Highveldt

Highveldt, a public listed company, acquired 75% of Samson's ordinary shares on 1 April 20X4. Highveldt paid an immediate $3·50 per share in cash and agreed to pay a further amount of $108 million on 1 April 20X5. Highveldt's cost of capital is 8% per annum. Highveldt has only recorded the cash consideration of $3·50 per share.

The summarised statements of financial position of the two companies at 31 March 20X5 are shown below:

	Highveldt		Samson	
	$m	$m	$m	$m
Property, plant and equipment (note (i))		420		320
Development costs (note (iv))		nil		40
Investments (note (ii))		300		20
		720		380
Current assets		133		91
Total assets		853		471
Equity and liabilities				
Ordinary shares of $1 each		270		80
Reserves:				
Share premium		80		40
Revaluation surplus		45		nil
Retained earnings – 1 April 20X4	160		134	
– year to 31 March 20X5	190		76	
		350		210
		745		330
Non-current liabilities				
10% intragroup loan (note (ii))		nil		60
Current liabilities		108		81
Total equity and liabilities		853		471

The following information is relevant:

(i) Highveldt has a policy of revaluing land and buildings to fair value. At the date of acquisition Samson's land and buildings had a fair value $20 million higher than their carrying amount and at 31 March 20X5 this had increased by a further $4 million (ignore any additional depreciation).

(ii) Included in Highveldt's investments is a loan of $60 million made to Samson at the date of acquisition. Interest is payable annually in arrears. Samson paid the interest due for the year on 31 March 20X5, but Highveldt did not receive this until after the year end. Highveldt has not accounted for the accrued interest from Samson.

(iii) Samson had established a line of products under the brand name of Titanware. Acting on behalf of Highveldt, a firm of specialists, had valued the brand name at a value of $40 million with an estimated life of 10 years as at 1 April 20X4. The brand is not included in Samson's statement of financial position.

(iv) Samson's development project was completed on 30 September 20X4 at a cost of $50 million. $10 million of this had been amortised by 31 March 20X5. Development costs capitalised by Samson at the date of acquisition were $18 million. Highveldt's directors are of the opinion that Samson's development costs do not meet the criteria in IAS 38 *Intangible assets* for recognition as an asset.

(v) Samson sold goods to Highveldt during the year at a profit of $6 million, one-third of these goods were still in the inventory of Highveldt at 31 March 20X5.

(vi) An impairment test at 31 March 20X5 on the consolidated goodwill concluded that it should be written down by $20 million. No other assets were impaired.

(vii) It is the group policy to measure non-controlling interest fair value. The fair value of the non-controlling interest in Samson at the acquisition date was $83 million.

Required

Calculate the following figures as they would appear in the consolidated statement of financial position of Highveldt at 31 March 20X5:

(i)	Goodwill	**(8 marks)**
(ii)	Non-controlling interest	**(4 marks)**
(iii)	The following consolidated reserves:	
	share premium, revaluation surplus and retained earnings.	**(8 marks)**

(20 marks)

MCQ bank – consolidated statement of profit or loss and other comprehensive income

107   Hillusion acquired 80% of Skeptik on 1 July 20X2. In the post-acquisition period Hillusion sold goods to Skeptik at a price of $12 million. These goods had cost Hillusion $9 million. During the year to 31 March 20X3 Skeptik had sold $10 million (at cost to Skeptik) of these goods for $15m million.

How will this affect group cost of sales in the consolidated statement of profit or loss of Hillusion for the year ended 31 March 20X3?

A   Increase by $11.5 million
B   Increase by $9.6 million
C   Decrease by $11.5 million
D   Decrease by $9.6 million   **(2 marks)**

108   On 1 July 20X7, Spider acquired 60% of the equity share capital of Fly and on that date made a $10 million loan to Fly at a rate of 8% per annum.

What will be the effect on group retained earnings at the year end date of 31 December 20X7 when this intragroup transaction is cancelled?

A   Group retained earnings will increase by $400,000.
B   Group retained earnings will be reduced by $240,000.
C   Group retained earnings will be reduced by $160,000.
D   There will be no effect on group retained earnings.   **(2 marks)**

109   Wiley acquired 80% of Coyote on 1 January 20X8. At the date of acquisition Coyote had a building which had a fair value $22 million and a carrying amount of $20 million. The remaining useful life was 20 years. At the year end date of 30 June 20X8 the fair value of the building was $23 million.

Coyote's profit for the year to 30 June 20X8 was $1.6 million which accrued evenly throughout the year.

Wiley measures non-controlling interest at fair value. At 30 June 20X8 it estimated that goodwill in Coyote was impaired by $500,000.

What is the total comprehensive income attributable to the non-controlling interest at 30 June 20X8?

A $250,000
B $260,000
C $360,000
D $400,000   **(2 marks)**

(6 marks)

CBE style OTQ bank – consolidated statement of profit or loss and other comprehensive income

110 Basil acquired 60% of Parsley on 1 March 20X9. In September 20X9 Basil sold $46,000 worth of goods to Parsley. Basil applies a 30% mark-up to all its sales. 25% of these goods were still held in inventory by Parsley at the end of the year.

An extract from the draft statements of profit or loss of Basil and Parsley at 31 December 20X9 is:

	Basil	Parsley
	$	$
Revenue	955,000	421,500
Cost of sales	(407,300)	(214,600)
Gross profit	547,700	206,900

All revenue and costs arise evenly throughout the year.

What will be shown as gross profit in the consolidated statement of profit or loss of Basil for the year ended 31 December 20X9?

$ ⬚

(2 marks)

111 Premier acquired 80% of Sanford on 1 June 20X1. Sales from Sanford to Premier throughout the year ended 30 September 20X1 were consistently $1 million per month. Sanford made a mark-up on cost of 25% on these sales. At 30 September 20X1 Premier was holding $2 million inventory that had been supplied by Sanford in the post-acquisition period.

By how much will the unrealised profit decrease the profit attributable to the non-controlling interest for the year ended 30 September 20X1?

$ ⬚

(2 marks)

112 Brigham has owned 70% of Dorset for many years. It also holds a $5 million 8% loan note from Dorset. One of Dorset's non-current assets has suffered an impairment of $50,000 during the year. There is a balance in the revaluation surplus of Dorset of $30,000 in respect of this asset. The impairment loss has not yet been recorded.

The entity financial statements of Dorset show a profit for the year of $1.3 million.

What is the amount attributable to the non-controlling interests in the consolidated statement of profit or loss?

$ ⬚

(2 marks)

113 On 1 January 20X3 Westbridge acquired all of Brookfield's 100,000 $1 shares for $300,000. The goodwill acquired in the business combination was $40,000, of which 50% had been written off as impaired by 31 December 20X5. On 31 December 20X5 Westbridge sold all of Brookfield's shares for $450,000 when Brookfield had retained earnings of $185,000.

What is the profit on disposal that should be included in the **consolidated** financial statements of Westbridge?

$ ⬚

(2 marks)

114   On 1 January 20X3 Westbridge acquired all of Brookfield's 100,000 $1 shares for $300,000. The goodwill acquired in the business combination was $40,000, of which 50% had been written off as impaired by 31 December 20X5. On 31 December 20X5 Westbridge sold all of Brookfield's shares for $450,000 when Brookfield had retained earnings of $185,000.

What is the profit on disposal that should be included in the **individual entity** financial statements of Westbridge?

$ [   ]   **(2 marks)**

---

115   Company A acquired a 70% holding in Company B on 1 January 20X4 for $600,000. At that date the fair value of the net assets of Company B was $700,000. Company A measures non-controlling interest at its share of net assets.

On 31 December 20X6 Company A sold all its shares in Company B for $950,000. At that date the fair value of Company B's net assets was $850,000. Goodwill was not impaired.

What was the profit or loss on disposal to be recognised in the consolidated financial statements of Company A?

$ [   ] profit / loss   **(2 marks)**

                                                                                                 (12 marks)

Section B

Port and Alfred OTQ case

Information relevant to questions 116-120

On 1 November 20X4 Port purchased 75% of the equity of Alfred for $650,000. The consideration was 35,000 $1 equity shares in Port with a fair value of $650,000.

Noted below are extracts from the draft statements of profit or loss for Port and its subsidiary Alfred for the year ending 31 December 20X4 along with the draft statements of financial position as at 31 December 20X4.

The profits of Alfred have been earned evenly throughout the year.

STATEMENTS OF PROFIT OR LOSS FOR THE YEAR ENDING 31 DECEMBER 20X4 (extract)

	Port	Alfred
	$'000	$'000
Gross profit	364	240
Profit for the year	330	96

STATEMENTS OF FINANCIAL POSITION AS AT 31 DECEMBER 20X4 (extracts)

	Port	Alfred
Equity		
$1 Equity shares	200	100
Share premium	500	85
Retained earnings	2,900	331
Revaluation surplus	30	–
	3,630	516

Port has not accounted for the issue of its own shares or for the acquisition of the investment in Alfred.

116   What amounts should appear as share capital and share premium in the consolidated statement of financial position as at 31 December 20X4?

	Share capital	Share premium
	$	$
☐	335,000	1,115,000
☐	235,000	585,000
☐	235,000	1,115,000
☐	335,000	585,000

117   What are the net assets of Alfred at acquisition?

☐ $420,000

☐ $500,000

☐ $516,000

☐ $596,000

118   The accountant of Port is finalising the consolidated financial statements. Which TWO of the following statements are true regarding consolidated financial statements?

☐ The non-controlling interest share of profit is part of the consolidated statement of profit or loss.

☐ Goodwill on acquisition should be amortised over a period not exceeding 20 years.

☐ If a subsidiary is acquired during the year, its results are apportioned over the year of acquisition.

☐ Only the group share of the subsidiary's non-current assets is shown in the statement of financial position.

119 What is the amount of group gross profit for the year ended 31 December 20X4?

$ [   ]

120 What is group retained earnings at 31 December 20X4?

☐ $2,912,000
☐ $2,916,000
☐ $2,972,000
☐ $2,996,000

(10 marks)

Section C

121 Viagem (12/12 amended)

39 mins

On 1 January 20X2, Viagem acquired 90% of the equity share capital of Greca in a share exchange in which Viagem issued two new shares for every three shares it acquired in Greca. Additionally, on 31 December 20X2, Viagem will pay the shareholders of Greca $1.76 per share acquired. Viagem's cost of capital is 10% per annum.

At the date of acquisition, shares in Viagem and Greca had a stock market value of $6.50 and $2.50 each respectively.

STATEMENTS OF PROFIT OR LOSS FOR THE YEAR ENDED 30 SEPTEMBER 20X2

	Viagem	Greca
	$'000	$'000
Revenue	64,600	38,000
Cost of sales	(51,200)	(26,000)
Gross profit	13,400	12,000
Distribution costs	(1,600)	(1,800)
Administrative expenses	(3,800)	(2,400)
Investment income	500	–
Finance costs	(420)	–
Profit before tax	8,080	7,800
Income tax expense	(2,800)	(1,600)
Profit for the year	5,280	6,200
Equity as at 1 October 20X1		
Equity shares of $1 each	30,000	10,000
Retained earnings	54,000	35,000

The following information is relevant:

(i) At the date of acquisition the fair values of Greca's assets were equal to their carrying amounts with the exception of two items:

   1 An item of plant had a fair value of $1.8 million above its carrying amount. The remaining life of the plant at the date of acquisition was three years. Depreciation is charged to cost of sales.

   2 Greca had a contingent liability which Viagem estimated to have a fair value of $450,000. This has not changed as at 30 September 20X2.

   Greca has not incorporated these fair value changes into its financial statements.

(ii) Viagem's policy is to value the non-controlling interest at fair value at the date of acquisition. For this purpose, Greca's share price at that date can be deemed to be representative of the fair value of the shares held by the non-controlling interest.

(iii) Sales from Viagem to Greca throughout the year ended 30 September 20X2 had consistently been $800,000 per month. Viagem made a mark-up on cost of 25% on these sales. Greca had $1.5 million of these goods in inventory as at 30 September 20X2.

(iv) Viagem's investment income is a dividend received from its investment in a 40% owned associate which it has held for several years. The underlying earnings for the associate for the year ended 30 September 20X2 were $2 million.

(v) Although Greca has been profitable since its acquisition by Viagem, the market for Greca's products has been badly hit in recent months and Viagem has calculated that the goodwill has been impaired by $2 million as at 30 September 20X2.

Required

(a) Calculate the goodwill arising on the acquisition of Greca **(6 marks)**

(b) Prepare the consolidated statement of profit or loss for Viagem for the year ended 30 September 20X2.

(14 marks)

(20 marks)

122 Prodigal (6/11 amended)

On 1 October 20X0 Prodigal purchased 75% of the equity shares in Sentinel. The acquisition was through a share exchange of two shares in Prodigal for every three shares in Sentinel. The stock market price of Prodigal's shares at 1 October 20X0 was $4 per share. The summarised statements of profit or loss and other comprehensive income for the two companies for the year ended 31 March 20X1 are:

	Prodigal	Sentinel
	$'000	$'000
Revenue	450,000	240,000
Cost of sales	(260,000)	(110,000)
Gross profit	190,000	130,000
Distribution costs	(23,600)	(12,000)
Administrative expenses	(27,000)	(23,000)
Finance costs	(1,500)	(1,200)
Profit before tax	137,900	93,800
Income tax expense	(48,000)	(27,800)
Profit for the year	89,900	66,000
Other comprehensive income		
Gain on revaluation of land (note(i))	2,500	1,000
Loss on fair value of investment in equity instrument	(700)	(400)
	1,800	600
Total comprehensive income for the year	91,700	66,600

The equity of Sentinel at 1 April 20X0 was:

	$'000
Equity shares of $1 each	160,000
Other equity reserve (re investment in equity instrument)	2,200
Retained earnings	125,000

The following information is relevant:

(i)   Prodigal's policy is to revalue the group's land to market value at the end of each accounting period. Prior to its acquisition, Sentinel's land had been valued at historical cost. During the post-acquisition period Sentinel's land had increased in value over its value at the date of acquisition by $1 million. Sentinel has recognised the revaluation within its own financial statements.

(ii)   Immediately after the acquisition of Sentinel on 1 October 20X0, Prodigal transferred an item of plant with a carrying amount of $4 million to Sentinel at an agreed value of $5 million. At this date the plant had a remaining life of two and half years. Prodigal had included the profit on this transfer as a reduction in its depreciation costs. All depreciation is charged to cost of sales.

(iii)   After the acquisition Sentinel sold goods to Prodigal for $40 million. These goods had cost Sentinel $30 million. $12 million of the goods sold remained in Prodigal's closing inventory.

(iv)   Prodigal's policy is to value the non-controlling interest of Sentinel at the date of acquisition at its fair value which the directors determined to be $100 million.

(v)   The goodwill of Sentinel has not suffered any impairment.

(vi)   All items in the above statements of profit or loss and other comprehensive income are deemed to accrue evenly over the year unless otherwise indicated.

Required

(a)   Calculate the goodwill on acquisition of Sentinel.   **(4 marks)**

(b)   Prepare the consolidated statement of profit or loss and other comprehensive income of Prodigal for the year ended 31 March 20X1.   **(16 marks)**

                                                                                                        (20 marks)

123 Plastik (12/14 amended)

39 mins

On 1 January 20X4, Plastik acquired 80% of the equity share capital of Subtrak. The consideration was satisfied by a share exchange of two shares in Plastik for every three acquired shares in Subtrak. At the date of acquisition, shares in Plastik and Subtrak had a market value of $3 and $2.50 each respectively. Plastik will also pay cash consideration of 27.5 cents on 1 January 20X5 for each acquired share in Subtrak. Plastik has a cost of capital of 10% per annum. None of the consideration has been recorded by Plastik.

Below are the summarised draft financial statements of both companies.

STATEMENTS OF PROFIT OR LOSS AND OTHER COMPREHENSIVE INCOME FOR THE YEAR ENDED 30 SEPTEMBER 20X4

	Plastik	Subtrak
	$'000	$'000
Revenue	62,600	30,000
Cost of sales	(45,800)	(24,000)
Gross profit	16,800	6,000
Distribution costs	(2,000)	(1,200)
Administrative expenses	(3,500)	(1,800)
Finance costs	(200)	–
Profit before tax	11,100	3,000
Income tax expense	(3,100)	(1,000)
Profit for the year	8,000	2,000
Other comprehensive income:		
Gain on revaluation of property	1,500	–
Total comprehensive income	9,500	2,000

STATEMENTS OF FINANCIAL POSITION AS AT 30 SEPTEMBER 20X4

	Plastik	Subtrak
	$'000	$'000
ASSETS		
Non-current assets		
Property, plant and equipment	18,700	13,900
Current assets		
Inventory (note(ii))	4,300	1,200
Trade receivables	5,700	2,500
Bank	-	300
	10,000	4,000
Total assets	28,700	17,900
EQUITY AND LIABILITIES		
Equity		
Equity shares of $1 each	10,000	9,000
Revaluation surplus (note(i))	2,000	-
Retained earnings	6,300	3,500
	18,300	12,500
Non-current liabilities		
10% loan notes (note(ii))	2,500	1,000
Current liabilities		
Trade payables (note(iv))	3,400	3,600
Bank	1,700	-
Current tax payable	2,800	800
	7,900	4,400
Total equity and liabilities	28,700	17,900

The following information is relevant:

(i) At the date of acquisition, the fair values of Subtrak's assets and liabilities were equal to their carrying amounts with the exception of Subtrak's property which had a fair value of $4 million above its carrying amount. For consolidation purposes, this led to an increase in depreciation charges (in cost of sales) of $100,000 in the post-acquisition period to 30 September 20X4. Subtrak has not incorporated the fair value property increase into its entity financial statements.

The policy of the Plastik group is to revalue all properties to fair value at each year end. On 30 September 20X4, the increase in Plastik's property has already been recorded, however, a further increase of $600,000 in the value of Subtrak's property since its value at acquisition and 30 September 20X4 has not been recorded.

(ii) Sales from Plastik to Subtrak throughout the year ended 30 September 20X4 had consistently been $300,000 per month. Plastik made a mark-up on cost of 25% on all these sales. $600,000 (at cost to Subtrak) of Subtrak's inventory at 30 September 20X4 had been supplied by Plastik in the post-acquisition period.

(iii) Plastik's policy is to value the non-controlling interest at fair value at the date of acquisition. For this purpose Subtrak's share price at that date can be deemed to be representative of the fair value of the shares held by the non-controlling interest.

(iv) Due to recent adverse publicity concerning one of Subtrak's major product lines, the goodwill which arose on the acquisition of Subtrak has been impaired by $500,000 as at 30 September 20X4. Goodwill impairment should be treated as an administrative expense.

(v) Assume, except where indicated otherwise, that all items of income and expenditure accrue evenly throughout the year.

Required

(a) Calculate the goodwill arising on the acquisition of Subtrak on 1 January 20X4. **(4 marks)**

(b) Calculate the following amounts for presentation in the consolidated statement of financial position:

(i) Group retained earnings
(ii) Non-controlling interest **(6 marks)**

(c) Prepare the consolidated statement of profit or loss and other comprehensive income for Plastik for the year ended 30 September 20X4. **(10 marks)**

(20 marks)

MCQ bank – accounting for associates

124 On 1 October 20X8 Pacemaker acquired 30 million of Vardine's 100 million shares in exchange for 75 million of its own shares. The stock market value of Pacemaker's shares at the date of this share exchange was $1.60 each.

Vardine's profit is subject to seasonal variation. Its profit for the year ended 31 March 20X9 was $100 million. $20 million of this profit was made from 1 April 20X8 to 30 September 20X8.

Pacemaker has one subsidiary and no other investments apart from Vardine.

What amount will be shown as 'investment in associate' in the consolidated statement of financial position of Pacemaker as at 31 March 20X9?

A $144 million
B $150 million
C $78 million
D $126 million **(2 marks)**

How should an associate be accounted for in the consolidated statement of profit or loss?

    A   The associate's income and expenses are added to those of the group on a line-by-line basis.

    B   The group share of the associate's income and expenses is added to the group figures on a line-by-line basis.

    C   The group share of the associate's profit after tax is recorded as a one-line entry.

    D   Only dividends received from the associate are recorded in the group statement of profit or loss.

(2 marks)

---

126   Jarvis owns 30% of McLintock. During the year to 31 December 20X4 McLintock sold $2 million of goods to Jarvis, of which 40% were still held in inventory by Jarvis at the year end. McLintock applies a mark-up of 25% on all goods sold.

What effect would the above transactions have on group inventory at 31 December 20X4?

    A   Debit group inventory $48,000
    B   Debit group inventory $160,000
    C   Credit group inventory $48,000
    D   No effect on group inventory

(2 marks)

(6 marks)

CBE style OTQ bank – accounting for associates

127   Wellington owns 30% of Boot, which it purchased on 1 May 20X7 for $2.5 million. At that date Boot had retained earnings of $5.3 million. At the year end date of 31 October 20X7 Boot had retained earnings of $6.4 million after paying out a dividend of $1 million. On 30 September 20X7 Wellington sold $700,000 of goods to Boot, on which it made 30% profit. Boot had resold none of these goods by 31 October.

At what amount will Wellington record its investment in Boot in its consolidated statement of financial position at 31 October 20X7?

$ [   ]

(2 marks)

---

128   On 1 February 20X1 Picardy acquired 35% of the equity shares of Avignon, its only associate, for $10 million in cash. The post-tax profit of Avignon for the year to 30 September 20X1 was $3 million. Profits accrued evenly throughout the year. Avignon made a dividend payment of $1 million on 1 September 20X1. At 30 September 20X1 Picardy decided that an impairment loss of $500,000 should be recognised on its investment in Avignon.

What amount will be shown as 'investment in associate' in the statement of financial position of Picardy as at 30 September 20X1?

$ [   ]

(2 marks)

---

129   An associate is an entity in which an investor has significant influence over the investee.

Which **TWO** of the following indicate the presence of significant influence?

    ☐   The investor owns 330,000 of the 1,500,000 equity voting shares of the investee.

    ☐   The investor has representation on the board of directors of the investee.

    ☐   The investor is able to insist that all of the sales of the investee are made to a subsidiary of the investor.

    ☐   The investor controls the votes of a majority of the board members.

(2 marks)

130 Ruby owns 30% of Emerald and exercises significant influence over it. Emerald sold goods to Ruby for $160,000. Emerald applies a one third mark up on cost. Ruby still had 25% of these goods in inventory at the year end.

What amount should be deducted from consolidated retained earnings in respect of this transaction?

$ [   ]

(2 marks)

(8 marks)

Section B

Plateau MCQ case

19 mins

The following information relates to questions 131-135

On 1 October 20X6 Plateau acquired the following non-current investments:

- 3 million equity shares in Savannah by an exchange of one share in Plateau for every two shares in Savannah plus $1.25 per acquired Savannah share in cash. The market price of each Plateau share at the date of acquisition was $6 and the market price of each Savannah share at the date of acquisition was $3.25.

- 30% of the equity shares of Axle at a cost of $7.50 per share in cash.

Only the cash consideration of the above investments has been recorded by Plateau.

Extracts from the summarised draft statements of financial position of the three companies at 30 September 20X7 are:

	Plateau $'000	Savannah $'000	Axle $'000
Equity shares of $1 each	10,000	4,000	4,000
Retained earnings			
– at 30 September 20X6	16,000	6,000	11,000
– for year ended 30 September 20X7	9,250	2,900	5,000
	35,250	12,900	20,000

The following information is relevant.

(i) At the date of acquisition Savannah had five years remaining of an agreement to supply goods to one of its major customers. The agreement has been consistently renewed when it expires. The directors of Plateau estimate that the value of this customer based contract has a fair value of £1 million and an indefinite life and has not suffered any impairment.

(ii) On 1 October 20X6, Plateau sold an item of plant to Savannah at its agreed fair value of $2.5 million. Its carrying amount prior to the sale was $2 million. The estimated remaining life of the plant at the date of sale was five years (straight-line depreciation).

(iii) During the year ended 30 September 20X7 Savannah sold goods to Plateau for $2.7 million. Savannah had marked up these goods by 50% on cost. Plateau had a third of the goods still in its inventory at 30 September 20X7. There were no intra-group payables/receivables at 30 September 20X7.

(iv) It is the group policy to value non-controlling interest at acquisition at full (or fair) value. For this purpose the share price of Savannah at the acquisition date should be used.

131 What is the total of the consideration paid by Plateau for Savannah?

A $3,750,000
B $9,750,000
C $12,750,000
D $21,750,000

132   How should the customer contract in note (i) be accounted for?

    A   Should not be recognised as item is internally-generated

    B   Group share of 75% should be recognised and not amortised

    C   Should be recognised at $1 million and not amortised

    D   Should be recognised at $1 million and amortised over five years

---

133   What amount will be shown as non-controlling interest in the consolidated statement of financial position at 30 September 20X7?

    A $3,900,000

    B $3,250,000

    C $3,225,000

    D $3,975,000

---

134   What is the correct journal to post the unrealised profit on the transfer of plant in note (ii)?

    A   DR Group retained earnings $0.3m DR Non-controlling interest $0.1m
           CR Property, plant and equipment $0.4m

    B   DR Group retained earnings $0.4m
           CR Property, plant and equipment $0.4m

    C   DR Property, plant and equipment $0.4m
           CR Group retained earnings $0.4m

    D   DR Property, plant and equipment $0.4m
           CR Group retained earnings $0.3m CR Non-controlling interest $0.1m

---

135   What amount will be shown in the consolidated statement of financial position at 30 September 20X7 in respect of the investment in Axle?

    A $9,000,000

    B $10,500,000

    C $14,000,000

    D $30,000,000

(10 marks)

136 Laurel   39 mins

Laurel acquired 80% of the ordinary share capital of Hardy for $160m and 40% of the ordinary share capital of Comic for $70m on 1 January 20X7 when the retained earnings balances were $64m in Hardy and $24m in Comic. Laurel, Comic and Hardy are public limited companies.

The statements of financial position of the three companies at 31 December 20X9 are set out below:

	Laurel	Hardy	Comic
	$m	$m	$m
Non-current assets			
Property, plant and equipment	220	160	78
Investments	230	-	-
	450	160	78
Current assets			
Inventories	384	234	122
Trade receivables	275	166	67
Cash at bank	42	10	34
	701	410	223
	1,151	570	301
Equity			
Share capital – $1 ordinary shares	400	96	80
Share premium	16	3	-
Retained earnings	278	128	97
	694	227	177
Current liabilities			
Trade payables	457	343	124
	1,151	570	301

You are also given the following information:

1   On 30 November 20X9 Laurel sold some goods to Hardy for cash for $32m. These goods had originally cost $22m and none had been sold by the year end. On the same date Laurel also sold goods to Comic for cash for $22m. These goods originally cost $10m and Comic had sold half by the year end.

2   On 1 January 20X7 Hardy owned some items of equipment with a book value of $45m that had a fair value of $57m. These assets were originally purchased by Hardy on 1 January 20X5 and are being depreciated over 6 years.

3   Group policy is to measure non-controlling interests at acquisition at fair value. The fair value of the non-controlling interests in Hardy on 1 January 20X7 was calculated as $39m.

4   Cumulative impairment losses on recognised goodwill amounted to $15m at 31 December 20X9. No impairment losses have been necessary to date relating to the investment in the associate.

Required

Prepare a consolidated statement of financial position for Laurel and its subsidiary as at 31 December 20X9, incorporating its associate in accordance with IAS 28.

(20 marks)

137 Tyson

Below are the statements of profit or loss and other comprehensive income of Tyson, its subsidiary Douglas and associate Frank at 31 December 20X8. Tyson, Douglas and Frank are public limited companies.

	Tyson $m	Douglas $m	Frank $m
Revenue	500	150	70
Cost of sales	(270)	(80)	(30)
Gross profit	230	70	40
Other expenses	(150)	(20)	(15)
Finance income	15	10	–
Finance costs	(20)	–	(10)
Profit before tax	75	60	15
Income tax expense	(25)	(15)	(5)
PROFIT FOR THE YEAR	50	45	10
Other comprehensive income:			
Gains on property revaluation, net of tax	20	10	5
TOTAL COMPREHENSIVE INCOME FOR THE YEAR	70	55	15

You are also given the following information:

1   Tyson acquired 80m shares in Douglas for $188m three years ago when Douglas had a credit balance on its reserves of $40m. Douglas has 100m $1 ordinary shares.

2   Tyson acquired 40m shares in Frank for $60m two years ago when that company had a credit balance on its reserves of $20m. Frank has 100m $1 ordinary shares.

3   During the year Douglas sold some goods to Tyson for $66m (cost $48m). None of the goods had been sold by the year end.

4   Group policy is to measure non-controlling interests at acquisition at fair value. The fair value of the non-controlling interests in Douglas at acquisition was $40m. An impairment test carried out at the year end resulted in $15m of the recognised goodwill relating to Douglas being written off and recognition of impairment losses of $2.4m relating to the investment in Frank.

Required

Prepare the consolidated statement of profit or loss and other comprehensive income for the year ended 31 December 20X8 for Tyson, incorporating its associate.

(20 marks)

138 Paladin (12/11 amended)

On 1 October 20X0, Paladin secured a majority equity shareholding in Saracen on the following terms.

An immediate payment of $4 per share on 1 October 20X0; and a further amount deferred until 1 October 20X1 of $5.4 million.

The immediate payment has been recorded in Paladin's financial statements, but the deferred payment has not been recorded. Paladin's cost of capital is 8% per annum, giving the deferred payment a current cost at 1 October 20X0 of $5 million.

On 1 February 20X1, Paladin also acquired 25% of the equity shares of Augusta paying $10 million in cash.

The summarised statements of financial position of the three companies at 30 September 20X1 are:

	Paladin $'000	Saracen $'000	Augusta $'000
Assets			
Non-current assets			
Property, plant and equipment	40,000	31,000	30,000
Intangible assets	7,500		
Investments – Saracen (8 million shares at $4 each)	32,000		
– Augusta	10,000	nil	nil
	89,500	31,000	30,000
Current assets			
Inventory	11,200	8,400	10,000
Trade receivables	7,400	5,300	5,000
Bank	3,400	nil	2,000
Total assets	111,500	44,700	47,000
Equity and liabilities			
Equity			
Equity shares of $1 each	50,000	10,000	10,000
Retained earnings – at 1 October 20X0	25,700	12,000	31,800
– for year ended 30 September 20X1	9,200	6,000	1,200
	84,900	28,000	43,000
Non-current liabilities			
Deferred tax	15,000	8,000	1,000
Current liabilities			
Bank	nil	2,500	nil
Trade payables	11,600	6,200	3,000
Total equity and liabilities	111,500	44,700	47,000

The following information is relevant:

(i) Paladin's policy is to value the non-controlling interest at fair value at the date of acquisition. The directors of Paladin considered the fair value of the non-controlling interest in Saracen to be $7 million.

(ii) At the date of acquisition, the fair values of Saracen's property, plant and equipment was equal to its carrying amount with the exception of Saracen's plant which had a fair value of $4 million above its carrying amount. At that date the plant had a remaining life of four years. Saracen uses straight-line depreciation for plant assuming a nil residual value.

Also at the date of acquisition, Paladin valued Saracen's customer relationships as a customer base intangible asset at fair value of $3 million. Saracen has not accounted for this asset. Trading relationships with Saracen's customers last on average for six years.

(iii) At 30 September 20X1, Saracen's inventory included goods bought from Paladin (at cost to Saracen) of $2.6 million. Paladin had marked up these goods by 30% on cost. Paladin's agreed current account balance owed by Saracen at 30 September 20X1 was $1.3 million.

(iv) Impairment tests were carried out on 30 September 20X1 which concluded that consolidated goodwill was not impaired, but, due to disappointing earnings, the value of the investment in Augusta was impaired by $2.5 million.

(v) Assume all profits accrue evenly through the year.

Required

Prepare the consolidated statement of financial position for Paladin as at 30 September 20X1.   **(20 marks)**

MCQ bank – financial instruments

139   An 8% $30 million convertible loan note was issued on 1 April 20X5 at par. Interest is payable in arrears on 31 March each year. The loan note is redeemable at par on 31 March 20X8 or convertible into equity shares at the option of the loan note holders on the basis of 30 shares for each $100 of loan. A similar instrument without the conversion option would have an interest rate of 10% per annum.

The present values of $1 receivable at the end of each year based on discount rates of 8% and 10% are:

		8%	10%
End of year	1	0.93	0.91
	2	0.86	0.83
	3	0.79	0.75
	Cumulative	2.58	2.49

What amount will be credited to equity on 1 April 20X5 in respect of this financial instrument?

    A $5,976,000
    B $1,524,000
    C $324,000
    D $9,000,000   **(2 marks)**

---

140   A 5% loan note was issued on 1 April 20X0 at its face value of $20 million. Direct costs of the issue were $500,000. The loan note will be redeemed on 31 March 20X3 at a substantial premium. The effective interest rate applicable is 10% per annum.

At what amount will the loan note appear in the statement of financial position as at 31 March 20X2?

    A $21,000,000
    B $20,450,000
    C $22,100,000
    D $21,495,000   **(2 marks)**

---

141   How does IFRS 9 *Financial Instruments* require investments in equity instruments to be measured and accounted for (in the absence of any election at initial recognition)?

    A   Fair value with changes going through profit or loss
    B   Fair value with changes going through other comprehensive income
    C   Amortised cost with changes going through profit or loss
    D   Amortised cost with changes going through other comprehensive income   **(2 marks)**

---

142   On 1 January 20X1 Penfold purchased a debt instrument for its fair value of $500,000. It had a principal amount of $550,000 and was due to mature in five years. The debt instrument carries fixed interest of 6% paid annually in arrears and has an effective interest rate of 8%. It is held at amortised cost.

At what amount will the debt instrument be shown in the statement of financial position of Penfold as at 31 December 20X2?

    A $514,560
    B $566,000
    C $564,560
    D $520,800   **(2 marks)**

                                                                                  (8 marks)

CBE style OTQ bank – financial instruments

143 Which of the following are **not** classified as financial instruments under IAS 32 *Financial instruments: presentation*?

- ☐ Share options
- ☐ Intangible assets
- ☐ Trade receivables
- ☐ Redeemable preference shares

(2 marks)

144 Dexon's draft statement of financial position as at 31 March 20X8 shows financial assets at fair value through profit or loss with a carrying amount of $12.5 million as at 1 April 20X7.

These financial assets are held in a fund whose value changes directly in proportion to a specified market index. At 1 April 20X7 the relevant index was 1,200 and at 31 March 20X8 it was 1,296.

What amount of gain or loss should be recognised at 31 March 20X8 in respect of these assets?

$ ☐

(2 marks)

145 On 1 January 20X8 a company purchased 40,000 $1 listed equity shares at a price of $3 per share. An irrevocable election was made to recognise the shares at fair value through other comprehensive income. Transaction costs were $3,000. At the year end of 31 December 20X8 the shares were trading at $6 per share.

What amount in respect of these shares will be shown under 'investments in equity instruments' in the statement of financial position as at 31 December 20X8?

$ ☐

(2 marks)

(6 marks)

Section B

Bertrand MCQ case

19 mins

Information relevant to questions 146-150

Bertrand issued $10 million convertible loan notes on 1 October 20X0 that carry a nominal interest (coupon) rate of 5% per annum. They are redeemable on 30 September 20X3 at par for cash or can be exchanged for equity shares in Bertrand on the basis of 20 shares for each $100 of loan. A similar loan note, without the conversion option, would have required Bertrand to pay an interest rate of 8%.

The present value of $1 receivable at the end of each year, based on discount rates of 5% and 8%, can be taken as:

End of year		5%	8%
	1	0.95	0.93
	2	0.91	0.86
	3	0.86	0.79
	cumulative	2.72	2.58

146   How should the convertible loan notes be accounted for?

    A   As debt
    B   As debt and equity
    C   As equity
    D   As debt until conversion, then as equity

147   What is the amount that will be recognised as finance costs for the year ended 30 September 20X1?

    A $500,000
    B $800,000
    C $735,000
    D   Nil

148   What is the amount that should be shown under liabilities at 30 September 20X1?

    A $9,425,000
    B $9,925,000
    C $9,690,000
    D   Nil

149   If Bertrand had incurred transaction costs in issuing these loan notes, how should these have been accounted for?

    A   Added to the proceeds of the loan notes
    B   Deducted from the proceeds of the loan notes
    C   Amortised over the life of the loan notes
    D   Charged to finance costs

150   Later that year Bertrand purchased a debt instrument which will mature in five years' time. Bertrand intends to hold the debt instrument to maturity to collect interest payments. How should this debt instrument be measured in the financial statements of Bertrand?

    A   As a financial liability at fair value through profit or loss
    B   As a financial liability at amortised cost
    C   As a financial asset at fair value through profit or loss
    D   As a financial asset at amortised cost

(10 marks)

MCQ bank – leasing

151 On 1 January 20X6 Fellini hired a machine under a finance lease. The cash price of the machine was $3.5 million and the present value of the minimum lease payments was $3.3 million. Instalments of $700,000 are payable annually in advance with the first payment made on 1 January 20X6. The interest rate implicit in the lease is 6%.

What amount will appear under non-current liabilities in respect of this lease in the statement of financial position of Fellini at 31 December 20X7?

    A $1,479,000
    B $2,179,000
    C $1,702,000
    D $2,266,000   **(2 marks)**

152 Which of the following situations does **not** suggest that a leasing arrangement constitutes a finance lease?
    A   The present value of the minimum lease payments is substantially less than the fair value of the asset.
    B   Ownership in the asset is transferred at the end of the lease term.
    C   The lease term is for a major part of the asset's useful life.
    D   The lease contains a purchase option at a price below fair value, which is reasonably certain to be exercised.   **(2 marks)**

153 A company acquired an item of plant under a finance lease on 1 April 20X7. The present value of the minimum lease payments was $15.6 million and the rentals are $6 million per annum paid in arrears for three years on 31 March each year.

The interest rate implicit in the lease is 8% per annum.

What amount will appear under current liabilities in respect of this lease in the statement of financial position at 31 March 20X8?

    A $5,132,000
    B $5,716,000
    C $6,000,000
    D $4,752,000   **(2 marks)**

154 At what amount does IAS 17 *Leases* require a lessee to capitalise an asset acquired under a finance lease?

    A   Cash price of the asset
    B   Fair value of the asset
    C   Present value of minimum lease payments
    D   Lower of fair value and present value of minimum lease payments   **(2 marks)**

155 On 1 October 20X3, Fresco acquired an item of plant under a five-year finance lease agreement. The plant had a cash purchase cost of $25 million. The agreement had an implicit finance cost of 10% per annum and required an immediate deposit of $2 million and annual rentals of $6 million paid on 30 September each year for five years.

What would be the current liability for the leased plant in Fresco's statement of financial position as at 30 September 20X4?

    A $19,300,000
    B $4,070,000
    C $5,000,000
    D $3,850,000   **(2 marks)**

         (10 marks)

CBE style OTQ bank – leasing

156 The objective of IAS 17 *Leases* is to prescribe the appropriate accounting treatment and required disclosures in relation to leases.

Which **TWO** of the following situations would normally lead to a lease being classified as a finance lease?

☐ The lease transfers ownership of the asset to the lessee by the end of the lease term

☐ The lease term is for approximately half of the economic life of the asset

☐ The lease assets are of a specialised nature such that only the lessee can use them without major modifications being made

☐ At the inception of the lease, the present value of the minimum lease payments is 60% of what the leased asset would cost to purchase

(2 marks)

157 Tourmalet sold an item of plant for $50 million on 1 April 20X4. The plant had a carrying amount of $40 million at the date of sale, which was charged to cost of sales. On the same date, Tourmalet entered into an agreement to lease back the plant for the next five years (being the estimated remaining life of the plant) at a cost of $14 million per annum payable annually in arrears. An arrangement of this type is normally deemed to have a financing cost of 10% per annum.

What amount will be shown as income from this transaction in the statement of profit or loss for the year ended 30 September 20X4?

$ ☐

(2 marks)

158 A sale and leaseback transaction involves the sale of an asset and the leasing back of the same asset. If the lease arrangement results in a finance lease, how should any 'profit' on the sale be treated?

☐ Recognise immediately in profit or loss
☐ Defer and amortise over the lease term
☐ Any excess above fair value to be deferred and amortised, rest to be recognised in profit or loss
☐ No profit should be recognised

(2 marks)

159 During the year ended 30 September 20X4 Hyper entered into two lease transactions:

On 1 October 20X3 a payment of $90,000, being the first of five equal annual payments of a finance lease for an item of plant which has a five-year useful life. The lease has an implicit interest rate of 10% and the fair value (cost to purchase) of the leased equipment on 1 October 20X3 was $340,000

On 1 January 20X4 a payment of $18,000 for a one-year lease of an item of excavation equipment.

What amount in total would be charged to Hyper's statement of profit or loss for the year ended 30 September 20X4 in respect of the above transactions?

$ ☐

(2 marks)

160 On 1 January 20X6 Platinum entered into a finance lease agreement. The cash price of the asset was $360,000 and the terms of the lease were a deposit of $120,000 payable on 1 January 20X6 and three further instalments of $100,000 payable on 31 December 20X6, 31 December 20X7 and 31 December 20X8. The rate of interest implicit in the lease is 12%.

What will be the amount of the finance charge arising from this lease which will be charged to profit or loss for the year ended 31 December 20X7?

$ ☐

(2 marks)

(10 marks)

Section B

Fino MCQ case

19 mins

Information relevant to questions 161-165

On 1 April 20X7, Fino increased the operating capacity of its plant. Due to a lack of liquid funds it was unable to buy the required plant which had a cost of $350,000. On the recommendation of the finance director, Fino entered into an agreement to lease the plant from the manufacturer. The lease required four annual payments in advance of $100,000 each commencing on 1 April 20X7. The rate of interest implicit in the lease is 10%. The plant would have a useful life of four years and would be scrapped at the end of this period. The finance director believes the lease to be an operating lease.

161 Assuming this is a finance lease, what is the total charge to profit or loss for the year ended 30 September 20X7 in respect of the plant?

    A $12,500
    B $25,000
    C $56,250
    D $68,750

162 The finance director thinks this an operating lease. Which TWO of the following, if true, would indicate that it was an operating lease?

    (i)   Ownership is transferred at the end of the lease term.
    (ii)   The lease is for a short part of the asset's life.
    (iii)   The present value of the minimum lease payments is considerably less than the asset's fair value.
    (iv)   The asset has been specially adapted for the use of the lessee.

    A   (i) and (ii)
    B   (ii) and (iii)
    C   (iii) and (iv)
    D   (i) and (iv)

163 What is the amount that should be shown under non-current liabilities at 30 September 20X7 in respect of this plant?

    A $175,000
    B $262,500
    C $250,000
    D $100,000

164 On 1 April 20X7 Fino also took out an operating lease on another piece of equipment. The lease runs for four years and payments of $1,000 per month are payable in arrears. As an incentive to enter into the lease, Fino received the first quarter rent free.

What amount should be recognised as payments under operating leases for the period up to 30 September 20X7?

    A $2,182
    B $3,000
    C $6,000
    D $5,625

165   The distinction between finance and operating leases is an illustration of the importance of accounting for transactions accordance to their 'substance' rather than just their legal form.

Which accounting concept or characteristic does this relate to?

A   Materiality
B   Faithful representation
C   Verifiability
D   Relevance

(10 marks)

MCQ bank – provisions and events after the reporting period

166   Candel is being sued by a customer for $2 million for breach of contract over a cancelled order. Candel has obtained legal opinion that there is a 20% chance that Candel will lose the case. Accordingly Candel has provided $400,000 ($2 million × 20%) in respect of the claim. The unrecoverable legal costs of defending the action are estimated at $100,000. These have not been provided for as the case will not go to court until next year.

What is the amount of the provision that should be made by Candel in accordance with IAS 37 *Provisions, contingent liabilities and contingent assets*?

A $2,000,000
B $2,100,000
C $500,000
D $100,000   (2 marks)

167   During the year Peterlee acquired an iron ore mine at a cost of $6 million. In addition, when all the ore has been extracted (estimated ten years' time) the company will face estimated costs for landscaping the area affected by the mining that have a present value of $2 million. These costs would still have to be incurred even if no further ore was extracted.

How should this $2 million future cost be recognised in the financial statements?

A   Provision $2 million and $2 million capitalised as part of cost of mine
B   Provision $2 million and $2 million charged to operating costs
C   Accrual $200,000 per annum for next ten years
D   Should not be recognised as no cost has yet arisen   (2 marks)

168   Which one of the following would **not** be valid grounds for a provision?

A   A company has a policy has a policy of cleaning up any environmental contamination caused by its operations, but is not legally obliged to do so.

B   A company is leasing an office building for which it has no further use. However, it is tied into the lease for another year.

C   A company is closing down a division. The Board has prepared detailed closure plans which have been communicated to customers and employees.

D   A company has acquired a machine which requires a major overhaul every three years. The cost of the first overhaul is reliably estimated at $120,000.   (2 marks)

169 Which one of the following events taking place after the year end but before the financial statements were authorised for issue would require adjustment in accordance with IAS 10 *Events after the reporting period*?

    A   Three lines of inventory held at the year end were destroyed by flooding in the warehouse.

    B   The directors announced a major restructuring.

    C   Two lines of inventory held at the year end were discovered to have faults rendering them unsaleable.

    D   The value of the company's investments fell sharply.   **(2 marks)**

170 Which of the following statements are correct in accordance with IAS 37 *Provisions, contingent liabilities and contingent assets*?

    (i)   Provisions should be made for both constructive and legal obligations.

    (ii)   Discounting may be used when estimating the amount of a provision.

    (iii)   A restructuring provision must include the estimated costs of retraining or relocating continuing staff.

    (iv)   A restructuring provision may only be made when a company has a detailed plan for the restructuring and has communicated to interested parties a firm intention to carry it out.

    A   All four statements are correct

    B   (i), (ii) and (iv) only

    C   (i), (iii) and (iv) only

    D   (ii) and (iii) only   **(2 marks)**

(10 marks)

CBE style OTQ bank – provisions and events after the reporting period

171 Tynan's year end is 30 September 20X4 and the following potential liabilities have been identified:

Which TWO of the above should Tynan recognise as liabilities as at 30 September 20X4?

☐ The signing of a non-cancellable contract in September 20X4 to supply goods in the following year on which, due to a pricing error, a loss will be made

☐ The cost of a reorganisation which was approved by the board in August 20X4 but has not yet been implemented, communicated to interested parties or announced publicly

☐ An amount of deferred tax relating to the gain on the revaluation of a property during the current year. Tynan has no intention of selling the property in the foreseeable future.

☐ The balance on the warranty provision which related to products for which there are no outstanding claims and whose warranties had expired by 30 September 20X4

(2 marks)

172 On 1 October 20X3 Xplorer commenced drilling for oil from an undersea oilfield. The extraction of oil causes damage to the seabed which has a restorative cost (ignore discounting) of $10,000 per million barrels of oil extracted. Xplorer extracted 250 million barrels in the year ended 30 September 20X4.

Xplorer is also required to dismantle the drilling equipment at the end of its five year licence. This has an estimated cost of $30 million on 30 September 20X8. Xplorer's cost of capital is 8% per annum and $1 has a present value of 68 cents in five years' time.

What is the total provision (extraction plus dismantling) which Xplorer would report in its statement of financial position as at 30 September 20X4 in respect of its oil operations?

$ ☐   **(2 marks)**

173   Hopewell sells a line of goods under a six-month warranty. Any defect arising during that period is repaired free of charge. Hopewell has calculated that if all the goods sold in the last six months of the year required repairs the cost would be $2 million. If all of these goods had more serious faults and had to be replaced the cost would be $6 million.

The normal pattern is that 80% of goods sold will be fault-free, 15% will require repairs and 5% will have to be replaced.

What is the amount of the provision required?

$ [   ]

(2 marks)

174   Which **TWO** of the following events which occur after the reporting date of a company but before the financial statements are authorised for issue are classified as **adjusting** events in accordance with IAS 10 *Events after the reporting period*?

☐   A change in tax rate announced after the reporting date, but affecting the current tax liability

☐   The discovery of a fraud which had occurred during the year

☐   The determination of the sale proceeds of an item of plant sold before the year end

☐   The destruction of a factory by fire

(2 marks)

(8 marks)

Section B

Rainbird MCQ case

19 mins

Information relevant to questions 175-179

Rainbird decided to reorganise a manufacturing facility during November 20X1 and commissioned a consulting engineer to carry out a feasibility study. A provision for the reorganisation was created at 31 December 20X1.

Staff functions will change following the reorganisation, so in December 20X1 Rainbird contracted with a training company to provide retraining to take place in January 20X2. A provision for this expenditure was created at 31 December 20X1.

Rainbird hopes that reorganising its manufacturing facility will improve quality control. It gives a one-year warranty with all products and the rate of returns under warranty is 12%. 5% of the returned items can be repaired at a cost of $5 (free of charge to the customer). The other 95% are scrapped and a full refund of $30 is given. Rainbird sold 525,000 units during the year to 31 December 20X1.

In five years' time Rainbird will have to dismantle its factory and return the site to the local authority. A provision was set up for the present value of the dismantling costs when the factory was first acquired. The opening balance on the provision at 1 January 20X1 was $2.63 million. Rainbird has a cost of capital of 8%.

175   Rainbird's accountant is preparing the financial statements for the year to 31 December 20X1 and is not too sure about the provisions set up for the reorganisation of the facility and the staff training.

     Which of these is a correct provision under IAS 37?

     A   The reorganisation

     B   The staff training

     C   The reorganisation and the staff training

     D   Neither the reorganisation nor the staff training

176   Rainbird's finance director is checking some of the financial estimates involved. In accordance with IAS 37 if the reporting entity is presently obliged to transfer economic benefit to another party, the occurrence is probable but the amount cannot be measured with sufficient reliability, this should give rise to:

     A   A provision

     B   A contingent liability

     C   A long-term liability

     D   A contingent asset

177   What is the amount of the provision that should be created at 31 December 20X1 for returns under warranty?

     A $1,890,000

     B $1,811,250

     C $1,795,500

     D $1,575,000

178   What is the amount of the provision that should be carried forward at 31 December 20X1 for the dismantling of the factory?

     A $2,630,000

     B $2,419,600

     C $2,435,185

     D $2,840,400

179   During January 20X2, before the financial statements for the year ended 31 December 20X1 had been finalised, a number of events took place.

Which one of these events would require an adjustment to the financial statements as at 31 December 20X1 in accordance with IAS 10 *Events after the reporting period*?

A   Rainbird's board announced a plan to discontinue one of its operations and dispose of the plant. The loss on disposal is estimated at $2 million.

B   The employees of the operation to be discontinued commenced a case against the company for constructive dismissal. The total cost could be $3 million.

C   A legal case for which Rainbird had provided $1.7 million at 31 December 20X1 to cover possible damages was unexpectedly settled in its favour.

D   One of Rainbird's warehouses was destroyed by fire and half of the inventory on hand at 31 December 20X1, valued at $2.5 million, was destroyed.

(10 marks)

MCQ bank – inventories and biological assets

180   Caminas has the following products in inventory at the year end.

Product	Quantity	Cost	Selling price	Selling cost
A	1,000	$40	$55	$8
B	2,500	$15	$25	$4
C	800	$23	$27	$5

At what amount should total inventory be stated in the statement of financial position?

A $95,900
B $103,100
C $95,100
D $105,100

(2 marks)

181   In which of the following situations is the net realisable value of an item of inventory likely to be lower than cost?

A   The production cost of the item has been falling.
B   The selling price of the item has been rising.
C   The item is becoming obsolete.
D   Demand for the item is increasing.

(2 marks)

182   At what amount is a biological asset measured on initial recognition in accordance with IAS 41 *Agriculture*?

A   Production cost
B   Fair value
C   Cost less estimated costs to sell
D   Fair value less estimated costs to sell

(2 marks)

183   Which of the following is **not** the outcome of a biological transformation according to IAS 41?

A   Growth
B   Harvest
C   Procreation
D   Degeneration

(2 marks)

184 How is a gain or loss arising on a biological asset recognised in accordance with IAS 41?

    A   Included in profit or loss for the year
    B   Adjusted in retained earnings
    C   Shown under 'other comprehensive income'
    D   Deferred and recognised over the life of the biological asset   **(2 marks)**

185 Which of the following statements about IAS 2 *Inventories* are correct?

    1   Production overheads should be included in cost on the basis of a company's actual level of activity in the period.

    2   In arriving at the net realisable value of inventories, settlement discounts must be deducted from the expected selling price.

    3   In arriving at the cost of inventories, FIFO, LIFO and weighted average cost formulas are acceptable.

    4   It is permitted to value finished goods inventories at materials plus labour cost only, without adding production overheads.

    A   1 only
    B   1 and 2
    C   3 and 4
    D   None of them   **(2 marks)**

(12 marks)

CBE style OTQ bank – inventories and biological assets

186 Isaac is a company which buys agricultural produce from wholesale suppliers for retail to the general public. It is preparing its financial statements for the year ending 30 September 20X4 and is considering its closing inventory.

In addition to IAS 2 *Inventories*, which of the following IFRSs may be relevant to determining the figure to be included in its financial statements for closing inventories?

    ☐ IAS 10 *Events after the reporting period*
    ☐ IAS 38 *Intangible assets*
    ☐ IAS 16 *Property, plant and equipment*
    ☐ IAS 41 *Agriculture*   **(2 marks)**

187 In preparing financial statements for the year ended 31 March 20X6, the inventory count was carried out on 4 April 20X6. The value of inventory counted was $36 million. Between 31 March and 4 April goods with a cost of $2.7 million were received into inventory and sales of $7.8 million were made at a mark-up on cost of 30%.

At what amount should inventory be stated in the statement of financial position as at 31 March 20X6?

$ ☐   **(2 marks)**

188 At 31 March 20X7 Tentacle had 12,000 units of product W32 in inventory, included at cost of $6 per unit. During April and May 20X7 units of W32 were being sold at a price of $5.40 each, with sales staff receiving a 15% commission on the sales price of the product.

At what amount should inventory of product W32 be recognised in the financial statements of Tentacle as at 31 March 20X7?

$ ☐   **(2 marks)**

(6 marks)

MCQ bank – accounting for taxation

189 A company's trial balance shows a debit balance of $2.1 million brought forward on current tax and a credit balance of $5.4 million on deferred tax. The tax charge for the current year is estimated at $16.2 million and the carrying amounts of net assets are $13 million in excess of their tax base. The income tax rate is 30%

What amount will be shown as income tax in the statement of profit or loss for the year?

A $15.6 million
B $12.6 million
C $16.8 million
D $18.3 million

(2 marks)

190 A company's trial balance at 31 December 20X3 shows a debit balance of $700,000 on current tax and a credit balance of $8,400,000 on deferred tax. The directors have estimated the provision for income tax for the year at $4.5 million and the required deferred tax provision is $5.6 million, $1.2 million of which relates to a property revaluation.

What is the profit or loss income tax charge for the year ended 31 December 20X3?

A $1 million
B $2.4 million
C $1.2 million
D $3.6 million

(2 marks)

191 The following information relates to an entity.

(i)   At 1 January 20X8 the carrying amount of non-current assets exceeded their tax written down value by $850,000.

(ii)   For the year to 31 December 20X8 the entity claimed depreciation for tax purposes of $500,000 and charged depreciation of $450,000 in the financial statements.

(iii)   During the year ended 31 December 20X8 the entity revalued a property. The revaluation surplus was $250,000. There are no current plans to sell the property.

(iv)   The tax rate was 30% throughout the year.

What is the provision for deferred tax required by IAS 12 *Income Taxes* at 31 December 20X8?

A $240,000
B $270,000
C $315,000
D $345,000

(2 marks)

(6 marks)

CBE style OTQ bank – accounting for taxation

192   The statements of financial position of Nedburg include the following extracts:

Statements of financial position as at 30 September

	20X2 $m	20X1 $m
Non-current liabilities		
Deferred tax	310	140
Current liabilities		
Taxation	130	160

The tax charge in the statement of profit or loss for the year ended 30 September 20X2 is $270 million.

What amount of tax was paid during the year to 30 September 20X2?

$ [   ]

(2 marks)

193   The trial balance of Highwood at 31 March 20X6 showed credit balances of $800,000 on current tax and $2.6 million on deferred tax. A property was revalued during the year giving rise to deferred tax of $3.75 million. This has been included in the deferred tax provision of $6.75 million at 31 March 20X6.

The income tax charge for the year ended 31 March 20X6 is estimated at $19.4 million.

What will be shown as the income tax charge in the statement of profit or loss of Highwood at 31 March 20X6?

$ [   ]

(2 marks)

(4 marks)

Section B

Julian MCQ case

Information relevant to questions 194-198

The carrying amount of Julian's property, plant and equipment at 31 December 20X3 was $310,000 and the tax written down value was $230,000.

The following data relates to the year ended 31 December 20X4:

(i) At the end of the year the carrying amount of property, plant and equipment was $460,000 and the tax written down value was $270,000. During the year some items were revalued by $90,000. No items had previously required revaluation. In the tax jurisdiction in which Julian operates revaluations of assets do not affect the tax base of an asset or taxable profit. Gains due to revaluations are taxable on sale.

(ii) Julian began development of a new product during the year and capitalised $60,000 in accordance with IAS 38. The expenditure was deducted for tax purposes as it was incurred. None of the expenditure had been amortised by the year end.

The corporate income tax rate is 30%. The current tax charge was calculated for the year as $45,000.

194 Julian's accountant is confused by the term 'tax base'. What is meant by 'tax base'?

    A   The amount of tax payable in a future period

    B   The tax regime under which an entity is assessed for tax

    C   The amount attributed to an asset or liability for tax purposes

    D   The amount of tax deductible in a future period

---

195 What is the taxable temporary difference to be accounted for at 31 December 20X4 in relation to property, plant and equipment and development expenditure?

	Property, plant and equipment	Development expenditure
A	$270,000	$60,000
B	$270,000	Nil
C	$190,000	$60,000
D	$190,000	Nil

---

196 What amount should be charged to the revaluation surplus at 31 December 20X4 in respect of deferred tax?

    A $60,000

    B $90,000

    C $18,000

    D $27,000

---

197 What amount will be shown as tax payable in the statement of financial position of Julian at 31 December 20X4?

    A $45,000

    B $72,000

    C $63,000

    D $75,000

198 Deferred tax assets and liabilities arise from taxable and deductible temporary differences. Which one of the following is **not** a circumstance giving rise to a temporary difference?

    A   Depreciation accelerated for tax purposes

    B   Development costs amortised in profit or loss but tax was deductible in full when incurred

    C   Accrued expenses which have already been deducted for tax purposes

    D   Revenue included in accounting profit when invoiced but only liable for tax when the cash is received.

(10 marks)

MCQ bank – presentation of published financial statements

199 Which one of the following would not **necessarily** lead to a liability being classified as a current liability?

    A   The liability is expected to be settled in the course of the entity's normal operating cycle.

    B   The liability has arisen during the current accounting period.

    C   The liability is held primarily for the purpose of trading.

    D   The liability is due to be settled within 12 months after the end of the reporting period.   **(2 marks)**

200 Which one of the following would be shown in the 'other comprehensive income' section of the statement of profit or loss and other comprehensive income?

    A   A revaluation gain on an investment property

    B   Profit on sale of an investment

    C   Receipt of a government grant

    D   Gain on revaluation of a factory building   **(2 marks)**

201 Which of the following are **not** items required by IAS 1 *Presentation of Financial Statements* to be shown on the face of the statement of financial position?

    A   Inventories

    B   Provisions

    C   Government grants

    D   Intangible assets   **(2 marks)**

202 How does IAS 1 define the 'operating cycle' of an entity?

    A   The time between acquisition of assets for processing and delivery of finished goods to customers

    B   The time between delivery of finished goods and receipt of cash from customers

    C   The time between acquisition of assets for processing and payment of cash to suppliers

    D   The time between acquisition of assets for processing and receipt of cash from customers   **(2 marks)**

203 Where are equity dividends paid presented in the financial statements?

    A   As a deduction from retained earnings in the statement of changes in equity

    B   As a liability in the statement of financial position

    C   As an expense in profit or loss

    D   As a loss in 'other comprehensive income'   **(2 marks)**

(10 marks)

Section C

204 Fresco (6/12 amended)

The following trial balance relates to Fresco at 31 March 20X2:

	$'000	$'000
Equity shares of 50 cents each (note (i))		45,000
Share premium (note (i))		5,000
Retained earnings at 1 April 20X1		5,100
Leased property (12 years) – at cost (note (ii))	48,000	
Plant and equipment – at cost (note (ii))	47,500	
Accumulated amortisation of leased property at 1 April 20X1		16,000
Accumulated depreciation of plant and equipment at 1 April 20X1		33,500
Inventory at 31 March 20X2	25,200	
Trade receivables (note (iii))	28,500	
Bank		1,400
Deferred tax (note (iv))		3,200
Trade payables		27,300
Revenue		350,000
Cost of sales	298,700	
Lease payments (note (ii))	8,000	
Distribution costs	16,100	
Administrative expenses	26,900	
Bank interest	300	
Current tax (note (iv))	800	
Suspense account (note (i))		13,500
	500,000	500,000

The following notes are relevant:

(i)   The suspense account represents the corresponding credit for cash received for a fully subscribed rights issue of equity shares made on 1 January 20X2. The terms of the share issue were one new share for every five held at a price of 75 cents each. The price of the company's equity shares immediately before the issue was $1.20 each.

(ii)   Non-current assets:

To reflect a marked increase in property prices, Fresco decided to revalue its leased property on 1 April 20X1. The directors accepted the report of an independent surveyor who valued the leased property at $36 million on that date. Fresco has not yet recorded the revaluation. The remaining life of the leased property is eight years at the date of the revaluation. Fresco makes an annual transfer to retained profits to reflect the realisation of the revaluation surplus. In Fresco's tax jurisdiction the revaluation does not give rise to a deferred tax liability.

On 1 April 20X1, Fresco acquired an item of plant under a finance lease agreement that had an implicit finance cost of 10% per annum. The lease payments in the trial balance represent an initial deposit of $2 million paid on 1 April 20X1 and the first annual rental of $6 million paid on 31 March 20X2. The lease agreement requires further annual payments of $6 million on 31 March each year for the next four years. Had the plant not been leased it would have cost $25 million to purchase for cash.

Plant and equipment (other than the leased plant) is depreciated at 20% per annum using the reducing balance method.

No depreciation/amortisation has yet been charged on any non-current asset for the year ended 31 March 20X2. Depreciation and amortisation are charged to cost of sales.

(iii)   In March 20X2, Fresco's internal audit department discovered a fraud committed by the company's credit controller who did not return from a foreign business trip. The outcome of the fraud is that $4 million of the company's trade receivables have been stolen by the credit controller and are not recoverable. Of this

BPP
LEARNING MEDIA

amount, $1 million relates to the year ended 31 March 20X1 and the remainder to the current year. Fresco is not insured against this fraud.

(iv)   Fresco's income tax calculation for the year ended 31 March 20X2 shows a tax refund of $2.4 million. The balance on current tax in the trial balance represents the under/over provision of the tax liability for the year ended 31 March 20X1. At 31 March 20X2, Fresco had taxable temporary differences of $12 million (requiring a deferred tax liability). The income tax rate of Fresco is 25%.

Required:

(a)   Prepare the statement of profit or loss and other comprehensive income for Fresco for the year ended 31 March 20X2.   **(10 marks)**

(b)   Prepare the statement of financial position of Fresco as at 31 March 20X2.   **(10 marks)**

                                                                                                                                        (20 marks)

205 Dexon   **39 mins**

Below is the summarised draft statement of financial position of Dexon, a publicly listed company, as at 31 March 20X8.

	$'000	$'000	$'000
ASSETS			
Non-current assets			
Property at valuation (land $20m; buildings $165m (note (i))			185,000
Plant (note (i))			180,500
Financial assets at fair value through profit or loss at 1 April 20X7 (note (ii))			12,500
			378,000
Current assets			
Inventory		84,000	
Trade receivables (note (iii))		52,200	
Bank		3,800	140,000
Total assets			518,000
EQUITY AND LIABILITIES			
Equity			
Ordinary shares of $1 each			250,000
Share premium		40,000	
Revaluation surplus		18,000	
Retained earnings – At 1 April 20X7	12,300		
– For the year ended 31 March 20X8	96,700	109,000	167,000
			417,000
Non-current liabilities			
Deferred tax – at 1 April 20X7 (note (iv))			19,200
Current liabilities			81,800
Total equity and liabilities			518,000

The following information is relevant.

(i)   The non-current assets have not been depreciated for the year ended 31 March 20X8.

Dexon has a policy of revaluing its land and buildings at the end of each accounting year. The values in the above statement of financial position are as at 1 April 20X7 when the buildings had a remaining life of 15 years. A qualified surveyor has valued the land and buildings at 31 March 20X8 at $180 million.

Plant is depreciated at 20% on the reducing balance basis.

(ii)   The financial assets at fair value through profit and loss are held in a fund whose value changes directly in proportion to a specified market index. At 1 April 20X7 the relevant index was 1,200 and at 31 March 20X8 it was 1,296.

(iii) In late March 20X8 the directors of Dexon discovered a material fraud perpetrated by the company's credit controller that had been continuing for some time. Investigations revealed that a total of $4 million of the trade receivables as shown in the statement of financial position at 31 March 20X8 had in fact been paid and the money had been stolen by the credit controller. An analysis revealed that $1.5 million had been stolen in the year to 31 March 20X7 with the rest being stolen in the current year. Dexon is not insured for this loss and it cannot be recovered from the credit controller, nor is it deductible for tax purposes.

(iv) During the year the company's taxable temporary differences increased by $10 million of which $6 million related to the revaluation of the property. The deferred tax relating to the remainder of the increase in the temporary differences should be taken to profit or loss. The applicable income tax rate is 20%.

(v) The above figures do not include the estimated provision for income tax on the profit for the year ended 31 March 20X8. After allowing for any adjustments required in items (i) to (iii), the directors have estimated the provision at $11.4 million (this is in addition to the deferred tax effects of item (iv)).

(vi) Dividends totaling $15.5 million were paid during the year.

Required

Taking into account any adjustments required by items (i) to (vi) above:

(a) Prepare a statement showing the recalculation of Dexon's profit for the year ended 31 March 20X8.

(8 marks)

(b) Redraft the statement of financial position of Dexon as at 31 March 20X8.

(12 marks)

Notes to the financial statements are not required.

(20 marks)

206 Xtol (6/14 amended)   39 mins

The following trial balance relates to Xtol at 31 March 20X4:

	$'000	$'000
Revenue		490,000
Cost of sales	290,600	
Distribution costs	33,500	
Administrative expenses	36,800	
Loan note interest and dividends paid (notes(iv) and (v))	13,380	
Bank interest	900	
20-year leased property at cost	100,000	
Plant and equipment at cost (note (ii))	155,500	
Accumulated amortisation/depreciation at 1 April 20X3:		
Leased property		25,000
Plant and equipment		43,500
Inventory at 31 March 20X4	61,000	
Trade receivables	63,000	
Trade payables		32,200
Bank		5,500
Equity shares of 25 cents each (note (iii))		56,000
Share premium		25,000
Retained earnings at 1 April 20X3		26,080
5% convertible loan note (note (iv))		50,000
Current tax (note (vi))	3,200	
Deferred tax (note (vi))		4,600
	757,880	757,880

The following notes are relevant:

(i) Revenue includes an amount of $20 million for cash sales made through Xtol's retail outlets during the year on behalf of Francais. Xtol, acting as agent, is entitled to a commission of 10% of the selling price of these goods. By 31 March 20X4, Xtol had remitted to Francais $15 million (of the $20 million sales) and recorded this amount in cost of sales.

(ii) Plant and equipment is depreciated at 12½% per annum on the reducing balance basis. All amortisation and depreciation of non-current assets is charged to cost of sales.

(iii) On 1 August 20X3, Xtol made a fully subscribed rights issue of equity share capital based on two new shares at 60 cents each for every five shares held. The issue has been fully recorded in the trial balance figures.

(iv) On 1 April 20X3, Xtol issued a 5% $50 million convertible loan note at par. Interest is payable annually in arrears on 31 March each year. The loan note is redeemable at par or convertible into equity shares at the option of the loan note holders on 31 March 20X6. The interest on an equivalent loan note without the conversion rights would be 8% per annum.

The present values of $1 receivable at the end of each year, based on discount rates of 5% and 8%, are:

	5%	8%
End of year 1	0.95	0.93
2	0.91	0.86
3	0.86	0.79

(v) An equity dividend of 4 cents per share was paid on 30 May 20X3 and, after the rights issue, a further dividend of 2 cents per share was paid on 30 November 20X3.

(vi) The balance on current tax represents the under/over provision of the tax liability for the year ended 31 March 20X3. A provision of $28 million is required for current tax for the year ended 31 March 20X4 and at this date the deferred tax liability was assessed at $8.3 million.

Required

(a) Prepare the statement of profit or loss for Xtol for the year ended 31 March 20X4 **(9 marks)**

(b) Prepare the statement of financial position for Xtol for the year ended 31 March 20X4 **(11 marks)**

(20 marks)

MCQ bank – reporting financial performance

207 Which one of the following would be treated under IAS 8 *Accounting policies, changes in accounting estimates and errors* as a change of accounting policy?

    A   A change in valuation of inventory from a weighted average to a FIFO basis

    B   A change of depreciation method from straight line to reducing balance

    C   Adoption of the revaluation model for non-current assets previously held at cost

    D   Capitalisation of borrowing costs which have arisen for the first time   **(2 marks)**

208 For an asset to be classified as 'held for sale' under IFRS 5 *Non-current assets held for sale and discontinued operations* its sale must be 'highly probable'. Which one of the following is **not** a requirement if the sale is to be regarded as highly probable?

    A   Management must be committed to a plan to sell the asset.

    B   A buyer must have been located for the asset.

    C   The asset must be marketed at a reasonable price.

    D   The sale should be expected to take place within one year from the date of classification.   **(2 marks)**

209 At what amount should an asset classified as 'held for sale' be measured?

A   Lower of carrying amount and fair value less costs of disposal
B   Lower of carrying amount and value in use
C   Higher of value in use and fair value less costs of disposal
D   Higher of carrying amount and recoverable amount   **(2 marks)**

---

210 Which of the following would be a change in accounting policy in accordance with IAS 8 *Accounting policies, changes in accounting estimates and errors*?

A   Adjusting the financial statements of a subsidiary prior to consolidation as its accounting policies differ from those of its parent
B   A change in reporting depreciation charges as cost of sales rather than as administrative expenses
C   Depreciation charged on reducing balance method rather than straight line
D   Reducing the value of inventory from cost to net realisable value due to a valid adjusting event after the reporting period   **(2 marks)**

---

211 Which of the following items is a change of accounting policy under IAS 8 *Accounting policies, changes in accounting estimates and errors*?

A   Classifying commission earned as revenue in the statement of profit or loss, having previously classified it as other operating income
B   Switching to purchasing plant using finance leases from a previous policy of purchasing plant for cash
C   Changing the value of a subsidiary's inventory in line with the group policy for inventory valuation when preparing the consolidated financial statements
D   Revising the remaining useful life of a depreciable asset   **(2 marks)**

(10 marks)

CBE style OTQ bank – reporting financial performance

212 As at 30 September 20X3 Dune's property in its statement of financial position was:
Property at cost (useful life 15 years) $45 million
Accumulated depreciation $6 million

On 1 April 20X4 Dune decided to sell the property. The property is being marketed by a property agent at a price of $42 million, which was considered a reasonably achievable price at that date. The expected costs to sell have been agreed at $1 million. Recent market transactions suggest that actual selling prices achieved for this type of property in the current market conditions are 10% less than the price at which they are marketed.

At 30 September 20X4 the property has not been sold.

At what amount should the property be reported in Dune's statement of financial position as at 30 September 20X4?

☐ $36 million
☐ $37.5 million
☐ $36.8 million
☐ $42 million   **(2 marks)**

213 Steeplechase sold a machine to a Greek company which it agreed to invoice in €. The sale was made on 1 October 20X6 for €250,000. €125,000 was received on 1 November 20X6 and the balance is due on 1 January 20X7.

The exchange rate moved as follows:

1 October 20X6 – €0.91 to $1
1 November 20X6 – €0.95 to $1
31 December 20X6 – €0.85 to $1

At what amount will the receivable be shown in the financial statements at 31 December 20X6?

$ [   ] (to the nearest $)   **(2 marks)**

---

214 IAS 21 sets out how entities that carry out transactions in a foreign currency should measure the results of these transactions at the year end.

At what exchange rate should non-monetary items carried at historical cost be measured?

A   The closing rate
B   The rate at the date of the transaction
C   The average rate for the year
D   The rate at the beginning of the year   **(2 marks)**

---

215 Miston buys goods priced at €50,000 from a Dutch company on 1 November 20X8. The invoice is due for settlement in two equal instalments on 1 December 20X8 and 1 January 20X9.

The exchange rate moved as follows:

1 November 20X8 - 1.63 to $1
1 December 20X8 – 1.61 to $1
31 December 20X8 – 1.64 to $1

What will be the net exchange gain or loss to be reported in the financial statements of Miston at 31 December 20X8?

$ [   ] gain / (loss) (to nearest $)   **(2 marks)**

                                                                       (8 marks)

Section B

Tunshill (12/10) MCQ case

19 mins

Information relevant to questions 216-220

The directors of Tunshill are disappointed by the draft profit for the year ended 30 September 20X3. The company's assistant accountant has suggested two areas where she believes the reported profit may be improved:

(i) A major item of plant that cost $20 million to purchase and install on 1 October 20X0 is being depreciated on a straight-line basis over a five-year period (assuming no residual value). The plant is wearing well and at the beginning of the current year (1 October 20X2) the production manager believed that the plant was likely to last eight years in total (ie from the date of its purchase). The assistant accountant has calculated that, based on an eight-year life (and no residual value) the accumulated depreciation of the plant at 30 September 20X3 would be $7.5 million ($20 million / 8 years × 3). In the financial statements for the year ended 30 September 20X2, the accumulated depreciation was $8 million ($20 million / 5 years × 2). Therefore, by adopting an eight-year life, Tunshill can avoid a depreciation charge in the current year and instead credit $0.5 million ($8 million – $7.5 million) to profit or loss in the current year to improve the reported profit.

(ii) Most of Tunshill's competitors value their inventory using the average cost (AVCO) basis, whereas Tunshill uses the first in first out (FIFO) basis. The value of Tunshill's inventory at 30 September 20X3 (on the FIFO basis) is $20 million, however on the AVCO basis it would be valued at $18 million. By adopting the same method (AVCO) as its competitors, the assistant accountant says the company would improve its profit for the year ended 30 September 20X3 by $2 million. Tunshill's inventory at 30 September 20X2 was reported as $15 million, however on the AVCO basis it would have been reported as $13.4 million.

216 What is the nature of the change being proposed by the assistant accountant in (i) and how should it be applied?

   A   Change of accounting policy : Retrospective application
   B   Change of accounting policy : Prospective application
   C   Change of accounting estimate : Retrospective application
   D   Change of accounting estimate : Prospective application

217 Adjusting for the change of useful life, what will be the carrying amount of the plant at 30 September 20X3?

   A $10 milliom
   B $12 million
   C $8 million
   D $18 million

218 Which one of the following would be treated as a change of accounting policy?

   A   Tunshill has received its first government grant and is applying the deferred income method.
   B   Tunshill has revalued its properties. Up to now they had all been carried at historical cost.
   C   Tunshill has reclassified development costs from other operating expenses to cost of sales.
   D   Tunshill has increased its irrecoverable debt allowance from 10% to 12%.

219 What will be the effect of the change in (ii) on profits for the year ended 30 September 20X3?

   A   Increased by $400,000
   B   Reduced by $400,000
   C   Increased by $1,600,000
   D   Reduced by $1,600,000

220   How would the change in inventory value for the year ended 30 September 20X3 be posted?

A   DR Revenue / CR Inventory
B   DR Inventory / CR Revenue
C   DR Inventory / CR Cost of sales
D   DR Cost of sales / CR Inventory

(10 marks)

MCQ bank – earnings per share

221   Barwell had 10 million ordinary shares in issue throughout the year ended 30 June 20X3. On 1 July 20X2 it had issued $2 million of 6% convertible loan stock, each $5 of loan stock convertible into 4 ordinary shares on 1 July 20X6 at the option of the holder.

Barwell had profit after tax for the year ended 30 June 20X3 of $1,850,000. It pays tax on profits at 30%.

What was diluted EPS for the year?

A $0.167
B $0.185
C $0.161
D $0.17

(2 marks)

222   At 30 September 20X2 the trial balance of Cavern includes the following balances:

	$'000
Equity shares of 20c each	50,000
Share premium	15,000

Cavern has accounted for a fully-subscribed rights issue of equity shares made on 1 April 20X2 of one new share for every four in issue at 42 cents each. This was the only share issue made during the year.

What were the balances on the share capital and share premium accounts at 30 September 20X1?

	Share capital	Share premium
	$'000	$'000
A	37,500	11,250
B	40,000	4,000
C	37,500	4,000
D	40,000	11,250

(2 marks)

223   Aqua has correctly calculated its basic earnings per share (EPS) for the current year.

Which of the following items need to be additionally considered when calculating the diluted EPS of Aqua for the year?

(i)   A 1 for 5 rights issue of equity shares during the year at $1.20 when the market price of the equity shares was $2.00

(ii)   The issue during the year of a convertible (to equity shares) loan note

(iii)   The granting during the year of directors' share options exercisable in three years' time

(iv)   Equity shares issued during the year as the purchase consideration for the acquisition of a new subsidiary company

A   All four
B   (i) and (ii) only
C   (ii) and (iii) only
D   (iii) and (iv) only

(2 marks)

224 Many commentators believe that the trend of earnings per share (EPS) is a more reliable indicator of underlying performance than the trend of net profit for the year.

Which of the following statements supports this view?

A   Net profit can be manipulated by the choice of accounting policies but EPS cannot be manipulated in this way

B   EPS takes into account the additional resources made available to earn profit when new shares are issued for cash, whereas net profit does not

C   The disclosure of a diluted EPS figure is a forecast of the future trend of profit

D   The comparative EPS is restated where a change of accounting policy affects the previous year's profits

(2 marks)

(8 marks)

CBE style OTQ bank – earnings per share

225 At 1 January 20X8 Artichoke had 5 million $1 equity shares in issue. On 1 June 20X8 it made a 1 for 5 rights issue at a price of $1.50. The market price of the shares on the last day of quotation with rights was $1.80.

Total earnings for the year ended 31 December 20X8 was $7.6 million.

What was EPS for the year?

☐ $1.35
☐ $1.36
☐ $1.27
☐ $1.06

(2 marks)

226 Waffle had share capital of $7.5 million in 50c equity shares at 1 October 20X6. On 1 January 20X7 it made an issue of 4 million shares at full market price immediately followed by a 1 for 3 bonus issue.

The financial statements at 30 September 20X7 showed profit for the year of $12 million.

What was EPS for the year?

$ ☐

(2 marks)

227 Plumstead had 4 million equity shares in issue throughout the year ended 31 March 20X7. On 30 September 20X7 it made a 1 for 4 bonus issue. Profit after tax for the year ended 31 March 20X8 was $3.6 million, out of which an equity dividend of 20c per share was paid. The financial statements for the year ended 31 March 20X7 showed EPS of $0.70.

What is the EPS for the year ended 31 March 20X8 and the restated EPS for the year ended 31 March 20X7?

20X8 $ ☐

20X7 $ ☐

(2 marks)

(6 marks)

MCQ bank – analysing and interpreting financial statements

228 An entity has an average operating profit margin of 23% and an average asset turnover of 0.8, which is similar to the averages for the industry.

The entity is likely to be:

A   An architectural practice
B   A supermarket
C   An estate agent
D   A manufacturer **(2 marks)**

229 Which of the following will increase the length of a company's operating cycle?

A   Reducing the receivables collection period
B   Reducing the inventory holding period
C   Reducing the payables payment period
D   Reducing time taken to produce goods **(2 marks)**

230 In the year to 31 December 20X9 Weston pays an interim equity dividend of 3.4c per share and declares a final equity dividend of 11.1c. It has 5 million $1 shares in issue and the ex div share price is $3.50.

What is the dividend yield?

A   4%
B   24%
C   3.2%
D   4.1% **(2 marks)**

231 Analysis of the financial statements of Capricorn at 31 December 20X8 yields the following information.

Gross profit margin	30%
Current ratio	2.14
ROCE	16.3%
Asset turnover	4.19
Inventory turnover	13.9

What is the net profit margin?

A   3.9%
B   7.6%
C   16.1%
D   7.1% **(2 marks)**

(8 marks)

CBE style OTQ bank – analysing and interpreting financial statements

232 Camargue is a listed company with four million 50c ordinary shares in issue. The following extract is from its financial statements for the year ended 30 September 20X4.

Statement of profit or loss

	$'000
Profit before tax	900
Income tax expense	(100)
Profit for the year	800

At 30 September 20X4 the market price of Camargue's shares was $1.50. What was the P/E ratio on that date?

[   ]

(2 marks)

233 Extracts from the financial statements of Persimmon are as follows:

Statement of profit or loss		Statement of financial position	
	$'000		$'000
Operating profit	230	Ordinary shares	2,000
Finance costs	(15)	Revaluation surplus	300
Profit before tax	215	Retained earnings	1,200
Income tax	(15)		3,500
Profit for the year	200	10% loan notes	1,000
		Current liabilities	100
		Total equity and liabilities	4,600

What is the return on capital employed?

[   ]

(2 marks)

(4 marks)

Section C

234 Bengal (6/11 amended)   39 mins

Bengal is a public company. Its most recent financial statements are shown below:

STATEMENTS OF PROFIT OR LOSS FOR THE YEAR ENDED 31 MARCH

	20X1 $'000	20X0 $'000
Revenue	25,500	17,250
Cost of sales	(14,800)	(10,350)
Gross profit	10,700	6,900
Distribution costs	(2,700)	(1,850)
Administrative expenses	(2,100)	(1,450)
Finance costs	(650)	(100)
Profit before taxation	5,250	3,500
Income tax expense	(2,250)	(1,000)
Profit for the year	3,000	2,500

STATEMENTS OF FINANCIAL POSITION AS AT 31 MARCH

	20X1 $'000	20X1 $'000	20X0 $'000	20X0 $'000
Non-current assets				
Property, plant and equipment		9,500		5,400
Intangibles		6,200		nil
		15,700		5,400
Current assets				
Inventory	3,600		1,800	
Trade receivables	2,400		1,400	
Bank	nil		4,000	
Non-current assets held for sale	2,000	8,000	nil	7,200
Total assets		23,700		12,600
Equity and liabilities				
Equity				
Equity shares of $1 each		5,000		5,000
Retained earnings		4,500		2,250
		9,500		7,250
Non-current liabilities				
5% loan notes		2,000		2,000
8% loan notes		7,000		nil
Current liabilities				
Bank overdraft	200		nil	
Trade payables	2,800		2,150	
Current tax payable	2,200	5,200	1,200	3,350
Total equity and liabilities		23,700		12,600

Additional information:

(i) There were no disposals of non-current assets during the period; however Bengal does have some non-current assets classified as 'held for sale' at 31 March 20X1.

(ii) Depreciation of property, plant and equipment for the year ended 31 March 20X1 was $640,000.

A disappointed shareholder has observed that although revenue during the year has increased by 48% (8,250 / 17,250 × 100), profit for the year has only increased by 20% (500 / 2,500 × 100).

Required

(a) Comment on the performance (including addressing the shareholder's observation) and financial position of Bengal for the year ended 31 March 20X1. Up to five marks are available for the calculation of appropriate ratios. **(15 marks)**

(b) Explain the limitations of ratio analysis. **(5 marks)**

(20 marks)

235 Woodbank (6/14 amended)   39 mins

Shown below are the financial statements of Woodbank for its most recent two years:

STATEMENTS OF PROFIT OR LOSS FOR THE YEAR ENDED 31 MARCH:

	20X4	20X3
	$'000	$'000
Revenue	150,000	110,000
Cost of sales	117,000	(85,800)
Gross profit	33,000	24,200
Distribution costs	(6,000)	(5,000)
Administrative expenses	(9,000)	(9,200)
Finance costs – loan note interest	(1,750)	(500)
Profit before tax	16,250	9,500
Income tax expense	(5,750)	(3,000)
Profit for the year	10,500	6,500

STATEMENTS OF FINANCIAL POSITION AS AT 31 MARCH

	20X4	20X3
	$'000	$'000
ASSETS		
Non-current assets		
Property, plant and equipment	118,000	85,000
Goodwill	30,000	-
	148,000	85,000
Current assets		
Inventory	15,500	12,000
Trade receivables	11,000	8,000
Bank	500	5,000
	27,000	25,000
Total assets	175,000	110,000

EQUITY AND LIABILITIES
Equity

Equity shares of $1 each	80,000	80,000
Retained earnings	15,000	10,000
	95,000	90,000
Non-current liabilities		
10% loan notes	55,000	5,000
Current liabilities		
Trade payables	21,000	13,000
Current tax payable	4,000	2,000
	25,000	15,000
Total equity and liabilities	175,000	110,000

The following information is available:

(i) On 1 January 20X4, Woodbank purchased the trading assets and operations of Shaw for $50 million and, on the same date, issued additional 10% loan notes to finance the purchase. Shaw was an unincorporated entity and its results (for three months from 1 January 20X4 to 31 March 20X4) and net assets (including goodwill not subject to any impairment) are included in Woodbank's financial statements for the year ended 31 March 20X4. There were no other purchases or sales of non-current assets during the year ended 31 March 20X4.

(ii) Extracts of the results (for three months) of the previously separate business of Shaw, which are included in Woodbank's statement of profit or loss for the year ended 31 March 20X4, are:

	$'000
Revenue	30,000
Cost of sales	(21,000)
Gross profit	9,000
Distribution costs	(2,000)
Administrative expenses	(2,000)

(iii) The following six ratios have been correctly calculated for Woodbank for the years ended 31 March:

	20X3
Return on capital employed (ROCE)	10.5%
(profit before interest and tax/year-end total assets less current liabilities)	
Net asset (equal to capital employed) turnover	1.16 times
Gross profit margin	22%
Profit before interest and tax margin	9.1%
Current ratio	1.7:1
Gearing (debt/(debt + equity))	5.3%

Required

(a) Calculate the ratios in (iii) above for Woodbank for the year ended 31 March 20X4. **(5 marks)**

(b) Calculate for the year ended 31 March 20X4 equivalent ratios to the first FOUR only for Woodbank excluding the effects of the purchase of Shaw. **(4 marks)**

(c) Assess the comparative financial performance and position of Woodbank for the year ended 31 March 20X4. Your answer should refer to the effects of the purchase of Shaw. **(11 marks)**

(20 marks)

236 Greenwood

39 mins

Greenwood is a public listed company. On 31 March 20X7 Greenwood sold its 80% -owned subsidiary – Deadwood - for $6 million. The directors have been advised that the disposal qualifies as a discontinued operation and it has been accounted for accordingly. The disposal proceeds were not collected until after the year end.

Extracts from Greenwood's financial statements are set out below.

CONSOLIDATED STATEMENTS OF PROFIT OR LOSS FOR THE YEAR ENDED 31 MARCH

	20X7	20X6
	$'000	$'000
Revenue	27,500	21,200
Cost of sales	(19,500)	(15,000)
Gross profit	8,000	6,200
Operating expenses	(2,900)	(2,450)
	5,100	3,750
Finance costs	(600)	(250)
Profit before taxation	4,500	3,500
Income tax expense	(1,000)	(800)
Profit for the year from continuing operations	3,500	2,700
Profit/(loss) from discontinued operations	(1,500)	320
Profit for the year	2,000	3,020
Profit attributable to:		
Owners of Greenwood	2,300	2,956
Non-controlling interest	(300)	64
	2,000	3,020

Analysis of discontinued operation:		
Revenue	7,500	9,000
Cost of sales	(8,500)	(8,000)
Gross profit/(loss)	(1,000)	1,000
Operating expenses	(400)	(550)
Profit/(loss) before tax	(1,400)	450
Tax (expense)/relief	300	(130)
	(1,100)	320
Loss on measurement to fair value of disposal group	(500)	–
Tax relief on disposal group	100	–
Profit/(loss) from discontinued operations	(1,500)	320

STATEMENTS OF FINANCIAL POSITION AS AT 31 MARCH

	20X7		20X6	
	$'000	$'000	$'000	$'000
Property, plant and equipment		17,500		17,600
Goodwill				1,500
Current assets				
Inventory	1,500		1,350	
Trade receivables	2,000		2,300	
Due on sale of subsidiary	6,000		nil	
Bank	nil	9,500	50	3,700
Total assets		27,000		22,800

	20X7		20X6	
	$'000	$'000	$'000	$'000
Equity and liabilities				
Equity shares of $1 each		10,000		10,000
Retained earnings		4,500		2,750
		14,500		12,750
Non-controlling interest				1,250
				14,000
Non-current liabilities				
5% loan notes		8,000		5,000
Current liabilities				
Bank overdraft	1,150		nil	
Trade payables	2,400		2,800	
Current tax payable	950	4,500	1,000	3,800
Total equity and liabilities		27,000		22,800

Note: the carrying amount of the assets of Deadwood at 31 March 20X6 was $6·25 million. Greenwood measures non-controlling interest at share of net assets.

Required

Analyse the financial performance and position of Greenwood for the two years ended 31 March 20X7. (Ignore working capital and gearing).

Note: Your analysis should be supported by appropriate ratios (up to 6 marks available) and refer to the effects of the disposal. **(20 marks)**

MCQ bank – limitations of financial statements and interpretation techniques

237   An entity carries its property at revalued amount. Property values have fallen during the current period and an impairment loss has been recognised on the property, however its carrying amount is still higher than its depreciated historical cost.

What is the effect of the impairment on these ratios?

	ROCE	Gearing
A	Decrease	Decrease
B	Decrease	Increase
C	Increase	Decrease
D	Increase	Increase

(2 marks)

238   A company has a current ratio of 1.5, a quick ratio of 0.4 and a positive cash balance. If it purchases inventory on credit, what is the effect on these ratios?

	Current ratio	Quick ratio
A	Decrease	Decrease
B	Decrease	Increase
C	Increase	Decrease
D	Increase	Increase

(2 marks)

239 Fritwell has an asset turnover of 2.0 and an operating profit margin of 10%. It is launching a new product which is expected to generate additional sales of $1.6 million and additional profit of $120,000. It will require additional assets of $500,000.

Assuming there are no other changes to current operations, how will the new product affect these ratios?

	Operating profit margin	ROCE
A	Decrease	Decrease
B	Decrease	Increase
C	Increase	Decrease
D	Increase	Increase

(2 marks)

240 Which of the following is a possible reason why a company's inventory holding period increases from one year to the next?

A An increase in demand for its products

B A reduction in selling prices

C Obsolete inventory lines

D Seasonal fluctuations in orders

(2 marks)

(8 marks)

CBE style OTQ bank – limitations of financial statements and interpretation techniques

241 Use of historical cost accounting means asset values can be reliably verified but it has a number of shortcomings which need to be considered when analysing financial statements.

Which one of these is a possible result of the use of historical cost accounting during a period of inflation?

☐ Overstatement of non-current asset values

☐ Overstatement of profits

☐ Understatement of interest costs

☐ Understatement of ROCE

(2 marks)

242 Creative accounting measures are often aimed at reducing gearing.

Which one of these is **not** a measure which can be used to reduce (or not increase) gearing?

☐ Re-negotiating a loan to secure a lower interest rate

☐ Treating a finance lease as an operating lease

☐ Repaying a loan just before the year end and taking it out again at the beginning of the next year.

☐ 'Selling' an asset under a sale and leaseback agreement

(2 marks)

243 If a company wished to maintain the carrying amount in the financial statements of its non-current assets, which one of the following would it be unlikely to do?

☐ Enter into a sale and operating leaseback

☐ Account for asset –based government grants using the deferral method

☐ Revalue its properties

☐ Change the depreciation method for new asset acquisitions from 25% reducing balance to ten years straight line

(2 marks)

244   Trent uses the formula: (trade receivables at year end/revenue for the year) × 365 to calculate how long on average (in days) its customers take to pay.

Which of the following would **not** affect the correctness of the above calculation of the average number of days a customer takes to pay?

☐   Trent experiences considerable seasonal trading

☐   Trent makes a number of cash sales through retail outlets

☐   Reported revenue does not include a 15% sales tax whereas the receivables do include the tax

☐   Trent factors with recourse the receivable of its largest customer   **(2 marks)**

(8 marks)

Section C

245 Quartile (12/12 amended) 39 mins

Quartile sells jewellery through stores in retail shopping centres throughout the country. Over the last two years it has experienced declining profitability and is wondering if this is related to the sector as a whole. It has recently subscribed to an agency that produces average ratios across many businesses. Below are the ratios that have been provided by the agency for Quartile's business sector based on a year end of 30 June 20X2

	Sector average
Return on year-end capital employed (ROCE)	16.8%
Net asset (total assets less current liabilities) turnover	1.4 times
Gross profit margin	35%
Operating profit margin	12%
Current ratio	1.25:1
Average inventory turnover	3 times
Trade payables' payment period	64 days
Debt to equity	38%

The financial statements of Quartile for the year ended 30 September 20X2 are:

STATEMENT OF PROFIT OR LOSS

	$'000	$'000
Revenue		56,000
Opening inventory	8,300	
Purchases	43,900	
Closing inventory	(10,200)	
Cost of sales		(42,000)
Gross profit		14,000
Operating costs		(9,800)
Finance costs		(800)
Profit before tax		3,400
Income tax expense		(1,000)
Profit for the year		2,400

STATEMENT OF FINANCIAL POSITION

	$'000
ASSETS	
Non-current assets	
Property and shop fittings	25,600
Deferred development expenditure	5,000
	30,600
Current assets	
Inventory	10,200
Bank	1,000
	11,200
Total assets	41,800
EQUITY AND LIABILITIES	
Equity	
Equity shares of $1 each	15,000
Property revaluation reserve	3,000
Retained earnings	8,600
	26,600

	$'000
Non-current liabilities	
10% loan notes	8,000
Current liabilities	
Trade payables	5,400
Current tax payable	1,800
	7,200
Total equity and liabilities	41,800

The deferred development expenditure relates to an investment in a process to manufacture artificial precious gems for future sale by Quartile in the retail jewellery market.

Required

(a)	Prepare for Quartile the equivalent ratios to those provided by the agency.	**(6 marks)**
(b)	Assess the financial and operating performance of Quartile in comparison to its sector averages.	**(10 marks)**
(c)	Explain four possible limitations on the usefulness of the above comparison.	**(4 marks)**

(20 marks)

MCQ bank – statement of cash flows

246   Extracts from the statements of financial position of Nedburg are as follows.

Statements of financial position as at 30 September:

	20X2	20X1
	$m	$m
Ordinary shares of $1 each	750	500
Share premium	350	100

On 1 October 20X1 a bonus issue of one new share for every 10 held was made, financed from the share premium account. This was followed by a further issue for cash.

What amount will appear under 'cash flows from financing activities' in the statement of cash flows of Nedburg for the year ended 30 September 20X2 in respect of share issues?

A $500 million
B $450 million
C $550 million
D $250 million   **(2 marks)**

247   The statement of financial position of Pinto at 31 March 20X7 showed property, plant and equipment with a carrying amount of $1,860,000. At 31 March 20X8 it had increased to $2,880,000.

During the year to 31 March 20X8 plant with a carrying amount of $240,000 was sold at a loss of $90,000, depreciation of $280,000 was charged and $100,000 was added to the revaluation surplus in respect of property, plant and equipment.

What amount should appear under 'investing activities' in the statement of cash flows of Pinto for the year ended 31 March 20X8 as cash paid to acquire property, plant and equipment?

A $1,640,000
B $1,440,000
C $1,260,000
D $1,350,000   **(2 marks)**

248   The following information is available for the property, plant and equipment of Fry as at 30 September:

	20X4	20X3
	$'000	$'000
Carrying amounts	23,400	14,400

The following items were recorded during the year ended 30 September 20X4:

(i)   Depreciation charge of $2.5 million

(ii)   An item of plant with a carrying amount of $3 million was sold for $1.8 million

(iii)   A property was revalued upwards by $2 million

(iv)   Environmental provisions of $4 million relating to property, plant and equipment were capitalised during the year

What amount would be shown in Fry's statement of cash flows for purchase of property, plant and equipment for the year ended 30 September 20X4?

A $8.5 million

B $12.5 million

C $7.3 million

D $10.5 million   (2 marks)

                                                                                                            (6 marks)

CBE style OTQ bank – statement of cash flows

249   The carrying amount of property, plant and equipment was $410 million at 31 March 20X1 and $680 million at 31 March 20X2. During the year, property with a carrying amount of $210 million was revalued to $290 million. The depreciation charge for the year was $115 million. There were no disposals.

What amount will appear on the statement of cash flows for the year ended 31 March 20X2 in respect of purchases of property, plant and equipment?

$ [   ]   (2 marks)

250   Extracts from Deltoid's statements of financial position are as follows.

Statement of financial position as at 31 March:

	20X1	20X0
	$'000	$'000
Non-current assets		
Property, plant and equipment		
Leased plant	6,500	2,500
Non-current liabilities		
Finance lease obligations	4,800	2,000
Current liabilities		
Finance lease obligations	1,700	800

During the year to 31 March 20X1 depreciation charged on leased plant was $1,800,000.

What amount will be shown in the statement of cash flows of Deltoid for the year ended 31 March 20X1 in respect of payments made under finance leases?

$ [   ]   (2 marks)

                                                                                                            (4 marks)

Section C

251 Dickson

39 mins

Below are the statements of financial position of Dickson as at 31 March 20X8 and 31 March 20X7, together with the statement of profit or loss and other comprehensive income for the year ended 31 March 20X8.

	20X8	20X7
	$'000	$'000
Non-current assets		
Property, plant and equipment	925	737
Development expenditure	290	160
	1,215	897
Current assets		
Inventories	360	227
Trade receivables	274	324
Investments	143	46
Cash	29	117
	806	714
Total assets	2,021	1,611
Equity		
Share capital – $1 ordinary shares	500	400
Share premium	350	100
Revaluation surplus	160	60
Retained earnings	229	255
	1,239	815
Non-current liabilities		
6% debentures	150	100
Finance lease liabilities	100	80
Deferred tax	48	45
	298	225
Current liabilities		
Trade payables	274	352
Finance lease liabilities	17	12
Current tax	56	153
Debenture interest	5	–
Bank overdraft	132	54
	484	571
Total equity and liabilities	2,021	1,611

STATEMENT OF PROFIT OR LOSS AND OTHER COMPREHENSIVE INCOME

	$'000
Revenue	1,476
Cost of sales	(962)
Gross profit	514
Other expenses	(157)
Finance costs	(15)
Profit before tax	342
Income tax expense	(162)
Profit for the year	180
Other comprehensive income:	
Gain on revaluation of property, plant and equipment	100
Total comprehensive income for the year	280

Notes

(i) During 20X8, amortisation of $60,000 was charged on development projects.

(ii) During 20X8 items of property, plant and equipment with a carrying amount of $103,000 were sold for $110,000. Profit on sale was netted off against 'other expenses'.

Depreciation charged in the year on property, plant and equipment totalled $57,000. Dickson purchased $56,000 of property, plant and equipment by means of finance leases, payments being made in arrears on the last day of each accounting period.

(iii) The current asset investments are government bonds and management has decided to class them as cash equivalents.

(iv) The new debentures were issued on 1 April 20X7. Finance cost includes debenture interest and finance lease finance charges only.

(v) During the year Dickson made a 1 for 8 bonus issue, capitalising its retained earnings, followed by a rights issue.

Required

(a) Prepare a statement of cash flows for Dickson in accordance with IAS 7 using the indirect method.

(b) Prepare (additionally) net cash from operating activities using the direct method.   **(20 marks)**

---

252 Mocha (12/11 amended)   39 mins

(a) The following information relates to the draft financial statements of Mocha.

SUMMARISED STATEMENTS OF FINANCIAL POSITION AS AT 30 SEPTEMBER

	20X1	20X0
	$'000	$'000
ASSETS		
Non-current assets		
Property, plant and equipment (note (i))	32,600	24,100
Financial asset: equity investments (note (ii))	4,500	7,000
	37,100	31,100
Current assets		
Inventory	10,200	7,200
Trade receivables	3,500	3,700
Bank	nil	1,400
	13,700	12,300
Total assets	50,800	43,400
EQUITY AND LIABILITIES		
Equity		
Equity shares of $1 each (note (iii))	14,000	8,000
Share premium (note (iii))	nil	2,000
Revaluation reserve (note (iii))	2,000	3,600
Retained earnings	13,000	10,100
	29,000	23,700

	20X1	20X0
	$'000	$'000
Non-current liabilities		
Finance lease obligations	7,000	6,900
Deferred tax	1,300	900
Current liabilities		
Tax	1,000	1,200
Bank overdraft	2,900	nil
Provision for product warranties (note (iv))	1,600	4,000
Finance lease obligations	4,800	2,100
Trade payables	3,200	4,600
Total equity and liabilities	50,800	43,400

SUMMARISED STATEMENTS OF PROFIT OR LOSS FOR THE YEARS ENDED 30 SEPTEMBER:

	20X1	20X0
	$'000	$'000
Revenue	58,500	41,000
Cost of sales	(46,500)	(30,000)
Gross profit	12,000	11,000
Operating expenses	(8,700)	(4,500)
Investment income (note (ii))	1,100	700
Finance costs	(500)	(400)
Profit before tax	3,900	6,800
Income tax expense	(1,000)	(1,800)
Profit for the year	2,900	5,000

The following additional information is available.

(i) Property, plant and equipment

	Cost	Accumulated depreciation	Carrying amount
	$'000	$'000	$'000
At 30 September 20X0	33,600	(9,500)	24,100
New finance lease additions	6,700		6,700
Purchase of new plant	8,300		8,300
Disposal of property	(5,000)	1,000	(4,000)
Depreciation for the year		(2,500)	(2,500)
At 30 September 20X1	43,600	(11,000)	32,600

The property disposed of was sold for $8.1 million.

(ii) Investments/investment income:

During the year an investment that had a carrying amount of $3 million was sold for $3.4 million. No investments were purchased during the year.

Investment income consists of:

Year to 30 September:	20X1	20X0
	$'000	$'000
Dividends received	200	250
Profit on sale of investment	400	nil
Increases in fair value	500	450
	1,100	700

(iii) On 1 April 20X1 there was a bonus issue of shares that was funded from the share premium and some of the revaluation reserve. This was followed on 30 April 20X1 by an issue of shares for cash at par.

(iv)   The movement in the product warranty provision has been included in cost of sales.

Required

Prepare a statement of cash flows for Mocha for the year ended 30 September 20X1, in accordance with IAS 7 *Statement of cash flows*, using the indirect method.   **(20 marks)**

MCQ bank – accounting for inflation

253   Historical cost accounting remains in use because of its practical advantages.

Which one of the following is **not** an advantage of historical cost accounting?

A   Amounts of transactions are reliable and can be verified.

B   Amounts in the statement of financial position can be matched to amounts in the statement of cash flows

C   It avoids the overstatement of profit which can arise during periods of inflation.

D   It provides fewer opportunities for creative accounting than systems of current value accounting.   **(2 marks)**

254   Overstatement of profits can arise during periods of inflation. This then leads to a number of other consequences. Which one of the following is **not** a likely consequence of overstatement of profits?

A   Higher wage demands from employees

B   Higher tax bills

C   Reduced dividends to shareholders

D   Overstated EPS   **(2 marks)**

255   Drexler acquired an item of plant on 1 October 20X2 at a cost of $500,000. It has an expected life of five years (straight line depreciation) and an estimated residual value of 10% of its historical cost or current cost as appropriate. As at 30 September 20X4, the manufacturer of the plant still makes the same item of plant and its current price is $600,000.

What is the correct carrying amount to be shown in the statement of financial position of Drexler as at 30 September 20X4 under historical cost and current cost?

	Historical cost	Current cost
	$	$
A	320,000	600,000
B	320,000	384,000
C	300,000	600,000
D	300,000	384,000

(2 marks)

(6 marks)

CBE style OTQ bank – accounting for inflation

256   The 'physical capital maintenance' concept states that profit is the increase in the physical productive capacity of the business over the period. This concept is applied in:

☐   Current cost accounting

☐   Historical cost accounting

☐   Current value accounting

☐   Current purchasing power accounting   **(2 marks)**

257 Which method of accounting adjusts income and capital values to allow for the effects of general price inflation?

☐ Historical cost accounting

☐ Current purchasing power accounting

☐ Current cost accounting

☐ Current value accounting **(2 marks)**

258 Under CCA goods sold are charged to profit or loss at:

☐ Historical cost

☐ Replacement cost

☐ Net realisable value

☐ Economic value **(2 marks)**

(6 marks)

MCQ bank – specialised, not-for-profit and public sector entities

259 Which of the following are unlikely to be stakeholders in a charity?

A Taxpayers
B Financial supporters
C Shareholders
D Government **(2 marks)**

260 The International Public Sector Accounting Standards Board regulates public sector entities and is developing a set of accounting standards which closely mirror IFRS.

Which of these is the main concept which needs to be introduced into public sector accounting?

A Materiality
B Accruals
C Relevance
D Faithful representation **(2 marks)**

261 Public sector entities have performance measures laid down by government, based on Key Performance Indicators. Which of the following are likely to be financial KPIs for a local council?

(i) Rent receipts outstanding
(ii) Interest paid
(iii) Interest received
(iv) Interest cover
(v) Dividend cover
(vi) Financial actuals against budget
(vii) Return on capital employed

A (i),(ii),(iii),(iv),(vi)
B (i),(ii),(vi),(vii)
C (ii),(iii),(iv),(v)
D All of them **(2 marks)**

262 Which one of the following is **not** true of entities in the charity sector?

    A   Their objective is to provide services to recipients and not to make a profit.

    B   They have to be registered.

    C   Their revenues arise mainly from contributions rather than sales.

    D   They have only a narrow group of stakeholders to consider.   **(2 marks)**

(8 marks)

CBE style OTQ bank – specialised, not-for-profit and public sector entities

263 Which one of the following is the main aspect in which public sector bodies differ from charities?

☐ Importance of budgeting

☐ Funded by government

☐ Performance measured by KPIs

☐ No requirement to earn a return on assets   **(2 marks)**

264 Although the objectives and purposes of not-for-profit entities are different from those of commercial entities, the accounting requirements of not-for-profit entities are moving closer to those entities to which IFRSs apply.

Which of the following IFRS requirements would **not** be relevant to a not-for-profit entity?

☐ Preparation of a statement of cash flows

☐ Requirement to capitalise a finance lease

☐ Disclosure of dividends per share

☐ Disclosure of non-adjusting events after the reporting date   **(2 marks)**

265 Which of the following statements about a not-for-profit entity is valid?

☐ There is no requirement to calculate an earnings per share figure as it is not likely to have shareholders who need to assess its earnings performance.

☐ The current value of its property, plant and equipment is not relevant as it is not a commercial entity.

☐ Interpretation of its financial performance using ratio analysis is meaningless.

☐ Its financial statements will not be closely scrutinised as it does not have any investors.   **(2 marks)**

(6 marks)

Answers

MCQ bank – conceptual framework

1   C   A resource controlled by an entity as a result of past events and from which future economic benefits are expected to flow to the entity

2   C   This is a valid liability.

             The licence payment could be avoided by ceasing manufacture.

             The fall in value of the investment is a loss chargeable to profit or loss.

             Planned expenditure does not constitute an obligation.

3   B   The amount that could be obtained from selling the asset, less any costs of disposal

4   A   The underlying assumption is going concern.

CBE style OTQ bank – conceptual framework

5   Comparability

        Disclosure of accounting policies is particularly important when comparing the results and performance of one entity against another which may be applying different policies.

6   To be authoritative where a specific IFRS conflicts with the *Conceptual Framework*

        Whenever there is a conflict between an IFRS and the *Conceptual Framework*, the IFRS takes precedence.

7   A receivable from a customer which has been sold (factored) to a finance company. The finance company has full recourse to the company for any losses.

        The receivable has been factored with recourse so should continue to be recognised as an asset. The other options do not meet the criteria to be recognised as an asset.

8   Applying an entity's current accounting policy to a transaction which an entity has not engaged in before

        As the transaction has not been engaged in before, comparability is not an issue.

Section B

Lisbon MCQ case

9   C   The *Conceptual Framework* requires information to be presented understandably, but without omitting complex issues.

10   A   Faithful representation. The substance of the transaction is likely to be that of a secured loan.

11   C   Relevance. The historical cost of the properties will be less relevant than their current value.

12   C   The financial statements should be prepared on a different basis. The basis of valuation of assets will be affected.

13   D   This is a change of accounting policy so the information will be amended retrospectively.

MCQ bank – regulatory framework

14   A   An Exposure Draft will be published following review of Discussion Paper comments.

15   C   Accountants and auditors may have **less** defence in case of litigation as they will not be able to demonstrate that they followed some precise rule, but will instead have to defend their application of judgement.

CBE style OTQ – regulatory framework

16   The correct answers are:

A rules-based system will require more detailed regulations than a principles-based system.
A rules-based system seeks to cover every eventuality.

A rules-based system has more detailed regulations because it seeks to cover every eventuality. A principles-based system gives rise to fewer accounting standards and requires the exercise of more judgement.

MCQ bank – tangible non-current assets

17   B

	$'000
Land	1,200
Materials	2,400
Labour	3,000
Architects fees	25
Surveyors fees	15
Site overheads	300
Testing fire alarms	10
	6,950

18   A   Weighted average capitalisation rate =

$(9\% \times 15 / 39) + (11\% \times 24 / 39) = 3.5\% + 7\% = 10.5\%$

		$
Borrowing costs =	$6m × 10.5% × 9/12	472,500
+	$2m × 10.5% × 5/12	87,500
		560,000

19   A

	$
Borrowing costs March – December ($2.4m × 8% × 10/ 12)	160,000
Less investment income ($1m × 6% × 6/12)	(30,000)
	130,000

20   C   A and B would be classified as inventory and WIP. The property leased out to a subsidiary would be regarded as an investment property in the single entity financial statements of Buildco but is treated as owner-occupied in the **consolidated** financial statements.

21   D   A gain or loss arising from a change in the fair value of an investment property is recognised in profit or loss. The other options are all correct.

22   D   Weighted capitalisation rate =

$(10\% \times 140 / 340) + (8\% \times 200 / 340) = 4.1\% + 4.7\% = 8.8\%$
$50 million × 8.8% × 6/12 = $2.2 million

CBE style OTQ bank – tangible non-current assets

23    $37,250

	$'000
Machine ((500,000 – 20,000) / 10 × 9/12)	36,000
Safety guard ((25,000/5) × 3/12)	1,250
	37,250

24   The correct answer is:

Capitalised and depreciated over the period to the next overhaul.

The expenditure should be capitalised when it takes place and depreciated over the period to the next overhaul. It should not be provided for in advance because there is no obligation arising from a past event – the overhaul could be avoided by ceasing to operate the aircraft.

25   $3,087

The machine has been owned for 2 years 3 months, so the remaining useful life at 31 March 20X7 was 9 years 9 months.

Prior to revaluation it was being depreciated at $2,500 pa (30,000/12), so the charge for the first three months of 20X7 was $625.

The machine will now be depreciated over the remaining 9 years 9 months = 117 months. So the charge for the remaining 9 months of 20X7 is $2,462 ((32,000 / 117) × 9).

So total depreciation for the year ended 31.12.X7 is (625 + 2,462) = $3,087

26   $203,000

	$
Cost 1.1.X0	900,000
Depreciation to 30.6.X8 (900,000 × 8.5 / 50)	(153,000)
Carrying amount 30.6.X8	747,000
Revaluation surplus	203,000
Fair value 30.6.X8	950,000

The increase of (1,200 – 950) = $250,000 arising between 30.6.X8 and 31.12.X8 will be credited to profit or loss in accordance with IAS 40.

Section B

Plethora plc MCQ case

27   B

Building transferred to investment property

	$'000
Original cost	600
Depreciation 1.1.X0 to 1.7.X9 ((600 / 50) × 9.5)	(114)
Carrying amount at 1.7.X9	486
Revaluation surplus	314
Fair value	800

28   A

The increase in value in this case of $190,000 (740,000 – 550,000) will be credited to profit or loss in accordance with IAS 40.

29   C   Recoverable amount. This is the higher of fair value less costs of disposal and value in use.

30   B   The impairment loss is not allocated to current assets.

31   D

	Prior to review $'000	After review $'000
Building	900	825
Plant and equipment	300	275
Inventory	70	70
Other current assets	130	130
Goodwill	40	–
	1,440	1,300
Recoverable amount	(1,300)	
Impairment loss	140	

The impairment loss is allocated first against goodwill and then pro-rata against the tangible non-current assets. This means writing $75,000 off the carrying amount of the building and $25,000 off plant and equipment.

Dearing MCQ case

32   B

Cost price

	$
Base price	1,050,000
Trade discount (1,050,000 × 20%)	(210,000)
	840,000
Freight charges	30,000
Electrical installation cost	28,000
Pre-production testing	22,000
	920,000

33   A   They should be added to the carrying amount of the machine

34   C   The cost of the overhaul should be capitalised and amortised over the period to the next overhaul.

35   A   The economic performance of the machine had declined.
The other options are **external** indicators of impairment.

36   B   Fair value less costs of disposal

MCQ bank – intangible assets

37   D   In order for capitalisation to be allowed it is not necessary for development to be completed, patents to be registered or sales contracts signed. However, an intangible asset can only be recognised if its cost can be reliably measured.

38   C

	$
Research costs	1,400,000
Expensed development Jan-Mar (800 × 3)	2,400,000
Depreciation on capitalised amount b/f (20m × 20%)	4,000,000
	7,800,000

Note that no depreciation is charged on the new project as it is still in development.

39   B   A pre-production prototype is classified as a development cost, so it is eligible to be capitalised. Internally-generated customer lists and goodwill cannot be capitalised. IAS 38 does not allow capitalisation of research costs.

CBE style OTQ bank – intangible assets

40 $12,500,000

	$m
Recoverable amount – fair value less costs of disposal	15.0
Less depreciation 1.4.X9 – 30.9.X9 (15m / 3 × 6/12)	(2.5)
	12.5

41 $88,000

	$
Expenses 1 January to 1 March (40,000 × 2)	80,000
4 months capitalised and amortised	
((40,000 × 4) / 5 years × 3/12)	8,000
	88,000

Section B

Dexterity MCQ case

42 A The training courses should be charged to profit or loss.

43 D The asset does not need to be completed or the proceeds reliably measured.

44 C This activity is still at the research stage.

45 B (10m – ((10m/8) × 6/12))

46 B It should be capitalised and reviewed for impairment every year.

CBE style OTQ bank – impairment of assets

47 $594,000

	$'000
Total impairment (1,010 – 750)	260
Goodwill	(90)
Damaged plant	(40)
Balance to allocate	130

The remaining $130,000 will be allocated pro rata as follows.

	Building	Plant
	$'000	$'000
	700	160
Impairment	(106)	(24)
	594	

48 The correct answer is:

The higher of fair value less costs of disposal and value in use.

49 $7,687

Fair value less costs of disposal (78,000 – 2,500)		$75,500
Value in use:	30,000 × 1 / 1.08 = 27,778	
	30,000 × 1 / 1.08^2 = 25,720	
	30,000 × 1 / 1.08^3 = 23,815	$77,313

Recoverable amount is $77,313 and carrying amount is $85,000, so impairment is $7,687.

50   The correct answers are:

An unusually significant fall in the market value of one or more assets
An increase in the market interest rates used to calculate value in use of the assets

The other options are internal indicators of impairment.

51        $350,000

	$
Fair value less costs of disposal (2.7m – 50,000)	2,650,000
Value in use	2,600,000
Recoverable amount is therefore:	2,650,000
Impairment loss (β)	350,000
Carrying amount	3,000,000

MCQ bank – impairment of assets

52   A

	$m	$m	$m
Goodwill	3	(3)	–
Patent	5	(3)	2
Property	10	(2)	8
Plant and equipment	15	(3)	12
Current assets	2	-	2
	35	(11)	24

The goodwill is written off, the patent is written down and the remaining $5m impairment is allocated pro-rata to the property and the plant.

53   A

	$
Carrying amount (100,000 × 5/10)	50,000
Fair value less costs to sell	30,000
Value in use (8,500 × 3.79)	32,215

Recoverable amount is $32,215 and impairment loss = 50,000 – 32,215 = $17,785

54   A

	Net assets prior to impairment	Impairment	Impaired net assets
	$	$	$
PPE	200,000	(45,455)	154,545
Goodwill	50,000	(50,000)	-
Patent	20,000	(4,545)	15,455
Net current assets	30,000	–	30,000
	300,000	(100,000)	200,000

Goodwill is written off in full and the balance of the loss is pro-rated between PPE and the patent.

55   D   If the NRV of inventory is greater than its carrying amount, no impairment has arisen.

Section B

Systria CBE style OTQ case

56 $40,000

	Original	Impairment	
	$'000	$'000	
Goodwill	50	(50)	
Patent	10	(10)	
Land and buildings	100	(20)	*Remaining 30*
Plant and machinery	50	(10)	*pro-rata*
Net current assets	10	-	
		(90)	

57 The correct answers are;

There are adverse changes to the use to which the asset is put.

The operating performance of the asset has declined.

Depreciation is irrelevant and the other options is an *external* indicator of impairment.

58 $1.5 million

Recoverable amount is $6 million, leaving an impairment loss of $4 million.

$2.5 million will be allocated to the destroyed assets and the remaining $1.5 million written off goodwill.

$3 million - $1.5 million = $1.5 million.

59 DR Accumulated depreciation $20,000

DR Property at cost $30,000 / CR Revaluation surplus $50,000

The depreciation is written off and the balance added to the cost of the property.

60 $3,250

Depreciation to date of $20,000 means the property has 40 years of useful life left at the revaluation date. Depreciation will be $130,000/40.

MCQ bank – revenue

61 A

	$
Costs incurred to date	740,000
Recognised profits (W)	231,000
Amounts invoiced	(700,000)
Contract asset	271,000

Working	
Total contract revenue	2,800,000
Costs to date	(740,000)
Costs to complete	(1,400,000)
Total expected profit	660,000
Profit to date (660,000 × 35%)	231,000

62   C   The grant can be treated as deferred income or deducted from the carrying amount of the asset. It cannot be credited directly to profit or loss.

63   A

	$'000
Total contract revenue	50,000
Costs to date	(12,000)
Specialist plant	(8,000)
Costs to complete	(10,000)
Total profit on contract	20,000

Profit to date = $20m × 22 / 50 = $8,800,000

64   A

	$
Costs incurred to date	48,000
Recognised profits (W)	10,800
Amounts invoiced	(50,400)
Contract asset	8,400

Working	
Total contract revenue	120,000
Costs to date	(48,000)
Costs to complete	(48,000)
Total expected profit	24,000
Profit to date (24,000 × 45%)	10,800

65   B   This feature suggests that the transaction is a genuine sale.

If the seller retains the right to use the asset or it remains on his premises, then the risks and rewards have not been transferred. If the sale price does not equal market value, then the transaction is likely to be a secured loan.

66   A

	$m
Contract price	12
Total costs (6 + 9)	(15)
Foreseeable loss	(3)

Costs to date	6
Foreseeable loss	(3)
Amounts invoiced	(4)
Contract liability	(1)

67   D   No sale has taken place as control of the goods has not been transferred, but Cambridge must show that it is holding $90,000 which belongs to Circus.

68   C   The amount to recognise in revenue is $150,000 as the servicing amount of $30,000 has not yet been earned. This would be recognised as deferred income.

CBE style OTQ bank – revenue

69    $160,000

Expected profit = ($5m – ($2.4m + $1.6m) = $1m
Profit to date = ($1m × (1.8m/5)) = $0.36m

Contract asset:

	$'000
Costs to date	1,600
Profit to date	360
Less amounts invoiced	(1,800)
	160

70 The correct answers are:

Manufacturer can require dealer to return the inventory
Manufacturer bears obsolescence risk

These both indicate that the manufacturer retains ownership of the inventory. The other options would indicate that the risks and rewards have been transferred to the dealer.

71 $105,000

	$
Grant received 1.4.X7	500,000
Recognised year to 31.3.X8 (500,000 × 30%)	(150,000)
Balance 31.3.X8	350,000
Recognised year to 31.3.X9 (350,000 × 30%)	105,000

72 $24,920,000

	$'000
Revenue per draft profit or loss	27,000
Servicing costs (800 × 2 × 130%)	(2,080)
	24,920

Section B

Derringdo MCQ case

73 C

	$
Operating expenses	
Depreciation charge (800,000 × 85% × 10% × 6/12))	34,000
Release of grant (240,000 × 10% × 6/12)	(12,000)
	22,000

74 D

	$
Deferred income	
Grant received ($800,000 × 30%)	240,000
Release for this year ($240,000 × 10% × 6/12)	(12,000)
Total balance at year-end	228,000
Presentation	
Current liability ($240,000 × 10%)	24,000
Non-current liability (balance)	204,000
	228,000

75 A

	$
Year 1	
Laptop (W)	158
Broadband (562 (W) /2)	281
	439

Working

Laptop	200	22%	158
Broadband (30 × 12 × 2)	720	78%	562
	920	100%	720

76 D Allocating the transaction price to the performance obligations

77 B The other options would all suggest that Derringdo was the principal.

Bridgenorth CBE style OTQ Case

78    $240,000

		$
Revenue	40% ×5,0000,000 =	2,000,000
Expenses	40% × (2,300,000 + 2,100,000) =	(1,760,000)
		240,000

79    $500,000   Work invoiced less cash received

80    $1,125,000

	$
Costs to date	3,600,000
Profit to date ((5,000,000 – 4,300,000) × 75%)	525,000
	4,125,000
Less amounts invoiced	(3,000,000)
	1,125,000

81   The correct answer is:

Costs incurred as a % of total expected costs.
This is a valid measure of the inputs expended to satisfy the performance obligation.

82    $400,000   Bridgenorth can recognise revenue to the extent of costs incurred to date.

CBE style OTQ bank – introduction to groups

83   The correct answer is:

There is no basis on which a subsidiary may be excluded from consolidation.

84   The correct answer is:

Credited to profit or loss

IFRS 3 requires negative goodwill to be credited to profit or loss.

85   The correct answer is:

Existence of significant influence. The other options indicate control over a subsidiary.

86   The correct answers are:

A subsidiary with a different reporting date may prepare additional statements up to the group reporting date for consolidation purposes.
When a subsidiary's financial statements are drawn up to a different reporting date from those of the parent, adjustments should be made for significant transactions or events occurring between the two reporting dates.
The allowable gap between reporting dates is three months, not five.

MCQ bank – introduction to groups

87   B   The present value of the future cash flows that the asset is expected to generate measures present value, not fair value. The other items would be considered in determining fair value.

88   B   This is the definition of **significant influence**, not control.

89   D   Consolidation is not appropriate in this case as the parent has lost control.

90 Preparation question: Group financial statements

(a) A parent need not present consolidated financial statements if one of the following exemptions applies.

- It is itself a wholly or partly-owned subsidiary of another entity and its other owners do not object to it not preparing consolidated financial statements.

- Its shares or debt instruments are not traded on any stock exchange.

- Its financial statements are not being filed with any regulatory organisation for the purpose of issuing any debt or equity instruments on any stock exchange.

- Its own or ultimate parent produces publicly-available financial statements that comply with IFRS.

(b) IFRS 10 *Consolidated financial statements* requires intragroup balances, transactions, income and expenses to be eliminated in full. The purpose of consolidated financial statements is to present the financial position of the parent and subsidiaries as that of a **single entity**, the group. This means that, in the consolidated statement of profit or loss, the only profits recognised should be those earned by the group in trading with entities outside the group. Similarly, inventory should be valued at cost to the group.

When a company sells goods to another company in the same group it will recognise revenue and profit in its individual financial statements. However, from the point of view of the group, no sale has taken place, because the goods are still held by the group. The sale must therefore be eliminated from revenue and the unrealised profit must be eliminated from group inventory.

Where one group company owes money to another group company or one company holds loan stock of another company, the asset and liability balances will be eliminated on consolidation. As far as the group is concerned, they do not represent amounts due to or from third parties.

Section C

91 Boo and Goose

BOO GROUP – CONSOLIDATED STATEMENT OF PROFIT OR LOSS AND OTHER COMPREHENSIVE INCOME
FOR THE YEAR ENDED 31 DECEMBER 20X8

	$'000
Revenue (5,000 + 1,000 – 100 (W5))	5,900
Cost of sales (2,900 + 600 – 100 + 20 (W5))	(3,420)
Gross profit	2,480
Other expenses (1,700 + 320)	(2,020)
Profit before tax	460
Tax (130 + 25)	(155)
Profit for the year	305
Other comprehensive income	
Gain on property revaluation	20
Total comprehensive income for the year	325
Profit attributable to	
Owners of the parent	294
Non-controlling interest (20% × 55)	11
	305
Total comprehensive income attributable to	
Owners of the parent (ß)	314
Non-controlling interest	11
	325

CONSOLIDATED STATEMENT OF FINANCIAL POSITION AS AT 31 DECEMBER 20X8

	$'000	$'000
Assets		
Non-current assets (1,940 + 200)		2,140
Goodwill (W2)		70
Current assets		
Inventory (500 + 120 + 80)	700	
Trade receivables (650 – 100 (W5) + 40)	590	
Bank and cash (170 + 35)	205	
		1,495
Total assets		3,705
Equity and liabilities		
Equity attributable to owners of the parent		
Share capital (Boo only)		2,000
Retained earnings (W3)		520
Revaluation surplus		20
		2,540
Non-controlling interest (W4)		70
Total equity		2,610
Current liabilities		
Trade payables (910 + 30)	940	
Tax (130 + 25)	155	
		1,095
Total equity and liabilities		3,705

Workings

1 *Group structure*

Boo

↓ 80%

Goose

2 *Goodwill*

	$'000	$'000
Consideration transferred		300
Fair value of non-controlling interest		60
		360
Fair value of net assets:		
Share capital	100	
Retained earnings	190	(290)
Goodwill		70

3 *Retained earnings*

	Boo $'000	Goose $'000
Per question	500	240
Unrealised profit (W5)	(20)	
	480	
Less pre acquisition		(190)
		50
Goose: 80% × 50	40	
Group total	520	

4   Non-controlling interest

	$'000
NCI at acquisition	60
NCI share of post - acquisition retained earnings (50 × 20%)	10
	70

5   Intragroup issues

Step 1: Record Goose's purchase

DEBIT Cost of sales	$100,000	
CREDIT Payables		$100,000
DEBIT Closing inventory (SFP)	$100,000	
CREDIT Cost of sales		$100,000

These transactions can be simplified to:

DEBIT Inventory	$100,000	
CREDIT Payables		$100,000

Step 2: Cancel unrealised profit

DEBIT COS (and retained earnings) in Boo	$20,000	
CREDIT Inventory (SFP)		$20,000

Step 3: Cancel intragroup transaction

DEBIT Revenue	$100,000	
CREDIT Cost of sales		$100,000

Step 4: Cancel intragroup balances

DEBIT Payables	$100,000	
CREDIT Receivables		$100,000

CBE style OTQ bank – consolidated statement of financial position

92 $193,125

	$
Fair value at acquisition (200,000 × 30% × $1.75)	105,000
Share of post-acquisition retained earnings ((750 − 450) × 30%)	90,000
Depreciation on fair value adjustment ((250 / 40) × 30%)	(1,875)
	193,125

93 $139,370

	$	$
Consideration transferred:		
Cash		250,000
Deferred consideration (400,000 / 1.08)		370,370
Shares (30,000 × $2.30)		69,000
		689,370
Fair value of non-controlling interest		400,000
		1,089,370
Fair value of net assets:		
Shares	100,000	
Retained earnings	850,000	
		(950,000)
		139,370

94   Increase $40,000

$($1.2 million / 8 × 4/12) × 80% = $40,000$

The adjustment will reduce depreciation over the next 8 years, so it will *increase* retained earnings.

$105 million

	$'000
Shares (18m × 2/3 × $5.75)	69,000
Deferred consideration (18m × $2.42 × 1 / 1.1^2)	36,000
	105,000

MCQ bank – consolidated statement of financial position

96   **D**   This adjustment reduces (debits) the liability and the credit is to retained earnings. The remeasurement relates to the post-acquisition period, so goodwill is not affected.

97   **D**

	$	$
Consideration transferred		800,000
Fair value of non-controlling interest		220,000
		1,020,000
Fair value of net assets:		
Shares	100,000	
Retained earnings	570,000	
Revaluation surplus	150,000	
Intangible	90,000	
		(910,000)
		110,000

98   **C**

	$	$
Consideration		200,000
NCI		82,800
Net assets:		
Shares	100,000	
Retained earnings	156,000	256,000
Goodwill		26,800
Phantom		275,000
Ghost:		
(177 – 156) × 70%		14,700
Goodwill impairment (26,800 / 2) × 70%		(9,380)
Group retained earnings		280,320

99   **A**   This combination results in negative goodwill of $1.2 million which should be credited to profit or loss.

Section B

Root and Branch CBE style OTQ case

100   **$268 million**

	$m
Cash	210
Shares (116m × 100/200)	58
	268

101 $5.6 million

	Acquisition $m	Movement (2 years) $m
Property	20	(2)
Brand	25	(5)
		(7)

$7 million × 80% = $5.6 million

102 $16 million

$56m × 40/140

103 The correct answer is:

DR Cost of sales / CR Inventories

The unrealised profit is added to cost of sales and removed from inventories.

104 The correct answer is:

Control of the subsidiary has been lost

Exclusion from consolidation is only allowed when control has been lost.

Section C

105 Pedantic (12/08 amended)

Text references. Chapters 8 and 9

Top tips. The first point to note here is that the subsidiary was acquired mid-year. Remember this when it comes to working out the depreciation on the fair value adjustment. This question had lots to do but no real problems. Get the formats down, note the adjustments on the question paper and then start working through.

Easy marks. There were lots of easy marks here. There were lots of marks available in the statement of financial position even if you did not get the goodwill quite right. Correctly calculating the figures from the share exchange would have gained you marks on goodwill, share capital and share premium.

			Marks
(a)	Statement of financial position:		
	Property, plant and equipment	2	
	Goodwill	5	
	Current assets	1½	
	Equity shares	1	
	Share premium	1	
	Retained earnings	2	
	Non-controlling interest	2	
	10% loan notes	½	
	Current liabilities	1	16
(b)	1 mark per valid point to maximum		4
			20

(a) PEDANTIC – CONSOLIDATED STATEMENT OF FINANCIAL POSITION AT 30 SEPTEMBER 20X8

	$'000
Non-current assets	
Property, plant and equipment (40,600 + 12,600 + 1,800 (W6))	55,000
Goodwill (W2)	4,500
	59,500
Current assets (16,000 + 6,600 – 800 – 600 + 200) (or see (W9))	21,400
Total assets	80,900
Equity attributable to owners of the parent	
Share capital (10,000 +1,600 (W5))	11,600
Share premium (W5)	8,000
Retained earnings (W3)	35,700
	55,300
Non-controlling interests (W4)	6,100
	61,400
Non-current liabilities	
10% loan notes (3,000 + 4,000)	7,000
Current liabilities (8,200 + 4,700 – 400 (W9))	12,500
	80,900

(b) Pedantic cannot take assurance from the Tradhat group financial statements that Trilby would be able to meet its liability in respect of the goods. The group financial statements will have aggregated the assets and liabilities of all the group companies and it will not be possible to use them to calculate liquidity ratios for any one company.

This is important, because Pedantic's contract would not be with the Tradhat group, it would be with Trilby. If Trilby defaulted on its obligations, the Tradhat group would be under no legal obligation to step in, so that the fact that the group has a strong financial position is not really relevant. It would only become relevant if Tradhat were willing to offer a parent company guarantee.

In the absence of a parent company guarantee, Pedantic must base its decision on the financial position of Trilby as shown in its individual company financial statements. It should also obtain references from other suppliers of Trilby, specifically those who supply it with large orders on 90-day credit terms.

Workings

1 Group structure

```
              Pedantic
1.4.X8          |          60%      Mid-year acquisition, six months before year end
                ↓
             Sophistic
```

2 Goodwill

	$'000	$'000
Consideration transferred (W5)		9,600
Fair value of non-controlling interests		5,900
Less: Fair value of net assets at acquisition:		
Share capital	4,000	
Retained earnings	5,000	
Fair value adjustment (W6)	2,000	
		(11,000)
Goodwill		4,500

3   *Retained earnings*

	Pedantic $'000	Sophistic $'000
Per question	35,400	6,500
Movement on FV adjustment (W6)		(200)
PUP (W7)		(800)
Pre- acquisition		(5,000)
		500
Group share (500 × 60%)	300	
	35,700	

4   *Non-controlling interests*

	$'000
NCI at acquisition	5,900
NCI share of post-acquisition retained earnings ((W3) 500 × 40%)	200
	6,100

5   *Share exchange*

	Dr $'000	Cr $'000
Consideration transferred (4,000 × 60% × 2/3 = 1,600 × $6)	9,600	
Share capital of Pedantic (1,600 × $1)		1,600
Share premium of Pedantic (1,600 × $5)		8,000

6   *Fair value adjustments*

	$,000 *Acq'n* 1.4.X8	$'000 *Mov't* 6/12	$'000 *Year end* 30.9.X8
Plant (*$2m / 5 × 6/12)	2,000	(200)*	1,800

7   *Intragroup trading*

	$'000	$'000
Eliminate unrealised profit		
Cost of sales/retained earnings ((8,000 − 5,200) × 40 / 140)	800	
Inventories (SOFP)		800

8   *Current assets (supplementary working)*

	$'000
Pedantic	16,000
Sophistic	6,600
Unrealised profit in inventory (W7)	(800)
Intercompany receivables (per question)	(600)
Cash in transit (W9)	200
	21,400

9   *Cash in transit*

	Dr	Cr
Receivables		600
Payables	400	
Cash	200	

106 Highveldt

Text reference. Chapter 9.

Top tips. Make sure that you read the question before doing anything. You are not asked to prepare a statement of financial position; just the goodwill and reserves. This makes the question easier to manage as effectively you are just doing the workings without having to tie it all together in a set of financial statements.

There are quite a few complications to consider. For each calculation go through each of the six additional pieces of information and make appropriate adjustments when relevant.

Examination Team's comments. This question was unusual in asking for extracts from the statement of financial position. Many candidates were confused by this and wasted time preparing a full statement of financial position. Other common errors were: fair value adjustments; consolidated reserves; revaluation and share premium reserves; and the cost of the investment.

Marking scheme

			Marks
(i)	*Goodwill*		
	– Consideration transferred	2	
	– Non-controlling interest	1	
	– Share capital and premium	1	
	– Retained earnings	1	
	– Fair value adjustments	2	
	– Goodwill impairment	1	
		Maximum	8
(ii)	*Non-controlling interest*		
	– Share capital and premium	1	
	– Retained earnings	2	
	– Fair value adjustment	1	
		Maximum	4
(iii)	*Consolidated reserves*		
	– Share premium	1	
	– Revaluation surplus	2	
	Retained earnings		
	– Post acquisition profit	2	
	– Interest receivable	1	
	– Finance cost	1	
	– Goodwill impairment	1	
		Maximum	8
		Maximum for question	20

(i) *Goodwill in Samson*

	$m	$m
Consideration transferred		
80m shares × 75% × $3.50		210
Deferred consideration; $108m × ¹/₁.₀₈		100
		310
Non-controlling interest		83
Fair value of net assets at acquisition:		
Carrying amount of net assets at 1.4.20X4:		
Ordinary shares	80	
Share premium	40	
Retained earnings	134	
Fair value adjustments (W)	42	
		(296)
		88
Impairment charge given in question		(20)
Carrying amount at 31 March 20X5		77

Working

	$m
Fair value adjustment:	
Revaluation of land	20
Recognition of fair value of brands	40
Derecognition of capitalised development expenditure	(18)
	42

(ii) *Non-controlling interest in Samson's net assets*

	$m
NCI at acquisition (per question)	83
NCI share of post-acquisition retained earnings (((iii)) 48 × 25%)	12
NCI share of post-acquisition revaluation surplus (((iii)) 4 × 25%)	1
NCI share of goodwill impairment ($20m x 25%)	(5)
	91

(iii) *Consolidated Reserves*

Share premium

The share premium of a group, like the share capital, is the share premium of the parent only ($80m)

Revaluation surplus

	$m
Parent's own revaluation surplus	45
Group share of Samson's post acquisition revaluation; $4m × 75%	3

Retained earnings attributable to owners of the parent

	Highveldt $m	Samson $m
Per question	350	76
Accrued interest from Samson ($60m × 10%)	6	–
Unwinding of discount on deferred consideration	(8)	–
Amortisation of brand ($40m/10 years)	–	(4)
Write off development expenditure as incurred ($50m – $18m)	–	(32)
Write back amortisation of development expenditure	–	10
Unrealised profit	–	(2)
	348	48
Group share (75%)	36	
Impairment of goodwill in Samson – group share (20 x 75%)	(15)	
	369	

MCQ bank – consolidated statement of profit or loss and other comprehensive income

			$m
107	C		
		Decrease	12.0
		Increase ($2m × 25% (profit margin))	0.5
		Net decrease	11.5

			$'000
108	C		
		Loss of investment income(10m × 8% × 6/12)	(400)
		Saving of interest payable (400 × 60%)	240
		Net reduction in group retained earnings	(160)

			$
109	A		
		Profit to 30 June 20X8 (1.6m × 6/12)	800,000
		Additional depreciation on FVA ((2m/20) × 6/12)	(50,000)
		Goodwill impairment	(500,000)
		Other comprehensive income – revaluation gain	1,000,000
			1,250,000
		NCI share 20%	250,000

CBE style OTQ bank – consolidated statement of profit or loss and other comprehensive income

110 $717,463

	$
Basil	547,700
Parsley (206,900 × 10/12)	172,417
PURP ((46,000 × 30 / 130) × 25%)	(2,654)
	717,463

111 $80,000 $2 million × 25 / 125 × 20% = $80,000

112 $264,000

	$'000
Profit for the year	1,300
Intra-group interest (5m × 8%)	(400)
Impairment (50,000 – 30,000)	(20)*
	880
× 30%	264

* The revaluation surplus is eliminated first and the remainder charged to profit or loss.

113 $145,000

	$	$
Sales proceeds		450,000
Share capital	100,000	
Retained earnings	185,000	
Goodwill	20,000	
		(305,000)
		145,000

114 $150,000 (450,000 – 300,000)

115 $245,000 profit

	$
Disposal proceeds	950,000
Goodwill on disposal (600,000 – (700,000 × 70%)	(110,000)
Share of net assets at disposal (850,000 × 70%)	(595,000)
	245,000

Section B

Port and Alfred CBE style OTQ case

116 The correct answer is:

Share capital $235,000 / Share premium $1,115,000

Issue of shares

	Draft $'000	New issue $'000	Revised $'000
Share capital	200	35	235
Share premium	500	615	1,115
Fair value of proceeds		650	

117 $500,000

	$'000
Net assets at date of acquisition	
Share capital	100
Share premium	85
Retained earnings (331 – (96 ×2/12)	315
	500

118 The correct answers are:

The non-controlling interest share of profit is part of the consolidated statement of profit or loss.

If a subsidiary is acquired during the year, its results are apportioned over the year of acquisition.

The statement of financial position shows all non-current assets. Goodwill is not amortised, it is subject to an annual impairment review.

119 $404,000   Port $364,000 and Alfred ($240,000 × 2/12) = $404,000

120 $2,912,000

	Port $'000	Alfred $'000
Port retained earnings	2,900	
Alfred post-acquisition (96,000 × 2/12)		16
Share of Alfred: (16 × 75%)	12	
	2,912	

Section C

121 Viagem (12/12 amended)

Text references. Chapter 9

Top tips. The goodwill impairment must be deducted from the consolidated profit or loss. The subsidiary has been owned for nine months so revenue and expenses must be apportioned. You have not been told that the parent has accounted for the unwinding of the discount on the deferred consideration, so you should assume that (as is normal for this paper) you have to make this adjustment.

Easy marks. There were plenty of marks available here for standard workings.

Marking scheme

	Marks
Goodwill	6
Consolidated statement of profit or loss:	
Revenue	2
Cost of sales	2
Distribution costs	1
Administrative expenses	2
Share of profit of associate	1½
Finance costs	2
Income tax	1
Profit for year – attributable to parent	½
– attributable to NCI	2
	20

(a)   Consolidated goodwill at acquisition

	$'000	$'000
Consideration transferred:		
Shares (9m x 2/3 x $6.50)		39,000
Deferred consideration ((9m x $1.76) / 1.1)		14,400
		53,400
Non-controlling interest ((10m x $2.50) x 10%)		2,500
		55,900
Fair value of net assets:		
Share capital	10,000	
Retained earnings: b/f	35,000	
three months to 1 Jan 20X2 (6,200 × 3/12)	1,550	
FVA on plant	1,800	
Contingent liability	(450)	
		(47,900)
Goodwill		8,000

(b)   CONSOLIDATED STATEMENT OF PROFIT OR LOSS FOR THE YEAR ENDED 30 SEPTEMBER 20X2

	$'000
Revenue (64,600 + (38,000 × 9/12) − 7,200 (W2))	85,900
Cost of sales (51,200 + (26,000 × 9/12) − 7,200 + 300 (W2) + 450 (W3))	(64,250)
Gross profit	21,650
Distribution costs (1,600 + (1,800 × 9/12))	(2,950)
Administrative expenses (3,800 + (2,400 × 9/12) + 2,000 (goodwill impairment))	(7,600)
Finance costs (W4)	(1,500)
Share of profit of associate (2,000 × 40%)	800
Profit before tax	10,400
Income tax expense (2,800 + (1,600 × 9/12))	(4,000)
Profit for the year	6,400
Profit attributable to	
Owners of the parent (ß)	6,180
Non-controlling interest (W5)	220
	6,400

Workings

1   Group structure

Viagem

1 Jan 20X2 ↓ 90%   Mid-year acquisition, nine months before year end

Greca

2   Intragroup trading

	$'000	$'000
Intragroup trading (800 × 9 months)		
DEBIT Revenue	7,200	
CREDIT Cost of sales		7,200
PURP (1,500 × 25/125)		
DEBIT Cost of sales	300	
CREDIT Group inventory (SFP)		300

3   *Fair value adjustment*

	Acquisition $'000	Movement $'000	Year end $'000
Plant	1,800	(450)*	1,350

*(1,800 / 3) × 9/12

4   *Finance costs*

	$'000
Viagem per statement of profit or loss	420
Unwinding of discount on deferred consideration:	
((14,400 × 10%) × 9/12)	1,080
	1,500

5   *Non-controlling interest*

	$'000
Profit for the year (6,200 × 9/12)	4,650
Depreciation on fair value adjustment (W3)	(450)
Goodwill impairment	(2,000)
	2,200
Non-controlling share 10%	220

122 Prodigal (6/11 amended)

Text reference. Chapter 9.

Top tips. The first point to note is that Sentinel was acquired mid-year. Always pay close attention to dates.

Easy marks. Revenue is relatively straightforward for two marks and for all of the expense categories apart from cost of sales it was only necessary to take Prodigal's balance plus 6/12 Sentinel. The other comprehensive income was also easy.

Examination Team's comments. There were many good scores here. Two problem areas were dealing with the elimination of intra-group sales and the additional depreciation on the asset transfer. Some candidates failed to calculate NCI in the total comprehensive income.

Marking scheme

			Marks
(a)	Goodwill on acquisition		
	Consideration transferred	2	
	Fair value of NCI	½	
	Fair value of net assets	1½	4
(b)	Statement of profit or loss and other comprehensive income		
	Revenue	2	
	Cost of sales	4	
	Distribution costs and administrative expenses	2	
	Finance costs	1½	
	Income tax expense	1	
	Non-controlling interest in profit for the year	1½	
	Other comprehensive income	2½	
	Non-controlling interest in other comprehensive income	1½	16
			20

(a)   Goodwill on acquisition of Sentinel

	$'000	$'000
Consideration (((160,000 × 75%) × 2/3) × $4)		320,000
Fair value of non-controlling interest		100,000
		420,000
Fair value of net assets:		
Shares	160,000	
Other equity reserve	2,200	
Retained earnings (125,000 + (66,000 × 6/12))	158,000	
		(320,200)
Goodwill		99,800

(b)   CONSOLIDATED STATEMENT OF PROFIT OR LOSS AND OTHER COMPREHENSIVE INCOME
FOR THE YEAR ENDED 31 MARCH 20X1

	$'000
Revenue (450,00 + (240,000 × 6/12) – (W4) 40,000)	530,000
Cost of sales (260,000 + (110,000 × 6/12) + (W3) 800 – (W4) 40,000 + 3,000)	(278,800)
Gross profit	251,200
Distribution costs (23,600 + (12,000 × 6/12))	(29,600)
Administrative expenses (27,000 + (23,000 × 6/12))	(38,500)
Finance costs (1,500 + (1,200 × 6/12))	(2,100)
Profit before tax	181,000
Income tax expense (48,000 + (27,800 × 6/12))	(61,900)
Profit for the year	119,100

	$'000
Other comprehensive income:	
Gain on land revaluation (2,500 + 1,000)*	3,500
Investments in equity instruments** (700 + (400 × 6/12))	(900)
Other comprehensive income, net of tax	2,600
Total comprehensive income for the year	121,700
Profit attributable to:	
Owners of the parent (bal)	111,600
Non-controlling interests (W2)	7,500
	119,100
Total comprehensive income attributable to:	
Owners of the parent (bal)	114,000
Non-controlling interests (W2)	7,700
	121,700

*All post - acquisition
**Could also be described as equity financial asset investments

Workings

1   *Group structure and timeline*

Prodigal

↓

Sentinel 1.10.20X0 75%

1.4.20X0   1.10.20X0   31.3.20X1

Prodigal   >

Sentinal × 6/12

2   *Non-controlling interests*

	Profit for year	Total comprehensive income
	$'000	$'000
Per question (66,000 × 6/12) ((66,000–400) × 6/12 + 1,000))	33,000	33,800
PUP (W4)	(3,000)	(3,000)
	30,000	30,800
×	25%	25%
	7,500	7,700

3   *Transfer of plant*

	$'000
1.10.20X0 Profit on transfer (5,000 – 4,000)	1,000
Proportion depreciated (½ / 2½)	(200)
Unrealised profit	800
Required adjustment:	
Dr Cost of sales (and retained earnings)	800
Cr Plant	800

4   *Intragroup trading*
     Cancel intragroup sales/purchases:

	$'000	$'000
Dr Group revenue	40,000	
Cr Group cost of sales		40,000
$((40,000 - 30,000) \times 12,000 / 40,000) = 3,000$		
DR Cost of sales (Sentinel) (NCI)	3,000	
CR Group inventories		3,000

123 Plastik (12/14 amended)

Text references Chapters 3, 4 and 14.

Top tips. This is quite a time-pressured question so you need to work fast. Get the proforma down for the statement of profit or loss and then go methodically through the workings, filling in the proforma as you go.

Easy marks. There are some marks available for figures that can be lifted straight from the question and good, clear workings will help you to fill in several gaps.

Marking scheme

			Marks
(a)	Goodwill		4
(b)	Group retained earnings	4	
	Non-controlling interest	2	
			6
(c)	Consolidated statement of profit or loss and other comprehensive income		
	Revenue	1½	
	Cost of sales	2½	
	Distribution costs	½	
	Administrative expenses (including goodwill impairment)	1	
	Finance costs	1	
	Income tax expense	½	
	Gain on revaluation of properties	1	
	Non-controlling interest - profit for the year	1	
	- total comprehensive income	1	
			10
	Total for question		20

(a) *Goodwill*

	$'000	$'000
Consideration transferred - 4.8m shares @ $3		14,400
Deferred consideration (7.2m × $0.275 × 1/1.1)		1,800
		16,200
Fair value of NCI (1.8m shares @ $2.50)		4,500
		20,700
Fair value of net assets:		
Shares	9,000	
Retained earnings (3,500 – (2,000 × 9/12))	2,000	
Fair value adjustment - property	4,000	
		(15,000)
Goodwill at acquisition		5,700

BPP
LEARNING MEDIA

(b)   *Retained earnings*

	Plastik	*Subtrak*
	$'000	$'000
Per question	6,300	3,500
Less pre-acquisition (1,500 + (2,000 × 3/12))		(2,000)
Goodwill impairment		(500)
Unwinding of discount on deferred consideration (1,800 (a) × 10% × 9/12)	(135)	
Depreciation on FVA		(100)
PURP (600,000 × 25/125)	(120)	
	6,045	900
Share of Subtrak (900 × 80%)	720	
	6,765	

Non-controlling interest

	$'000
NCI at acquisition (see goodwill)	4,500
Share of post-acquisition retained earnings (900 × 20%)	180
Share of property revaluation gain (600 × 20%)	120
	4,800

(c)   CONSOLIDATED STATEMENT OF PROFIT OR LOSS AND OTHER COMPREHENSIVE INCOME FOR THE YEAR ENDED 30 SEPTEMBER 20X4

	$'000
Revenue (62,600 + (30,000 × 9/12) – 2,700 (W2))	82,400
Cost of sales (45,800 + (24,000 × 9/12) – 2,580 (W2) + 100 (b))	61,320
Gross profit	21,080
Distribution costs (2,000 + (1,200 × 9/12))	(2,900)
Administrative expenses (3,500 + (1,800 × 9/12) + 500 (goodwill))	(5,350)
Finance costs (200 + 135 (see retained earnings))	(335)
Profit before tax	12,495
Income tax (3,100 + (1,000 × 9/12))	(3,850)
	8,645
Other comprehensive income	
Gain on revaluation of property (1,500 + 600)	2,100
Total comprehensive income	10,745
Profit for the year attributable to:	
Owners of the parent (β)	8,465
Non-controlling interest (W1)	180
	8,645
Total comprehensive income attributable to:	
Owners of the parent (β)	10,445
Non-controlling interest (W1)	300
	10,745

Workings

1   *Non-controlling interests*

	Profit for year	*Total comprehensive income*
	$'000	$'000
Per (b) above	900	900
Gain on property revaluation		600
	900	1,500
NCI 20%	180	300

2   *Intragroup trading*

		$'000	$'000
(1)	*Cancel intragroup sales/purchases*		
	DEBIT Group revenue (300,000 × 9)	2,700	
	CREDIT Group cost of sales		2,700
(2)	*Eliminate unrealised profit*		
	DEBIT Cost of sales (600,000 × 25/125)	120	
	CREDIT Group inventories		120

MCQ bank – accounting for associates

124   A

	$m
Cost (75m × $1.60)	120
Share of post-acquisition retained earnings (100 – 20) × 30%	24
	144

125   C   The group's share of the associate's profit after tax is recorded as a one-line entry. Line by line treatment would be correct for a subsidiary, not an associate. The dividends received from the associate are all that is recorded in the individual entity financial statements of the parent, but in the consolidated financial statements this is replaced by the group share of profit after tax.

126   C   (($2m × 40%) × 25 / 125) × 30% = $48,000

This adjustment is removing profit from inventory so it is a credit entry.

CBE style OTQ bank – accounting for associates

127   $2,767,000

	$'000
Cost of investment	2,500
Share of post-acquisition profit (6,400 – 5,300) × 30%)	330
PURP (700 × 30% ×30%)	(63)
	2,767

128   $9,850,000

	$'000
Cost of investment	10,000
Share of post-acquisition profit (3,000 × 8/12) – 1,000) × 35%	350
Impairment	(500)
	9,850

129   The correct answers are:

The investor owns 330,000 of the 1,500,000 equity voting shares of the investee.
The investor has representation on the board of directors of the investee.

The present of significant influence is indicated by a shareholding of 20% or more or representation on the board. Regarding the third option, material transactions would need to be between the investor itself and the investee. The final option denotes control, not significant influence.

130   $3,000   ($160,000 / 4) × 25% × 30% = $3,000

Section B

Plateau MCQ case

131   C $12,750,000 $((3m / 2 \times \$6) + (3m \times \$1.25))$

132   C   The contract is estimated to have an indefinite life.

133   A

	$'000
NCI at acquisition (1m shares @ $3.25)	3,250
NCI share of post-acquisition retained earnings ((W) 2,600 × 25%)	650
	3,900

Working

	$'000
Retained earnings per draft	2,900
Less unrealised profit ($2.7m × 50/150 × 1/3)	(300)
	2,600

134   B   Plateau is the seller so there is no charge to NCI

135   B $10,500,000

	$'000
Cost (4m × 30% × $7.50)	9,000
Share of post-acquisition retained earnings (5,000 × 30%)	1,500
	10,500

Section C

136 Laurel

STATEMENT OF FINANCIAL POSITION AS AT 31 DECEMBER 20X9

	$m
Non-current assets	
Property, plant and equipment (220 + 160 + (W7) 3)	383
Goodwill (W2)	9
Investment in associate (W3)	96.8
	488.8
Current assets	
Inventories (384 + 234 – (W6) 10)	608
Trade receivables (275 + 166)	441
Cash (42 + 10)	52
	1,101
	1,589.8
Equity attributable to owners of the parent	
Share capital – $1 ordinary shares	400
Share premium	16
Retained earnings (W4)	326.8
	742.8
Non-controlling interests (W5)	47
	789.8
Current liabilities	
Trade payables (457 + 343)	800.0
	1,589.8

Workings

1   *Group structure*

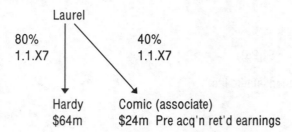

Laurel

80%   40%
1.1.X7   1.1.X7

Hardy   Comic (associate)
$64m $24m Pre acq'n ret'd earnings

2   *Goodwill*

	$'m	$'m
Consideration transferred		160
Non-controlling interests (at fair value)		39
Fair value of net assets at acq'n:		
Share capital	96	
Share premium	3	
Retained earnings	64	
Fair value adjustment (W7)	12	
		(175)
		24
Impairment losses		(15)
		9

3   *Investment in associate*

	$'m
Cost of associate	70
Share of post acquisition retained reserves (W4)	29.2
Unrealised profit (W6)	(2.4)
Impairment losses	(0)
	96.8

4   *Consolidated retained earnings*

	Laurel	Hardy	Comic
	$'m	$'m	$'m
Per question	278	128	97
Less: PUP re Hardy (W6)	(10)		
PUP re Comic (W6)	(2.4)		
Fair value adjustment movement (W7)		(9)	
Less pre-acquisition retained earnings		(64)	(24)
		55	73
Group share of post-acquisition retained earnings:			
Hardy (55 × 80%)	44		
Comic (73 × 40%)	29.2		
Less group share of impairment losses (15 × 80%)	(12.0)		
	326.8		

5   *Non-controlling interests*

	$'m
Non-controlling interests at acquisition (W2)	39
NCI share of post-acquisition retained earnings:	
Hardy (55 × 20%)	11
Less NCI share of impairment losses (15 × 20%)	(3)
	47

6   *Unrealised profit*

Laurel's sales to Hardy: $32m – $22m = $10m

DR Retained earnings (Laurel)	$10m
CR Group inventories	$10m

Laurel's sales to Comic (associate) ($22m – $10m) × ½ × 40% share = $2.4m.

DR Retained earnings (Laurel)	$2.4m
CR Investment in associate	$2.4m

7   *Fair value adjustments*

	At acquisition date	Movement	At year end
	$'m	$'m	$'m
PPE (57 – 45)	+12	(9)*	+3
	↓	↓	↓
	Goodwill	Ret'd earnings	PPE

*Extra depreciation $12m × ¾

137 Tyson

STATEMENT OF PROFIT OR LOSS AND OTHER COMPREHENSIVE INCOME FOR THE YEAR ENDED
31 DECEMBER 20X8

	$'m
Revenue (500 + 150 – 66)	584
Cost of sales (270 + 80 – 66 + (W3) 18)	(302)
Gross profit	282
Other expenses (150 + 20 + 15)	(185)
Finance income (15 + 10)	25
Finance costs	(20)
Share of profit of associate [(10 × 40%) – 2.4*]	1.6
Profit before tax	103.6
Income tax expense (25 + 15)	(40)
Profit for the year	63.6
Other comprehensive income:	
Gains on property revaluation, net of tax (20 + 10)	30
Share of other comprehensive income of associate (5 × 40%)	2
Other comprehensive income for the year, net of tax	32.0
Total comprehensive income for the year	95.6
Profit attributable to:	
Owners of the parent (63.6 – 2.4)	61.2
Non-controlling interests (W2)	2.4
	63.6
Total comprehensive income attributable to:	
Owners of the parent (95.6 – 4.4)	91.2
Non-controlling interests (W2)	4.4
	95.6

*Impairment losses could either be included in expenses or deducted from the share of profit of associates figure.
  IAS 28 is not prescriptive.

Workings

1   *Group structure*

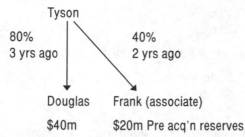

2   *Non-controlling interests*

	PFY	TCI
	$'m	$'m
PFY/TCI per question	45	55
Unrealised profit (W3)	(18)	(18)
Impairment loss	(15)	(15)
	12	22
× NCI share (20%)	2.4	4.4

3   *Unrealised profit*

	$'m
Selling price	66
Cost	(48)
PUP	18

138 Paladin (12/11 amended)

Text references. Chapters 4 and 8.

Top tips. This is a pretty straightforward consolidated statement of financial position. Set out the proformas and then work methodically through the numbers. There are quite a few adjustments to retained earnings, so make sure your retained earnings working is very clear.

Easy marks. There are a lot of easy marks in this question. The complications are dealing with the deferred payment and the unwinding of the discount, capitalising and amortising the intangible asset and remembering to deduct the intercompany balance from receivables and payables. Most of the rest of it is quite easy, the PURP is only in the parent and two marks are available for investment in associate, which is not a complicated working. Part (b) is easy marks for correctly assessing the situation.

Examination Team's comments. The parts of this question that related to basic consolidation adjustments were well dealt with by most candidates. Errors occurred in the more complex aspects. Some candidates failed to discount the deferred consideration and some did not treat the customer relationship as an intangible asset. Others deducted the post-acquisition additional depreciation from the goodwill. Some students only deducted 25% of the impairment loss on the investment in associate, when the loss applied to the whole of the investment. A common error was to offset the subsidiary's overdraft against the parent's bank balance. No such right of offset exists.

Marks

Consolidated statement of financial position	
Property, plant and equipment	2
Goodwill	4
Other intangibles	2
Investment in associate	2
Inventory	1
Receivables	1
Bank	½
Equity shares	½
Retained earnings	4
Non-controlling interest	2
Deferred tax	½
Bank overdraft	½
Deferred consideration	1
Trade payables	1
	22
Maximum	20

CONSOLIDATED STATEMENT OF FINANCIAL POSITION AS AT 30 SEPTEMBER 20X1

ASSETS	$'000
Non-current assets	
Property, plant and equipment (40,000 + 31,000 + 3,000 (W6))	74,000
Goodwill (W2)	15,000
Intangible assets (7,500 + 2,500 (W6))	10,000
Investment in associate (W3)	7,700
	106,700
Current assets	
Inventories (11,200 + 8,400 – 600 (W7))	19,000
Trade receivables (7,400 + 5,300 – 1,300 (W7))	11,400
Bank	3,400
	33,800
Total assets	140,500
EQUITY AND LIABILITIES	
Equity attributable to owners of Paladin	
Share capital	50,000
Retained earnings (W4)	35,200
	85,200
Non-controlling interests (W5)	7,900
	93,100
Non-current liabilities	
Deferred tax (15,000 + 8,000)	23,000
Current liabilities	
Overdraft	2,500
Payables (11,600 + 6,200 – 1,300 (W7))	16,500
Deferred consideration (5,000 + 400 (W2))	5,400
	24,400
Total equity and liabilities	140,500

Workings

1   *Group structure*

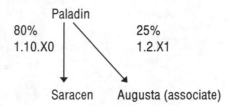

Paladin

80%   25%
1.10.X0   1.2.X1

Saracen   Augusta (associate)

2   *Goodwill*

	$'000	$'000
Consideration transferred:		
Cash		32,000
Deferred consideration		5,000
		37,000
Non-controlling interest		7,000
		44,000
Fair value of net assets:		
Share capital	10,000	
Retained earnings	12,000	
Fair value adjustment on plant	4,000	
Intangible asset	3,000	
		(29,000)
Goodwill		15,000

3   *Investment in associate*

	$'000
Cost of investment	10,000
Share of post-acquisition retained earnings (800 (W4) × 25%)	200
Impairment	(2,500)
	7,700

4   *Retained earnings*

	Paladin	Saracen	Augusta
	$'000	$'000	$'000
Per question – 1.10.20X0	25,700	12,000	31,800
– year to 30.9.20X1	9,200	6,000	1,200
		18,000	33,000
PURP (W7)	(600)		
Depreciation on fair value adjustments (W6)		(1,500)	
Unwinding of discount (5,400 – 5,000 (W2))	(400)		
Less pre-acquisition retained earnings to		(12,000)	(31,800)
1.10.20X0			
Less pre-acquisition to 1.2.X1 (1,200 × 4/12)		–	(400)
		4,500	800
Saracen (4,500 × 80%)	3,600		
Augusta (800 × 25%)	200		
Impairment of investment in associate (W3)	(2,500)		
	35,200		

5   *Non-controlling interests*

	$'000
NCI at acquisition (W2)	7,000
Share of post-acquisition retained earnings (4,500 (W4) × 20%)	900
	7,900

6   *Fair value adjustments*

	Acquisition $'000		*Movement* $'000	*Year end* $'000
Plant	4,000	1/4	(1,000)	3,000
Intangible asset (customer relationships)	3,000	1/6	(500)	2,500
	7,000		(1,500)	5,500

7   *Intragroup trading*

Unrealised profit:

	$'000	$'000
Dr Cost of sales/retained earnings (2,600 × 30/130)	600	
Cr Inventories		600
Current account:		
Dr Group trade payables	1,300	
Cr Group trade receivables		1,300

MCQ bank – financial instruments

139   B

	$'000
Interest years 1–3 (30m × 8% × 2.49)	5,976
Repayment year 3 (30m × 0.75)	22,500
Debt component	28,476
Equity option (β)	1,524
	30,000

140   D

	$'000
Proceeds (20m – 0.5m)	19,500
Interest 10%	1,950
Interest paid (20m × 5%)	(1,000)
Balance 30 March 20X1	20,450
Interest 10%	2,045
Interest paid (20m × 5%)	(1,000)
	21,495

141   A   Fair value with changes going through profit or loss. Fair value through OCI would be correct if an election had been made to recognise changes in value through other comprehensive income. Amortised cost is used for debt instruments, not equity instruments.

142   A

	$
1 January 20X1	500,000
Interest 8%	40,000
Interest received (550,000 × 6%)	(33,000)
31 December 20X1	507,000
Interest 8%	40,560
Interest received	(33,000)
31 December 20X2	514,560

CBE style OTQ bank – financial instruments

143   The correct answer is:

Intangible assets.

These do not give rise to a present right to receive cash or other financial assets. The other options are financial instruments.

144 $1,000,000 gain

	$'000
$12,500 × 1,296 / 1,200	13,500
Carrying amount	(12,500)
Gain	1,000

145 $243,000

	$
40,000 shares @ $6	240,000
Transaction costs	3,000
	243,000

Section B

Bertrand MCQ case

146 B   As debt and equity

147 C

	$'000
Interest payable ($10m × 5% × 2.58*)	1,290
Capital repayable ($10m × 0.79)	7,900
Debt element	9,190
Finance costs for year = 9,190 × 8%	735

148 A

	$'000
1 October 20X0	9,190
Finance charge 8%	735
Interest paid (10,000 × 5%)	(500)
Balance 30 September 20X1	9,425

149 B   Deducted from the proceeds of the loan notes. The effective interest rate is then applied to the net amount.

150 D   As a financial asset at amortised cost

MCQ bank – leasing

151 A

	$,000
PVMLPs	3,300
Payment	(700)
	2,600
Interest 6%	156
Balance 31.12.X6	2,756
Payment	(700)
	2,056
Interest 6%	123
Balance 31.12.X7	2,179
Current	700
Non-current	1,479
	2,179

152 A   This would suggest that the lease is an operating lease. The other options all point to a finance lease.

153	A		$'000
		PVMLPs	15,600
		Interest 8%	1,248
		Payment	(6,000)
		Balance 31.3.X8	10,848
		Interest 8%	868
		Payment	(6,000)
		Balance 31.3.X9	5,716

Current liability = 10,848 – 5,716 = 5,132

154   D   An asset acquired under a finance lease should be capitalised at the lower of fair value and the present value of minimum lease payments. These amounts will often be the same.

155	B		$'000
		Liability 1 October 20X3 (25m – 2m)	23,000
		Interest 10%	2,300
		Rental	(6,000)
		Balance 30 September 20X4	19,300
		Interest 10%	1,930
		Rental	(6,000)
		Balance 30 September 20X5	15,230

So current liability = (19,300,000 – 15,230,000) = $4,070,000

CBE style OTQ bank – leasing

156   The correct answers are:

The lease transfers ownership of the asset to the lessee by the end of the lease term.
The lease assets are of a specialised nature such that only the lessee can use them without major modifications being made.

The lease term would need to be for 'the major part' (not approximately half) of the economic life of the asset if the criterion in the second option were being used. Regarding the final option, the present value of the minimum lease payments would have to amount to 'substantially all' of the fair value of the asset.

157    $1 million

This is in substance a secured loan, so the asset will be recognised at its new carrying amount of $50m and a lease liability will be set up for the same amount.

The $10m increase in carrying amount will be treated as other income deferred over the life of the asset. The amount which can be recognised for the year to 30 September 20X4 is:

($10m / 5) × 6/12 = $1m

158   The correct answer is:

Defer and amortise over the lease term.

Immediate recognition in profit or loss would apply if there was no leaseback. Deferral of the excess over FV would apply if the leaseback involved an operating lease.

159    $106,500

	$
Finance lease interest ((340,000 -90,000) × 10%)	25,000
Plant depreciation (340,000 / 5)	68,000
Operating lease (18,000 × 9/12)	13,500
Total charge to profit or loss	106,500

160

$20,256

	$
Cash price	360,000
Deposit	(120,000)
	240,000
Interest 12%	28,800
Payment	(100,000)
Balance 3.12.X6	168,800
Interest to 31.12.X7 12%	20,256

Section B

Fino MCQ case

161   C

	$
Depreciation (350,000/4 × 6/12)	43,750
Finance costs ((350,000 − 100,000) ×10% × 6/12)	12,500
	56,250

162   B   A finance lease is normally for a substantial portion of the asset's life and the PV of the MLPs would be close to or above the fair value of the asset.

163   A

	$
Cost 1.4.X7	350,000
1.4.X7 payment	(100,000)
Balance 1.4.X7	250,000
Interest to 30.9.X7 (250,000 × 10% × 6/12)	12,500
Balance 30.9.X7	262,500
Interest to 1.4.X8 (250,000 × 10% × 6/12)	12,500
1.4.X8 payment	(100,000)
Capital balance due 30.9.X8	175,000

164   D   ((48,000 − 3,000) / 48) × 6)) = $5,625

165   B   The principle of substance over form relates to faithful representation.

MCQ bank – provisions and events after the reporting period

166   D   Loss of the case is not 'probable', so no provision is made, but the legal costs will have to be paid so should be provided for.

167   A $2 million should be provided for and capitalised as part of the cost of the mine. It will then be depreciated over the useful life.

168   D   The cost of the overhaul will be capitalised when it takes place. No obligation exists before the overhaul is carried out. The other options would all give rise to valid provisions.

169   C   We can assume that these faults also existed at the year end, so this is the only option which would require adjustment. The others have all taken place after the year end.

170   B   A restructuring provision must not include the costs of retraining or relocating staff.

CBE style OTQ bank – provisions and events after the reporting period

171   The correct answers are:

The signing of a non-cancellable contract in September 20X4 to supply goods in the following year on which, due to a pricing error, a loss will be made.

An amount of deferred tax relating to the gain on revaluation of a property during the current year. Tynan has no intention of selling the property in the foreseeable future.

The reorganisation does not meet the criteria for a provision and a provision is no longer needed for the warranties.

172     $24,532,000

	$'000
Restoration of seabed (10,000 × 250)	2,500
Dismantling of equipment (30m × 0.68)	20,400
Unwinding of discount (20,400 × 8%)	1,632
	24,532

173     $0.6 million

	$m
$2 million × 15%	0.3
$6 million × 5%	0.3
	0.6

174   The correct answers are:

The discovery of a fraud which occurred during the year
The determination of the sale proceeds of an item of plant sold before the year end

These both provide evidence of conditions that existed at the end of the reporting period. The other options refer to conditions which arose after the reporting period.

Section B

Rainbird MCQ case

175   D   The reorganisation cannot be provided for because it has only gone as far as a feasibility study.

Staff training is not a valid provision.

176   B   This is a contingent liability. The outcome is probable but cannot be reliably measured.

177   B $1,811,250
Total returns = 525,000 × 12% = 63,000
Expected cost:

	$
63,000 × 95% × 30	1,795,500
63,000 × 5% × 5	15,750
	1,811,250

178   D $2.63 million × 108% = $2,840,400. This is the unwinding of the discount.

179   C   This is a favourable event after the reporting period because it provides evidence regarding conditions that existed at the end of the reporting period ie the legal case that was ongoing.

The other events have all taken place after the reporting period.

MCQ bank – inventories and biological assets

180 C

Product	$
A 1,000 × 40	40,000
B 2,500 × 15	37,500
C 800 × 22	17,600
	95,100

181 C As the item becomes obsolete we can expect its market price to fall – and eventually fall below cost. The other options would all maintain or improve the net realisable value of the item.

182 D IAS 41 *Agriculture* requires biological assets to be measured on initial recognition at fair value less estimated costs to sell.

183 B Harvest is an intervention, not a biological process. Growth, procreation and degeneration are natural biological processes.

184 A A gain or loss on a biological asset is included in profit or loss for the year.

185 D None of these statements is correct. Production overheads are allocated on the basis of a company's *normal* level of activity. Settlement discounts are not deducted to arrive at NRV. The LIFO formula is not allowed under IAS 2 *Inventories*. Valuation of finished goods should include production overheads.

CBE style OTQ bank – inventories and biological assets

186 The correct answer is:

IAS 10 *Events after the reporting period*

This may be relevant as agricultural produce is perishable and if prices have to be reduced after the year end, this will affect the year end valuation.

187 $39.3 million

	$m
Per inventory count	36.0
Received after year end	(2.7)
Sold after year end (7.8m / 1.3)	6.0
	39.3

188 $55.080   NRV – (12,000 × (5.4 × 85%)) = $55,080

MCQ bank – taxation

189   C
	$'000
Charge for year	16,200
Underprovision	2,100
Adjust deferred tax (W)	(1,500)
Profit or loss charge	16,800

Working
Provision needed (13m × 30%)	3,900
Provision b/f	(5,400)
Reduce provision	(1,500)

190   C
	$'000
Prior year underprovision	700
Current provision	4,500
Movement of deferred tax (8.4 – 5.6)	(2,800)
Deferred tax on revaluation surplus	(1,200)
Tax charge for the year	1,200

191   D
	$'000
B/f	850
Year to 31.12.X8 (500 – 450)	50
Revaluation surplus	250
	1,150
× 30%	345

CBE style OTQ bank – taxation

192 $130 million
	$m
B/f (140 + 160)	300
Charge for year	270
C/f (310 + 130)	(440)
Tax paid	130

193 $19 million
	$'000
Current charge	19,400
Overprovision	(800)
Deferred tax (W)	400
	19,000

Working
Required provision	6,750
Less revaluation	(3,750)
	3,000
Balance b/f	(2,600)
Charge to income tax	400

Section B

Julian MCQ case

194	C	The amount attributed to an asset or liability for tax purposes
195	C	PPE (460 – 270)
196	D	(90,000 × 30%) will go to the revaluation surplus
197	A	$45,000. The tax charge for the year.
198	C	Accrued expenses which have already been deducted for tax purposes will not give rise to a temporary difference.

MCQ bank – presentation of published financial statements

199	B	The fact that a liability has arisen during the current accounting period does not make it a current liability. The other options would all lead to classification as a current liability.
200	D	The revaluation gain on the factory will be presented under 'other comprehensive income'. The other items will be recognised in profit or loss. Note that gains on investment properties go through profit or loss.
201	C	Inventories, provisions and intangible assets are shown separately. There is no such requirement for government grants.
202	D	The time between acquisition of assets for processing and receipt of cash from customers
203	A	Equity dividends are presented in the statement of changes in equity.

Section C

204 Fresco (6/12 amended)

> **Text references.** Chapters 4 and 16.
>
> **Top tips.** There was a lot to get through in this question. Get the formats down quickly and then go through the question and transfer any figures that can go straight from the trial balance to the financial statements. You needed to do workings for PPE and for the leased plant but these were not complicated.
>
> **Easy marks.** The statement of changes in equity was all straightforward. If you had remembered the transfer to retained earnings it was possible to score full marks on this. The PPE working made it possible to score marks on both the statement of profit or loss and other comprehensive income and the statement of financial position, so it was worth spending a bit of time on this. The lease working, on the other hand, carried very few marks.
>
> **Examination Team's comments.** Most candidates showed a sound knowledge of preparing financial statements. Most of the errors arose in the adjustments:
>
> Some candidates deducted the loss on the fraud from revenue for the year rather adding it to expenses and treating it as a prior year adjustment, with the other entry being a deduction from receivables.
>
> There were some difficulties with the finance lease, mainly involving the timing of the lease payments and the initial deposit. Many candidates were confused with the tax, especially failing to realise that the tax for the year was a refund.

	Marks	
Statement of profit or loss and other comprehensive income:		
Revenue	½	
Cost of sales	3	
Distribution costs	½	
Administrative expenses	½	
Finance costs	1½	
Income tax	1	
Other comprehensive income	1	8
Statement of financial position:		
Property, plant and equipment	2½	
Inventory	½	
Trade receivables	½	
Share capital	1	
Share premium	1	
Revaluation surplus	1	
Retained earnings	2	
Current tax	½	
Non-current lease obligation	½	
Deferred tax	1	
Trade payables	½	
Current lease obligation	½	
Bank overdraft	½	12
		20

(a)   STATEMENT OF PROFIT OR LOSS AND OTHER COMPREHENSIVE INCOME
       FOR THE YEAR ENDED 31 MARCH 20X2

	$'000
Revenue	350,000
Cost of sales (W1)	(311,000)
Gross profit	39,000
Distribution costs (W1)	(16,100)
Administrative expenses (W1)	(29,900)
Finance costs (300 + 2,300 (W3))	(2,600)
Loss before tax	(9,600)
Income tax (W5)	1,800
Loss for the year	(7,800)
Other comprehensive income:	
Gain on revaluation of property (W2)	4,000
Total comprehensive loss for the year	(3,800)

(b)　　　STATEMENT OF FINANCIAL POSITION AS AT 31 MARCH 20X2

	$'000
ASSETS	
Non-current assets	
Property, plant and equipment (W2)	62,700
Current assets	
Inventory	25,200
Receivables (28,500 – 4,000 (W4))	24,500
Tax asset (W5)	2,400
Total assets	114,800
EQUITY AND LIABILITIES	
Equity	
Share capital 50c shares(45,000 + 9,000(W6))	54,000
Share premium (5,000 + 4,500(W6))	9,500
Revaluation surplus (4,000 – 500 (W2))	3,500
Retained earnings (5,100 – 1,000(W4) - 7,800 + 500(W2))	(3,200)
	63,800
Non-current liabilities	
Deferred tax (W5)	3,000
Lease payable (W3)	15,230
Current liabilities	
Trade payables	27,300
Lease payable (19,300 – 15,230 (W3))	4,070
Bank overdraft	1,400
Total equity and liabilities	114,800

Workings

1　　　*Expenses*

	Cost of sales	Distribution costs	Administrative expenses
	$'000	$'000	$'000
Per trial balance	298,700	16,100	26,900
Depreciation (W2)	7,800	–	–
Amortisation (W2)	4,500	–	–
Fraud – current year cost (W4)	–	–	3,000
	311,000	16,100	29,900

2　　　*Property, plant and equipment*

	Leased property	Plant and equipment	Leased plant	Total
	$'000	$'000	$'000	$'000
Cost	48,000	47,500		
Acc. amortisation/depreciation	(16,000)	(33,500)		
Balance 1 April 20X1	32,000	14,000	25,000	
Revaluation surplus	4,000			
Revised carrying amount	36,000			
Depreciation / amortisation:				
36,000 / 8	(4,500)			
14,000 × 20%		(2,800)		
25,000 / 5			(5,000)	
	31,500	11,200	20,000	62,700

The transfer to retained earnings = 4,000/8 = 500

BPP LEARNING MEDIA

3   *Finance lease*

	$'000
Cost	25,000
Deposit	(2,000)
Balance 1.4.X1	23,000
Interest 10%	2,300
Instalment 31.3.X2	(6,000)
Balance 31.3.X2	19,300
Interest 10%	1,930
Instalment 31.3.X3	(6,000)
Balance 31.3.X3	15,230

4   *Fraud*

	DEBIT	CREDIT
	$'000	$'000
Retained earnings – prior year	1,000	
Current year profit	3,000	
Receivables		4,000

5   *Tax credit*

	$'000
Underprovided in prior year	800
Tax refund due (asset in SFP)	(2,400)
Reduction in deferred tax provision (3,200 – (12,000 × 25%))	(200)
Current tax (credit to profit or loss)	(1,800)

6   *Share issue*

Shares issued = 13.5m / 0.75 = 18m

		$'000
Share capital	18m × 50c	9,000
Share premium	18m × 25c	4,500
		13,500

205 Dexon

(a)

	$'000	$'000
Draft retained profit		96,700
Dividends paid		15,500
Draft profit for the year		112,200
Depreciation:		
Buildings (165,000 / 15)	11,000	
Plant (180,500 × 20%)	36,100	
		(47,100)
Gain on investment (W2)		1,000
Current year fraud loss		(2,500)
Increase in deferred tax provision (W4)		(800)
Current year tax		(11,400)
		51,400

(b) DEXON – STATEMENT OF FINANCIAL POSITION AS AT 31 MARCH 20X8

	$'000	$'000
Non-current assets		
Property (W1)		180,000
Plant (W1)		144,400
Investments (W2)		13,500
		337,900
Current assets		
Inventory	84,000	
Trade receivables (W5)	48,200	
Bank	3,800	
		136,000
Total assets		473,900
Equity and liabilities		
Share capital		250,000
Share premium		40,000
Revaluation surplus (W6)		22,800
Retained earnings(12,300 – 1,500(W3) + 51,400 – 15,500)		46,700
Total equity		359,500
Non-current liabilities		
Deferred tax (19,200 + 2,000 (W4))		21,200
Current liabilities		
As per draft SFP	81,800	
Tax payable	11,400	
		93,200
Total equity and liabilities		473,900

Workings

1   *Property, plant and equipment*

	Property $'000	Plant $'000	Total $'000
Per question	185,000	180,500	365,500
Depreciation (165,000 / 15)	(11,000)	(36,100)	(47,100)
	174,000	144,400	318,400
Revaluation	6,000	–	6,000
Balance c/d	180,000	144,400	324,400

2   *Financial assets at FV through profit or loss*

	$'000
FV at year end (12,500 × 1,296 / 1,200)	13,500
Per draft SOFP	(12,500)
Gain – to profit or loss	1,000

3   *Fraud*

	$'000	$'000
DR Retained earnings re prior year	1,500	
DR Current year profit	2,500	
CR Receivables		4,000

4   *Deferred tax*

	$'000	$'000
DR Revaluation surplus (6,000 × 20%)	1,200	
DR Profit or loss (tax charge) (4,000 × 20%)	800	
CR Deferred tax liability (10,000 × 20%)		2,000

5	*Trade receivables*	$'000
	Per draft SFP	52,200
	Adjustment re fraud	(4,000)
		48,200

6	*Revaluation surplus*	$'000
	B/f	18,000
	Surplus re land and buildings	6,000
		24,000
	Deferred tax provision (6,000 × 20%)	(1,200)
	Net surplus	4,800

206 Xtol (6/14 amended)

Text references Chapters 16, 17 and 18.

Top tips. You have two financial statements to produce here, so be very organised. Note that you will have to work out the effects of the rights issue to get the dividend payments.

Examination Team's comments. This question was generally well answered. Most of the errors that occurred involved the agency sale, the rights issue (such as failing to notice that the shares were 25c, not $1), the convertible loan note, and the tax.

Marking scheme

		Marks	
(a)	Statement: of profit or loss		
	Revenue	1	
	Cost of sales	2	
	Distribution costs	½	
	Administrative expenses	½	
	Agency sales	1	
	Finance costs	1½	
	Income tax	1½	
			8
(b)	Statement of financial position		
	Property, plant and equipment	1½	
	Inventory	½	
	Trade receivables	½	
	Share capital	½	
	Share premium	½	
	Equity option	1	
	Retained earnings	2	
	Deferred tax	1	
	Loan note	1½	
	Trade payables	1½	
	Bank overdraft	½	
	Current tax payable	1	
			12
	Total for question		20

(a)   STATEMENT OF PROFIT OR LOSS FOR THE YEAR ENDED 31 MARCH 20X4

	$'000
Revenue (490,000 – 20,000(W3))	470,000
Cost of sales (W1)	(294,600)
Gross profit	175,400
Distribution costs (W1)	(33,500)
Administrative expenses (W1)	(36,800)
Other operating income – agency sales (W3)	2,000
Finance costs (13,380 + 900 + 1,176 (W4) – 10,880 (W5))	(4,576)
Profit before tax	102,524
Income tax expense (28,000 + 3,200 + 3,700 (W6))	(34,900)
Profit for the year	67,624

(b)   STATEMENT OF FINANCIAL POSITION AS AT 31 MARCH 20X4

	$'000	$'000
ASSETS		
Non-current assets		
Property, plant and equipment (W2)		168,000
Current assets		
Inventory	61,000	
Trade receivables	63,000	
		124,000
Total assets		292,000
EQUITY AND LIABILITIES		
Equity		
Equity shares 25c		56,000
Share premium		25,000
Other component of equity – equity option (W4)		4,050
Retained earnings (26,080 – 10,880 (W5) + 67,624)		82,824
		167,874
Non-current liabilities		
Deferred tax (4,600 + 3,700 (W6))	8,300	
5% convertible loan note (50,000 – 4,050 (W4) + 1,176)	47,126	
		55,426
Current liabilities		
Trade payables (32,200 + 3,000 (W3))	35,200	
Bank overdraft	5,500	
Current tax payable	28,000	
		68,700
Total equity and liabilities		292,000

Workings

1   *Expenses*

	Cost of sales $'000	Distribution costs $'000	Administrative expenses $'000
Per question	290,600	33,500	36,800
Agent not principal	(15,000)		
Depreciation – property (W2)	5,000		
Depreciation – plant and equipment (W2)	14,000		
	294,600	33,500	36,800

2 *Property, plant and equipment*

	Property $'000	Plant and equipment $'000	Total $'000
Cost per TB	100,000	155,500	255,500
Acc depreciation b/d per TB	(25,000)	(43,500)	(68,500)
	75,000	112,000	187,000
Depreciation property (100,000/20 years)	(5,000)		(5,000)
Depreciation P&E (112,000 ×12.5%)		(14,000)	(14,000)
	70,000	98,000	168,000

3 *Agency transaction*

Should have been:

	$'000
DR Cash	20,000
CR Other income (10%)	2,000
CR Trade payables	18,000
DR Trade payables	15,000
CR Cash	15,000

Did:

	$'000
DR Cash	20,000
CR Revenue	20,000
DR Cost of sales	15,000
CR Cash	15,000

Correction:

	$'000
DR Revenue	20,000
CR Cost of sales	15,000
CR Other income	2,000
CR Trade payables	3,000

4 *Loan notes*

		$'000	$'000
PV of principal	(50,000 × 0.79)		39,500
PV interest flows:			
20X4	50,000 × 5% = 2,500 × 0.93 =	2,325	
20X5	50,000 × 5% = 2,500 × 0.86 =	2,150	
20X6	50,000 × 5% = 2,500 × 0.79 =	1,975	
			6,450
Debt component			45,950
Equity component (β)			4,050
Cash received			50,000
Liability component b/d	1.4.20X3	45,950	
Effective interest	(45,950 × 8%)	3,676	
Cash coupon paid		(2,500)	
Liability component c/d	31.3.20X4	47,126	

Adjustment required:

		$'000	$'000
DR Loan notes		4,050	
CR Other components of equity			4,050
DR Finance costs (3,676 – 2,500)		1,176	
CR Loan notes			1,176

5 *Dividend paid*

		$'000	$'000
Before rights issue (56,000 × $1/25c × 5/7 = 160m × 4c)			6,400
After rights issue (56,000 × $1/25c × 2c)			4,480
			10,880
DR Retained earnings		10,880	
CR Loan note interest and dividends paid			10,880

6 *Tax*

		$'000	$'000
Current tax: DR Current tax (P/L)		28,000	
CR Current tax payable			28,000
Deferred tax:			
B/d (per TB)			4,600
To P/L			3,700
C/d			8,300

MCQ bank – reporting financial performance

207   A   A change of depreciation method is treated as a change of accounting estimate. Adoption of the revaluation method is dealt with under IAS 16. Application of a new accounting policy (such as capitalisation of borrowing costs) for transactions that did not previously occur is not a change in accounting policy according to IAS 8.

208   B   It is not necessary for a buyer to have been located for the asset.

209   A   Lower of carrying amount and fair value less costs of disposal. As the assets are to be sold, value in use is not relevant and recoverable amount will be fair value less costs of disposal.

210   B   This is a change in presentation which will affect calculation of gross profit and will be retrospectively adjusted when presenting comparatives. A and D are simply adjustments made during preparation of the financial statements, C is a change of accounting estimate.

211   A   This is a change in presentation so qualifies as a change in accounting policy.

CBE style OTQ bank – reporting financial performance

212   $36.8 million

Selling price × 90% minus selling costs.

213   $147,059   €125,000 / 0.85

214   The correct answer is:

The rate at the date of the transaction

215   $98 loss

Date	Rate	$	€	Gain/ (loss)
1/11	1.63	30,675	50,000	
1/12	1.61	(15,528)	(25,000)	(191)
31/12	1.64	15,244	25,000	<u>93</u>
				<u>98</u>

Section B

Tunshill (12/10) MCQ case

216   D   This is a change of accounting estimate so does not need to be retrospectively applied.

217   A

	$m
Original cost 1 October 20X0	20
Two years depreciation ((20/5) × 2)	(8)
Carrying amount at 1 October 20X2	12
Depreciation to 30 September 20X3 (12/6)	(2)
Carrying amount at 30 September 20X3	10

218   C   This is a change in presentation so it is a change of accounting policy.

219 B

	FIFO $m	AVCO $m	Current year profit $m
Year to 30 September 20X2	15	13.4	(1.6)
B/f 1 October 20X2			1.6
Year to 30 September 20X3	20	18	(2.0)
At 30 September 20X3			(0.4)

The net effect at 30 September 20X3 of this proposal will be to reduce current year profits by $400,000.

220 D DR Cost of sales / CR Inventory

The credit entry reduces inventory

MCQ bank – earnings per share

221 A

Earnings on dilution:	$'000
Basic	1,850
Add back interest (2,000 × 6% × 70%)	84
	1,934

Shares on dilution:	'000
Existing	10,000
Conversion (2m × 4/5)	1,600
	11,600

Basic EPS = 1,850 / 10,000 = $0.185

Diluted EPS = 1,934 / 11,600 = $0.167

222 B

	Share capital $'000	Share premium $'000
Balance 30 September X2 (250m shares)	50,000	15,000
Rights issue:		
Share capital (50m × 20c)	(10,000)	
Share premium (50m × 22c)	–	(11,000)
Balance 30 September X1 (200m shares)	40,000	4,000

223 C The convertible loan note and the share options should be taken into account when calculating diluted EPS.

224 B EPS takes into account the additional resources made available to earn profit when new shares are issued for cash, whereas net profit does not.

CBE style OTQ bank – earnings per share

225 $1.35

TERP

5 × 1.8 =	9.0	
1 × 1.5 =	1.5	
	10.5	/ 6 = $1.75

Shares		'000
5,000 × 5/12 × 1.8 / 1.75		2,143
6,000 × 7/12		3,500
		5,643

EPS = 7,600 / 5,643 = $1.35

226	$0.50	Shares
		'000
	B/f (7,500 / 0.5)	15,000
	Full market price issue (4,000 × 9/12)	3,000
	Bonus issue (18,000 / 3)	6,000
		24,000

EPS = 12 / 24 = $0.50

227	$0.72 / $0.56	Shares
		'000
	B/f	4,000
	Bonus issue	1,000
		5,000

EPS 20X8 = 3.6 / 5 = $0.72

EPS 20X7 = $0.70 × 4,000 / 5,000 = $0.56

MCQ bank – analysing and interpreting financial statements

228 D The low asset turnover suggests a capital-intensive industry. This rules out the estate agency or architectural practice. Supermarkets can also be capital-intensive but tend to operate on low profit margins.

229 C This will reduce working capital and means that it will take longer to build up working capital needed for production. The other options will all speed up the operating cycle.

230 D (Dividends (3.4 + 11.1) / Share price) × 100 = 14.5 / 350 × 100 = 4.1%

231 A Net profit margin is a component of ROCE, so 16.3% / 4.19 = 3.9%

CBE style OTQ bank – analysing and interpreting financial statements

232 7.5 EPS = 800 / 4,000 = $0.20. P/E ratio = 150 / 20 = 7.5

233 5.1%

	$'000
Profit before interest and tax	230 %
Capital employed (3,500 + 1,000)	4,500
	= 5.1%

Section C

234 Bengal (6/11 amended)

Text references. Chapters 19 and 20.

Top tips. Note that only five marks are available for ratios – the rest is for your analysis, so it needs to make sense. Review the information you have in the context of profitability, gearing and liquidity. This will tell you which ratios need to be included.

Easy marks. Most marks here are for reviewing all the information and making as many useful points as you can, not just calculating loads of ratios. Try to bear in mind the shareholder's comments and arrive at a conclusion.

Examination Team's comments. Most did well on the ratios but not so well on the performance analysis, often failing to see that the decline in profit was due to the finance costs and the tax charge.

(a) It is correct that revenue has increased by 48% while profit for the year has only increased by 20%. However, on closer inspection, we can see that this is to a large degree attributable to the tax charge for the year. The tax charge was 28.6% of the profit before tax in the year ended 31.3.20X0 and 42.8% of the profit before tax in the year ended 31.3.20X1. We do not have a breakdown of the tax charge but it could include underpayments in previous years, which distorts the trading results.

A better comparison between the two years is the profit before tax % and the gross profit %. Both of these are higher in 20X1 than in 20X0. The shareholders will also be interested in the ROCE. There has been a significant increase in capital employed during the year ended 31.3. 20X1. Bengal has acquired nearly $13m in tangible and intangible assets, financed from cash reserves and a new issue of 8% loan notes. An additional $2m of non-current assets have been reclassified as held for sale. This suggests that Bengal has taken over the trade of another business and is disposing of the surplus assets. This is a long-term project which may take time to show a return and the ROCE does show a significant drop in 20X1. However, if we disregard the loan capital and look at the ROE we can see a considerable increase in 20X1.

The increase in loan capital does have significance for shareholders. The interest charge has increased from $100,000 to $650,000, which reduces the amount available for dividend. Gearing has increased significantly. The rate that Bengal has to offer to loan note holders has already increased from 5% to 8%. If it required further borrowing, with this high gearing, it would have to pay substantially more. Shares in Bengal have become a riskier investment. One indicator of this is the interest cover, which has fallen from 36 times to 9 times. The acquisition could presumably have been financed from a share issue or share exchange, rather than loan capital. However, this would have diluted the return available to shareholders.

The area in which there is most cause for concern is liquidity. As we can see from the statement of cash flows, cash and cash equivalents have fallen by $4.2m and the company is now running an overdraft. It has tax to pay of $2.2m and this will incur penalties if it is not paid on time. The current ratio has declined from 2.1:1 to 1.5:1 and this is including the non-current assets held for sale as part of non-current assets. The quick ratio, excluding inventory and non-current assets held for sale, indicates the immediate cash situation and this shows a fall from 1.6:1 to 0.46:1. Bengal needs to remedy this by disposing of the non-current assets held for sale as soon as possible and selling off surplus inventory, which may have been acquired as part of the acquisition.

Overall, the shareholder should be reassured that Bengal is profitable and expanding. The company has perhaps overstretched itself and significantly raised its gearing, but it is to be hoped that the investment will bring in future returns. This is no doubt the picture the company wants to give to shareholders, which is why it has paid a dividend in spite of having very little cash with which to do so.

(b) While ratio analysis is a useful tool, it has a number of limitations, particularly when comparing ratios for different companies.

Some ratios can be calculated in different ways. For instance, gearing can be expressed using debt as a proportion of debt and equity or simply debt as a proportion of equity. Ratios can be distorted by inflation, especially where non-current assets are carried at original cost.

Ratios are based upon financial statements which may not be comparable due to the adoption of different accounting policies and different estimation techniques. For instance, whether non-current assets are carried at original cost or current value will affect ROCE, as will the use of different depreciation rates. In addition, financial statements are often prepared with the key ratios in mind, so may have been subject to creative accounting. The year-end values also may not be representative of values during the year, due to seasonal trading.

Appendix: Ratios

		20X1	20X0
Net profit %	(3,000 / 25,500) / (2,500 / 17,250)	11.8%	14.5%
Net profit % (pre-tax)	(5,250 / 25,500) / (3,500 / 17,250)	20.6%	20.3%
Gross profit %	(10,700 / 25,500) / (6,900 / 17,250)	42%	40%
ROCE	(5,900 / 18,500) / (3,600 / 9,250)	31.9%	38.9%
ROE	(5,250 / 9,500) / (3,500 / 7,250)	55.3%	48.3%
Gearing	(9,000 / 9,500) / (2,000 / 7,250)	94.7%	27.6%
Interest cover	(5,900 / 650) / (3,600 / 100)	9 times	36 times
Current ratio	(8,000 / 5,200) / (7,200 / 3,350)	1.5:1	2.1:1
Quick ratio	(2,400 / 5,200) / (5,400 / 3,350)	0.5:1	1.6:1

235 Woodbank (6/14 amended)

Text reference. Chapter 19.

Top tips. The question makes it very clear where your analysis should be heading – the effect of the purchase of Shaw – so concentrate on this and review the information from this angle.

Easy marks. The ratios were easy marks and a thorough reading of the question would have given you some obvious points to make.

Examination Team's comments. Many candidates paid too little attention to the incremental effect of the acquisition of Shaw and few commented on the fact that profit or loss only included the results of Shaw for three months. This led a lot of candidates to conclude that the acquisition was not advantageous, which is not the conclusion borne out by taking into account the expected profits of Shaw over 12 months.

Marking scheme

	Marks
1 mark per valid point (including 9 for ratios)	<u>20</u>

(a) **Ratios for 20X4**

	20X4
Return on capital employed (ROCE)	12%
(profit before interest and tax/year-end total assets less current liabilities)	
Net asset (equal to capital employed) turnover	1.0 times
Gross profit margin	22%
Profit before interest and tax margin	12%
Current ratio	1.08:1
Gearing (debt/(debt + equity))	36.7%

(b)   **Equivalent ratios for Woodbank without Shaw.**

ROCE	((18 - 5)/(150 - 50))	13%
Net asset turnover	((150 – 30)/100)	1.2 times
Gross profit margin	((33-9)/(150 – 30))	20%
Profit before interest and tax %	((18 – 5)/(150 – 30))	10.8%

(c)   **Analysis of performance and position**

The acquisition of Shaw has materially affected the results of Woodbank for the year ended 31 March 20X4. In order to meaningfully compare the performance of Woodbank during the year to 31 March 20X4 with its performance during the year to 31 March 20X3 it is therefore necessary to isolate the effects of the acquisition and consider how Woodbank's performance would have looked without Shaw.

Profitability

Shaw has contributed significantly to profitability with its gross profit margin of 30% and PBIT% of 16.6%. However the $50 million of loan notes which financed the acquisition have increased capital employed and so exerted a downward pull on ROCE. With Shaw ROCE is 12%. Without Shaw it would have been 13%. If we check the ROCE for Shaw alone we can see that it is only 10% (5,000/50,000). But this is based on the total net assets of Shaw and only three months profits. If twelve months profits were used, we could expect the return to be correspondingly higher.

During the three months to 31 March 20X4 Shaw had a gross profit margin of 30%. Combined with Woodbank, it raises Woodbank gross profit margin from 20% to 22%. Woodbank's individual gross profit has therefore declined by 2% since 20X3. While revenue has risen by 9%, cost of sales has increased by 11%. However, Woodbank has done well at keeping down expenses and its PBIT margin without Shaw (10.8%) would have been up on 20X3 (9.1%). It is important to remember that Shaw was only owned for the final three months of the financial year, not much time for the additional assets to show a return. It is likely that the acquisition will enhance profitability to a greater extent over the next twelve months.

Liquidity

The current ratio of Woodbank has fallen from 1.7:1 to 1.08:1. This is a steep drop. We can see immediately that cash reserves have declined by $4.5 million and trade payables have increased by $8 million. This suggests that Woodbank is having trouble paying its suppliers on time. Payables days have increased from 55 to 66. The retained earnings balance shows that Woodbank paid a dividend of $5.5 million during 20X4. This was perhaps unwise when working capital was needed to finance expansion and pay the additional loan interest. Had the dividend not been paid the current ratio for 20X4 would be 1.3:1 – still a fall from 20X3, but less alarming.

Gearing

Gearing has risen from 5.3% to 36.7%, attributable to an additional $50 million loan notes issued to finance the acquisition of Shaw. The interest payments each year will be $5.5 million – the amount of the dividend paid in 20X4. Shareholders may expect to receive less in future years as the servicing of the debt will take priority, but had the acquisition been funded by a share issue their returns would have been diluted. Gearing of 36.7% is still within acceptable limits and future good returns from the acquisition will build up retained earnings and keep gearing in check.

Conclusion

Woodbank's performance would have been broadly comparable to the previous year had no acquisition taken place. The acquisition of Shaw has had a detrimental effect on liquidity and gearing for 20X4 but appears from three months results to have the capacity to significantly increase profits for Woodbank. It seems likely that over a longer period this will also improve liquidity and gearing, giving an overall positive result for shareholders.

236 Greenwood

		Marks
Up to 6 marks for relevant ratios		6
Up to 5 marks for effect of disposal		5
Up to 1 mark per relevant interpretive comment	Maximum	9
	Total for questions	20

The application of IFRS 5 *Non-current assets held for sale and discontinued operations* makes it possible to separate out the results of continuing and discontinued operations. This is important for analysts as discontinued operations will not be contributing to future performance and non-current assets held for sale will be disposed of in the near future. As the disposal is treated as a discontinued operation and this was Greenwood's only subsidiary, the profits attributable to the non-controlling interest form part of the results of the discontinued operation.

We can see in comparing the statements of financial position for 20X6 and 20X7 that Deadwood had no property, plant or equipment, but it will have had some current assets and liabilities. The value disposed of will have been based on the group share of Deadwood's share capital and retained earnings and the $1.5m goodwill. Looking at the analysis of discontinued operations for both years, it is likely that Deadwood did not have a large balance on retained earnings and the value of the goodwill is questionable on the same basis, so Greenwood probably did well to obtain $6m for its shareholding.

In the case of Greenwood we have excluded the results of the disposal and the disposal proceeds from ratios where applicable. Non-controlling interest is normally included in ROCE based on consolidated financial statements. It has been excluded here in order to facilitate comparison with the year of disposal.

Greenwood's ROCE based on continuing operations has declined from 32.6% to 29.7% between 20X6 and 20X7. Separating this ratio into its component parts, we can see that there has been a slight improvement in the profit before interest and tax ratio, from 17.7% to 17.8%. The problem therefore lies with the asset turnover, which has declined from 1.84 to 1.67. This means that Greenwood made less effective use of its assets in 20X7 than in 20X6. An additional $3m of loan notes were issued during the year, but this capital has not yet generated a commensurate return.

There has been a healthy increase in revenue in 20X7 and gross profit % has almost kept pace, but the margin has been eroded by an increase in operating expenses and finance costs which have increased by 140%. These are due to the additional $3m loan notes and the overdraft, on which Greenwood appears to be paying about 17% per annum (200/1,150 = 17.4%).

The analysis of discontinued operations demonstrates why Deadwood has been sold. A gross profit of $1m in 20X6 represented a return of 11%, compared with the 29% gross profit percentage on the continuing operations. In 20X6 the discontinued operation made a pre-tax profit of $450,000 which represents a ROCE of about 7% on its $6.3m assets. In 20X7 the ROCE was of course negative. The loss on disposal indicates that a goodwill impairment loss should probably have been recognised at the end of 20X6.

At first sight Greenwood's current ratio of 2.11 for 20X7 looks healthy, but this has been distorted by the assets relating to Deadwood. Adjusted for this, we get a current ratio of 0.77. This is alarming in itself and is a decline from 0.97 in 20X6. The quick ratio, similarly adjusted, stands at 0.62 in 20X6 and 0.44 in 20X7. During 20X7 Greenwood's cash balances have declined by $1.2m, despite the further $3m loan, and it has a tax bill of $950,000, which will presumably accrue interest if it is not paid by the due date.

What we cannot see from the consolidated financial statements is the level of intercompany trading as these transactions and balances will have been eliminated on consolidation. Greenwood could have been selling to Deadwood on favourable terms and providing management services free of charge in order to make the financial statements of Deadwood look better (or less disastrous) and boost the chances of a sale. Or it could have been using transfer pricing to move across profits from Deadwood in order to boost its own profits and be able to pay higher dividends to its own shareholders. We would need to have sight of the individual company financial statements of Greenwood and Deadwood in order to make a judgement about this.

Overall, Greenwood's results do not inspire confidence. Disposing of the unprofitable subsidiary was no doubt the correct action and management now needs to collect the proceeds and do whatever else can be done to handle the liquidity situation.

Appendix

Ratios	20X7	20X6
ROCE – continuing operations		
(4,500 + 400*)/(14,500 + 8,000 - 6,000**)	29.7%	
(3,750/(12,750 + 5,000 – 6,250))		32.6%

*Note that of the finance costs shown for 20X7 only $400,000 is loan note interest
** Due on sale of subsidiary

Gross profit % - continuing operations		
(8,000/27,500)	29.1%	
(6,200/21,200)		29.2%
Net profit before interest and tax %		
(4,900/27,500)	17.8%	
(3,750/21,200)		17.7%
Asset turnover		
(27,500/(14,500 + 8,000 – 6,000))	1.67	
(21,200/(12750 + 5,000 – 6,250))		1.84
Current ratio		
Including disposal assets (9,500/4,500)	2.11	
Excluding disposal assets (3,500/4,500)	0.78	
(3,700/3,800)		0.97

Quick ratio (acid test)

Including disposal assets (8,000/4,500)	1.78
Excluding disposal assets (2,000/4,500)	0.44
(2,350/3,800)	0.62

MCQ bank – limitations of financial statements and interpretation techniques

237   D   Capital employed (assets) would decrease, increasing ROCE. The impairment loss will reduce equity (revaluation surplus) and so increase gearing.

238   A   The value of the inventory will be added to both current assets and current liabilities. It will add proportionately more to liabilities and so reduce the current ratio. The effect on the quick ratio will be even greater as inventory is excluded from assets.

239   B   The new product will have an operating profit of 120 / 1,600 = 7.5%, so will reduce the current margin. It will have an ROCE of 120 / 500 = 24%, higher than the current 20%.

240   C   Obsolete goods can lead to a build-up of unsold inventory, thereby increasing the holding period. A reduction in selling price or an increase in demand could increase sales leading to a fall in the holding period. Seasonal fluctuations will change the holding period throughout the year, but should not affect the year-on-year picture.

CBE style OTQ bank – limitations of financial statements and interpretation techniques

241   The correct answer is:
Overstatement of profits

The use of historical cost accounting during a period of inflation can lead to overstatement of profits. Non-current assets carried at historical cost may be presented at a value well below their fair value, leading to understated depreciation and consequently overstated profits. This can be compounded by the use of FIFO, if inventory is held at an original cost which is significantly below replacement cost. The charge to cost of sales will be understated and profit overstated.

The use of historical cost accounting will lead to understatement rather than overstatement of non-current asset values and will not affect interest costs. It is likely to lead to overstatement rather than understatement of ROCE.

242   The correct answer is:
Renegotiating a loan to secure a lower interest rate.

This may save interest costs but will have no effect on gearing. The other options are methods that could be resorted to in order to reduce or avoid any increase in gearing.

243   The correct answer is:
A sale and operating leaseback

This would be an unlikely transaction as it would remove the asset from the statement of financial position.

The deferral method of accounting for government grants leaves the carrying amount of the asset intact, rather than deducting the amount of the grant from the asset amount.

Revaluing assets is the obvious way of increasing the carrying amount of assets.

Under the reducing balance method, more depreciation is charged in the earlier years of the life of an asset, so a change to 10% straight line would reduce the depreciation charge for the first few years. Of course this effect is only temporary as the charge will catch up after a few years.

244   The correct answer is:

Trent factors with recourse the receivable of its largest customer.

A receivable factored with recourse will still be included in trade receivables at the year end. Seasonal trading will create particular distortion if the busiest period is just before the year end. Cash sales will need to be removed from the calculation and an adjustment will have to be made for sales tax.

Section C

245 Quartile (12/12 amended)

Text references. Chapters 19 and 20

Top tips. A bit of planning is useful for a question like this and the categories of profitability, liquidity and gearing give you a structure around which to base your analysis. Note that this is a retail business, so this will affect the ratios.

Easy marks. Analysis of the ratios is straightforward and some useful points on the limitations on usefulness of a sector average comparison could have earned four marks.

Marking scheme

		Marks
(a)	Ratios	6
(a)	1 mark per valid comment	10
(b)	1 mark per issue	4
Total for question		20

(a)

Return on year-end capital employed (ROCE)	12.1%
Net asset (total assets less current liabilities) turnover	1.6 times
Gross profit margin	25%
Operating profit margin	7.5%
Current ratio	1.55:1
Average inventory turnover	4.5 times
Trade payables' payment period	45 days
Debt to equity	30%

(b)   **Analysis of financial and operating performance of Quartile compared to sector average**

Profitability

Quartile has a ROCE **significantly lower** at 12.1% than the sector average of 16.8%. This is mainly due to the lower than average gross profit margin and consequent **low operating profit margin**. The operating expenses are actually lower (17.5%) as a percentage of revenue than the sector average of 23% (35% – 12%) so the problem lies between revenue and cost of sales. Inventory turnover is quite brisk (4.5 times compared to a sector average of three times) but Quartile's mark-up of 33.3% ((25 / 75) × 100) is significantly below the sector average of 54% (35 / 65) × 100). Quartile is maintaining turnover **by keeping prices down**.

The other component of ROCE, net asset turnover, is slightly higher than the sector average. This is due to the buoyant turnover, as the ratio will have been depressed by the property revaluation and the capitalisation of the development expenditure, which have increased the asset base. It is to be hoped that the development expenditure will generate the expected revenue. If it had been necessary to expense it for the year ended 30 September 20X2 Quartile would have reported a loss before tax of $1.6m.

Liquidity

Quartile has a current ratio of 1.55:1 compared to the sector average of 1.25:1. Both appear low, but satisfactory for the retail sector as the cash cycle is fairly rapid. Inventory can be turned into immediate cash and this is particularly true for Quartile with its high inventory turnover level. The lower than average payables days (45 compared to 64) and the absence of an overdraft suggest that **Quartile is not suffering liquidity problems**.

Gearing

Quartile's debt to equity ratio is 30%, well below the sector average of 38% and the interest rate on the loan notes is below the ROCE of 12.1%, meaning that the **borrowings are earning a good return** for the business. The interest cover of 5.25 times (4,200 / 800) is satisfactory. Quartile is not having any problems servicing its loan and is unlikely to give lenders any particular concern,

Conclusion

There are no going concern worries for Quartile but it does have an issue with **low profitability**. It appears to be positioned at the bottom end of the jewellery market selling high volume cheap items rather than more valuable pieces on which there would be significantly higher profit margins. This may or may not be the most advantageous strategy in a period of recession.

(c)   The following factors may limit the usefulness of comparisons based on business sector averages.

   (i)   The companies included in the average may have used different accounting policies. Some may be applying the revaluation basis to their assets and some may not. This will affect asset turnover and ROCE.

   (ii)   Some companies in the average may have used some form of creative accounting, such as sale and leaseback transactions, which will have boosted both profit for the year and ROCE.

   (iii)   The average may include a wide variety of entities with different trading methods and risk profiles. Very high-end jewellers may even operate on an invoice rather than a cash basis and will have receivables included in their current assets. Very large chains will probably have more access to cheap borrowing.

   (iv)   Some ratios, in particular ROCE and gearing, can be calculated in different ways. It is up to the organisation carrying out the comparison to ensure that a standard definition is used, and they may or may not do this.

MCQ bank – statement of cash flows

246	A		$m
		B/f (500 + 100)	600
		Cash received (β)	500
		C/f (750 + 350)	1,100

247	B		$'000
		Balance b/f	1,860
		Revaluation	100
		Disposal	(240)
		Depreciation	(280)
			1,440
		Additions (β)	1,440
		Balance c/f	2,880

248   A

	$'000
Carrying amount 20X3	14,400
Depreciation	(2,500)
Sale of plant	(3,000)
Revaluation	2,000
Environmental provision	4,000
	14,900
Purchases (β)	8,500
	23,400

CBE style OTQ bank – statement of cash flows

249    $305 million

	$m
B/f	410
Depreciation	(115)
Revaluation	80
Purchases (β)	305
C/f	680

250    $2,100,000

	$'000
B/f (2,000 + 800)	2,800
Additions (6,500 – 2,500 + 1,800)	5,800
Payments made (β)	(2,100)
C/f (4,800 + 1,700)	6,500

Section C

251 Dickson

(a) STATEMENT OF CASH FLOWS FOR YEAR ENDED 31 MARCH 20X8

Cash flows from operating activities	$'000	$'000
Profit before taxation	342	
Adjustments for:		
Depreciation	57	
Amortisation (W1)	60	
Interest expense	15	
Profit on disposal of assets (110 – 103)	(7)	
	467	
Increase in inventories (W4)	(133)	
Decrease in trade receivables (W4)	50	
Decrease in trade payables (W4)	(78)	
Cash generated from operations	306	
Interest paid (W3)	(10)	
Income taxes paid (W3)	(256)	
Net cash from operating activities		40
Cash flows from investing activities		
Development expenditure	(190)	
Purchase of property, plant & equipment (W1)	(192)	
Proceeds from sale of property, plant & equipment	110	
Net cash used in investing activities		(272)
Cash flows from financing activities		
Proceeds from issue of shares (W2)	300	
Proceeds from issue of debentures	50	
Payment of finance lease liabilities (W3)	(31)	
Dividends paid (W2)	(156)	
Net cash from financing activities		163
Net decrease in cash and cash equivalents		(69)
Cash and cash equivalents at beginning of period		109
Cash and cash equivalents at end of period		40

Workings

1 Assets

	Property, plant and equipment	Development expenditure
	$'000	$'000
B/d	737	160
Disposals	(103)	
P/L	(57)	
OCI	100	
Purchase under F/L	56	
Additions (β)		190
Amortisation		(60)
Cash additions (β)	192	–
C/d	925	290

2   Equity

	Share capital and premium	Revaluation surplus	Retained earnings
	$'000	$'000	$'000
B/d	500	60	255
P/L			180
OCI		100	
Bonus issue	50		(50)
Rights issue (β)	300		
Dividend paid (β)	–	–	(156)
C/d	850	160	229

3   Liabilities

	Debentures	Finance leases	Taxation	Interest
	$'000	$'000	$'000	$'000
B/d	100	92*	198**	–
SPLOCI			162	15
New lease		56		
Cash received (paid) (β)	50	(31)	(256)	(10)
C/d	150	117	104	5

*Non-current + current

**Deferred + current

4   Working capital

	Inventories	Receivables	Payables
	$'000	$'000	$'000
B/d	227	324	352
Movement (β)	133	(50)	(78)
C/d	360	274	274

(b)   CASH FLOWS FROM OPERATING ACTIVITIES (direct method)

	$'000
Cash received from customers (W2)	1,526
Cash paid to suppliers and employees (W1)	(1,220)
Cash generated from operations	306
Interest paid	(10)
Income taxes paid	(256)
Net cash from operating activities	40

Workings

1   Payables

	$'000
Payables balance b/d	352
Purchases (W3)	1,095
Other expenses (W4)	47
Payments (β)	1,220
Payables balance c/d	274

2   Receivables

	$'000
Receivables balance b/d	324
Sales revenue	1,476
Cash received (β)	(1,526)
	274

3   Purchases

	$'000
Inventory balance b/d	227
Transfer to cost of sales	(962)
Purchases (β)	1,095
Inventory balance c/d	360

4   Other expenses

	$'000
Balance per statement of profit or loss	157
Depreciation	(57)
Amortisation	(60)
Profit on disposal	7
	47

252 Mocha (12/11)

Text references. Chapter 21.

Top tips. Statements of cash flow are popular questions with students. This one has a few complications, but is basically straightforward. As always, get the proforma down and do the standard workings.

Easy marks. There are plenty of easy marks available for dealing with the usual adjustments – working capital, tax, finance lease and share capital and 1½ marks just for showing that interest charged is the same as interest paid.

Examination Team's comments. The statement of cash flows was very well answered, with many candidates scoring full marks. The main errors involved the profit on disposal, the warranty provision, the tax calculation, the finance lease and the share issue. The bonus issue is not a cash flow.

Marking scheme

	Marks
Profit before tax	½
Depreciation	1
Profit on disposal of property	1
Investment income deducted	½
Interest expense added back	½
Working capital items	1½
Decrease in product warranty	1½
Interest paid	1
Income tax paid	2
Purchase of PPE	1½
Disposal of PPE	1
Disposal of investment	1
Dividends received	1
Share issue	2½
Payments under finance lease	2½
Cash b/f / c/f	1
	20

(a) STATEMENT OF CASH FLOWS FOR THE YEAR ENDED 30 SEPTEMBER 20X1

	$'000	$'000
Cash flows from operating activities		
Profit before tax	3,900	
Adjustments for:		
Depreciation	2,500	
Profit on sale of property	(4,100)	
Investment income	(1,100)	
Interest expense	500	
	1,700	
Increase in inventories (W4)	(3,000)	
Decrease in receivables (W4)	200	
Decrease in payables (W4)	(1,400)	
Decrease in warranty provision (4,000 – 1,600)	(2,400)	
Cash used in operations	(4,900)	
Interest paid	(500)	
Income tax paid (W3)	(800)	
Net cash used in operating activities		(6,200)
Cash flows from investing activities		
Sale of property	8,100	
Purchase of plant	(8,300)	
Sale of investment	3,400	
Dividends received	200	
Net cash from investing activities		3,400
Cash flows from financing activities		
Issue of share capital (W2)	2,400	
Payments under finance leases (W3)	(3,900)	
Net cash from financing activities		(1,500)
Decrease in cash and cash equivalents		(4,300)
Cash and cash equivalents b/f		1,400
Cash and cash equivalents c/f		(2,900)

Workings

1 Assets

	PPE $'000	Financial asset $'000
B/d	24,100	7,000
New F/L additions	6,700	
Purchase of new plant	8,300	
Disposal	(4,000)	(3,000)
Depreciation	(2,500)	
Increase in fair value		500
	32,600	4,500

2 Equity

	Share capital $'000	Share premium $'000	Revaluation surplus $'000	Retained earnings $'000
B/d	8,000	2,000	3,600	10,100
Bonus issue:	3,600	(2,000)	(1,600)	
SPLOCI				2,900
Issued for cash (β)	2,400	–		–
C/d	14,000	–	2,000	13,000

3   Liabilities

	Finance leases	Income tax
	$'000	$'000
B/d	9,000*	2,100**
Additions	6,700	
SPLOCI		1,000
Paid (β)	(3,900)	(800)
	11,800*	2,300**

*Non-current + current
**Deferred + current

4   Working capital

	Inventories	Receivables	Payables
	$'000	$'000	$'000
B/d	7,200	3,700	4,600
Movement	3,000	(200)	(1,400)
C/d	10,200	3,500	3,200

MCQ bank – accounting for inflation

253   C   Historical cost accounting does not avoid the overstatement of profit which arises during periods of inflation, which is why alternative models have been proposed.

254   C   A,B and D are all likely consequences of overstatement of profits. In the case of C, what tends to happen when profits are overstated is that **too much** cash is paid out in dividends to shareholders, depleting funds needed for investment.

255   B

	Historical cost	Current cost
	$'000	$'000
Cost/valuation	500	600
Depreciation ((500,000 × 90%) /5) × 2	(180)	
Depreciation ((600,000 × 90%) /5) × 2		(216)
Carrying amount	320	384

CBE style OTQ bank – accounting for inflation

256   The correct answer is:

Current cost accounting

The concept of 'physical capital maintenance' is applied in current cost accounting.

257   The correct answer is:

Current purchasing power accounting

Current purchasing power accounting adjusts for general price inflation.

258   The correct answer is:

Replacement cost

Under CCA goods sold are charged to profit or loss at replacement cost.

MCQ bank – specialised, not-for-profit and public sector entities

259   C   Charities do not usually have shareholders, in the commercial sense of the term.

260   B   Public sector accounting needs to move from cash-based accounting to application of the accruals concept.

261   A   A local council would not pay dividends and would be unlikely to measure ROCE, which deals with return to investors.

262   D   Charities have to consider a very wide group of shareholders, which can include donors, beneficiaries, volunteers, local organisations, government bodies and the public at large.

CBE style OTQ bank – specialised, not-for-profit and public sector entities

263   The correct answer is:
Funding by government

Public sector bodies have a major advantage not generally enjoyed by charities – government funding.

264   The correct answer is:
Disclosure of dividends per share

Not-for-profit entities do not have share capital so dividends per share is not relevant. The other requirements could be relevant to a not-for-profit entity.

265   The correct answer is:
There is no requirement to calculate an earnings per share figure as it is not likely to have shareholders who need to assess its earnings performance.

The objectives of a not-for-profit entity do not include making a profit so it would not calculate earnings per share or report to shareholders.

Mock Exams

ACCA

Fundamentals Level

Paper F7

Financial Reporting

Mock Examination 1

Time allowed: 3 hours 15 minutes

This question paper is divided into three sections:

Section A – ALL 15 questions are compulsory and MUST be attempted

Section B – ALL 15 questions are compulsory and MUST be attempted

Section C – BOTH questions are compulsory and MUST be attempted

Do NOT open this question paper until instructed by the supervisor.

Do NOT record any of your answers on the question paper.

This question paper must not be removed from the examination hall.

BPP
LEARNING MEDIA

Section A – ALL 15 questions are compulsory and MUST be attempted

1   Monty had profit before tax of $3 million for the year ended 31 March 20X3, after charging loan interest of $150,000 and interest on a finance lease of $250,000. Extracts from the equity and liabilities section of the statement of financial position of Monty at 31 March 20X3 are as follows.

	$'000	$'000
Total equity		12,550
Non-current liabilities		
8% loan notes	1,400	
Deferred tax	1,500	
Finance lease obligation	1,200	
		4,100
Current liabilities		
Finance lease obligation	750	
Trade payables	2,650	
Current tax	1,250	
		4,650

What is the return on year-end capital employed?

A   16.3%
B   21.4%
C   18.6%
D   24.3%   (2 marks)

---

2   How can ROCE be further analysed into its component ratios?

A   Gross profit margin / net asset turnover
B   Gross profit margin × net asset turnover
C   Net profit margin / net asset turnover
D   Net profit margin × net asset turnover   (2 marks)

---

3   At 1 April 20X2 Atlas had in issue 80 million 50c equity shares. On 1 July 20X2 Atlas made and recorded a fully subscribed rights issue of 1 for 4 at $1.20 each. Immediately before this issue the stock market value of Atlas's shares was $2 each, giving a theoretical ex-rights price of $1.84. Earnings for the year amounted to $31.2 million.

What is the basic earnings per share of Atlas for the year ended 31 March 20X3?

A $0.328
B $0.312
C $0.323
D $0.334   (2 marks)

---

4   At 31 March 20X2 Monty had equity of $9.75 million, loan notes of $3.125 million and finance lease obligations totalling $1.5 million.

During the year to 31 March 20X3 equity increased by $2.8 million, $1.725 million of the loan notes were repaid and finance lease obligations increased by $450,000.

What was gearing (debt / debt + equity) at 31 March 20X3?

A   10%
B   35%
C   28%
D   21%   (2 marks)

5   On 1 October 20X2 Atlas sold $10 million of maturing inventory to Xpede. The cost of the goods at the date
     of sale was $7 million and Atlas has the option to repurchase these goods at any time within three years of
     the sale at a price of $10 million plus accrued interest from the date of sale at 10% per annum. At 31 March
     20X3 the option had not been exercised but it is highly likely that it will be before the date it lapses.

     What should be the net effect on profit or loss of this transaction for the year ended 31 March 20X3?

     A   Credit $3,000,000
     B   Charge $500,000
     C   Credit $2,500,000
     D   Credit $2,000,000   (2 marks)

6   Radar's sole activity is the operation of hotels all over the world. After a period of declining profitability,
     Radar's management took the following steps during the year ended 31 March 20X3:

     (i)   It entered into negotiations with a buyer to sell all of its hotels in country A
     (ii)   It disposed of two loss-making hotels in country B

     Which of these decisions meet the criteria for being classified as discontinued operations in the financial
     statements for the year ended 31 March 20X3?

     A   (i)
     B   (ii)
     C   Both of them
     D   Neither of them   (2 marks)

7   Which of the following is **not** an advantage which could be expected to follow from global harmonisation of
     accounting standards?

     A   Elimination of exchange differences
     B   Easier transfer of accounting staff across national borders
     C   Ability to comply with the requirements of overseas stock exchanges
     D   Better access to foreign investor funds   (2 marks)

8   At a year-end board meeting on 31 March 20X2, Pulsar's directors made the decision to close down one of
     its factories at the end of the following year, on 31 March 20X3. The factory and its related plant would then
     be sold. A formal plan was formulated and the factory's employees were given three months' notice of
     redundancy on 1 January 20X3. Customers and suppliers were also informed of the closure at this date.

     How should the closure be accounted for?

     A   Discontinued operation as at 31 March 20X2
     B   Discontinued operation during the year to 31 March 20X3
     C   No discontinued operation, but restructuring provision at 31 March 20X3
     D   No discontinued operation or restructuring provision   (2 marks)

9   Which of the following would **not** give rise to a valid provision in accordance with IAS 37 *Provisions,
     contingent liabilities and contingent assets*?

     A   A company's operations have caused environmental damage. It is not legally obliged to rectify this
          but always does so in order to maintain its eco-credentials.

     B   A company is vacating a factory building that it was occupying under an operating lease. It is moving
          to a new building on 1 July but the lease on the existing building runs up to 1 September and cannot
          be cancelled.

     C   A company has decided to change one of its current raw materials for a substitute which is more
          environmentally friendly. This material is more expensive and it is estimated that this will lead to a $2
          million reduction in profit in the coming year.

     D   A company sells a product with a six-month guarantee which provides customers with free repairs or
          replacement for any defect which arises within that period.   (2 marks)

10   Speculate owned an office building with a depreciated historical cost of $2 million and a remaining useful life of 20 years at 1 April 20X2. On 1 October 20X2 Speculate ceased to occupy the building and let it out to a third party. The property was reclassified as an investment property, applying the fair value model in accordance with IAS 40 *Investment property*. The value of the property was independently assessed at $2.3 million at 1 October 20X2 and had risen to $2.34 million by 31 March 20X3.

What amount will be charged/credited to profit or loss in respect of this property for the year ended 31 March 20X3?

A   Credit $40,000
B   Charge $50,000
C   Charge $10,000
D   No charge or credit   (2 marks)

11   At what amount does IAS 41 *Agriculture* generally require biological assets to be measured upon initial recognition?

A   Cost
B   Fair value
C   Market value
D   Fair value less costs to sell   (2 marks)

12   What are the two fundamental qualitative characteristics of financial information according to the *Conceptual Framework*?

A   Relevance and faithful representation
B   Accruals and going concern
C   Going concern and faithful representation
D   Relevance and accruals   (2 marks)

13   The *Conceptual Framework* describes a number of different measurement bases. One of them is described as follows.

'Assets are carried at the amount of cash or cash equivalents that would have to be paid if the same or an equivalent asset was acquired currently. Liabilities are carried at the undiscounted amount of cash or cash equivalents that would be required to settle the obligation currently.'

Which measurement basis is being described?

A   Historical cost
B   Current cost
C   Realisable (settlement) value
D   Present value   (2 marks)

14   A company purchased a machine for $50,000 on 1 January 20X1. It was judged to have a five-year life with a residual value of $5,000. On 1 January 20X3 $15,000 was spent on an upgrade to the machine. his extended its remaining useful life to 5 years with the same residual value. During 20X3 the market for the product declined and the machine was sold on 1 January 20X4 for $7,000.

What was the loss on disposal?

A $30,600
B $40,000
C $31,600
D $29,000   (2 marks)

15   Which one of the following would require adjustment to the financial statements according to IAS 10 *Events after the reporting period* if they took place between the end of the reporting period and the date the financial statements were authorised for issue?

A   A decision to discontinue an operation
B   A collapse in property prices, affecting the company's portfolio
C   Sale of inventory in its year-end condition at a price below its year end carrying amount
D   Legal action commenced by a supplier   **(2 marks)**

Section B questions

Each question is worth 2 marks

The following scenario relates to questions 16-20

Sandbag is a listed manufacturing company. Its summarised statement of financial position is given below.

STATEMENT OF FINANCIAL POSITION AS AT 31 DECEMBER 20X4

	$m
Non-current assets	610
Inventories	96
Trade receivables	29
Current asset investments	5
Cash	3
	133
	743
Equity and liabilities	
$1 ordinary shares	400
Retained earnings	190
	590
Non-current liabilities – loans	50
Trade payables	103
	743

16   What is Sandbag's current ratio at 31 December 20X4?

    A   0.37
    B   1.29
    C   0.87
    D   1.26

17   The finance director of Sandbag is worried about its current ratio. He is considering a number of actions that he hopes will improve Sandbag's current ratio.
Which of the following would increase Sandbag's current ratio?

    A   Offer a settlement discount to customers
    B   Make a bonus issue of ordinary shares
    C   Make a rights issue of ordinary shares
    D   Sell current asset investments at the carrying amount

18   What is Sandbag's acid test (quick) ratio at 31 December 20X4?

    A   0.36
    B   0.29
    C   0.93
    D   0.24

19   The finance director of Sandbag knows that the acid test ratio is below 1. He is planning two changes:
Proposal 1: Offering a 2% early settlement discount to credit customers
Proposal 2: Delaying payment to all trade payables by one extra month

What effect would each of these proposals have on the acid test ratio?

A   Proposal 1 – increase ratio / Proposal 2 – decrease ratio
B   Proposal 1 – increase ratio / Proposal 2 – increase ratio
C   Proposal 1 – decrease ratio / Proposal 2 – decrease ratio
D   Proposal 1 – decrease ratio / Proposal 2 – increase ratio

20   Sandbag is a manufacturing company. Which one of the following ratios would best assess the efficiency of Sandbag?

A   Price/earnings ratio
B   Gearing ratio
C   Non-current asset turnover
D   Current ratio

The following scenario relates to questions 21-25

Apex is a publicly listed supermarket chain. During the current year it started the building of a new store. The directors are aware that in accordance with IAS 23 *Borrowing costs* certain borrowing costs have to be capitalised.

Details relating to construction of Apex's new store:

Apex issued a $10 million unsecured loan with a coupon (nominal) interest rate of 6% on 1 April 20X8. The loan is redeemable at a premium which means the loan has an effective finance cost of 7·5% per annum. The loan was specifically issued to finance the building of the new store which meets the definition of a qualifying asset in IAS 23. Construction of the store commenced on 1 May 20X8 and it was completed and ready for use on 28 February 20X9, but did not open for trading until 1 April 20X9.

21   Apex's new store meets the definition of a qualifying asset. Which of the following describes a qualifying asset?

A   An asset that is ready for use or sale when purchased
B   An asset that takes over 12 months to get ready for use or sale
C   An asset that is intended for use rather than sale
D   An asset that takes a substantial period of time to get ready for use or sale

22   Apex issued the loan stock on 1 April 20X8. Three events or transactions must be taking place for capitalisation of borrowing costs to commence. Which one of the following is **not** one of these?

A   Expenditure on the asset is being incurred
B   Borrowing costs are being incurred
C   Physical construction of the asset is nearing completion
D   Necessary activities are in progress to prepare the asset for use or sale

23   What is the total of the finance costs which can be capitalised in respect of Apex's new store?

A $625,000
B $750,000
C $600,000
D $500,000

24   Rather than take out a loan specifically for the new store Apex could have funded the store from existing borrowings which are:

(i)   10% bank loan $50 million
(ii)   8% bank loan $30 million

In this case it would have applied a 'capitalisation rate' to the expenditure on the asset. What would that rate have been?

A   10%
B   8.75%
C   9%
D   9.25%

---

25   If Apex had been able to temporarily invest the proceeds of the loan from 1 April to 1 May when construction began, how would the proceeds be accounted for?

A   Deducted from finance costs
B   Deducted from the cost of the asset
C   Recognised as investment income in the statement of profit or loss
D   Deducted from administrative expenses in the statement of profit or loss

---

The following scenario relates to questions 26-30

Advent is a publicly listed company. Details of Advent's non-current assets at 1 October 20X8 were:

	Land and building $m	Plant $m	Telecommunications licence $m	Total $m
Cost/valuation	280	150	300	730
Accumulated depreciation/amortisation	(40)	(105)	(30)	(175)
Carrying amount	240	45	270	555

The following information is relevant:

(i)   The land and building were revalued on 1 October 20X3 with $80 million attributable to the land and $200 million to the building. At that date the estimated remaining life of the building was 25 years. A further revaluation was not needed until 1 October 20X8 when the land and building were valued at $85 million and $180 million respectively. The remaining estimated life of the building at this date was 20 years.

(ii)   Plant is depreciated at 20% per annum on cost with time apportionment where appropriate. On 1 April 20X9 new plant costing $45 million was acquired. In addition, this plant cost $5 million to install and commission. No plant is more than four years old.

(iii) The telecommunications licence was bought from the government on 1 October 20X7 and has a 10 year life. It is amortised on a straight line basis. In September 20X9, a review of the sales of the products related to the licence showed them to be very disappointing. As a result of this review the estimated recoverable amount of the licence at 30 September 20X9 was estimated at only $100 million.

There were no disposals of non-current assets during the year to 30 September 20X9.

---

26   What is the carrying amount of the land and buildings at 30 September 20X9?

A $256m
B $265m
C $240m
D $271m

27   What is the depreciation charge on the plant for the year ended 30 September 20X9?

    A $30m
    B $25m
    C $20m
    D $35m

28   Having revalued its property Advent is required to make certain disclosures in respect of the revaluation.

Which one of the following is **not** one of these disclosures?

    A   Effective date of revaluation
    B   Professional qualifications of valuer
    C   Basis used to revalue assets
    D   Carrying amount of assets if no revaluation had taken place

29   What is the amount of the impairment loss on the licence?

    A $200m
    B $170m
    C $140m
    D $60m

30   Advent's licence is now carried at its recoverable amount. How should the recoverable amount be treated?

    A   Deducted from finance costs
    B   Deducted from the cost of the asset
    C   Recognised as investment income in the statement of profit or loss
    D   Deducted from administrative expenses in the statement of profit or loss

(30 marks)

Section C

Both questions are compulsory and must be attempted

31 The following trial balance relates to Atlas at 31 March 20X3.

	$'000	$'000
Equity shares of 50 cents each		50,000
Share premium		20,000
Retained earnings at 1 April 20X2		11,200
Land and buildings – at cost (land $10 million) (Note (i))	60,000	
Plant and equipment – at cost (Note (i))	94,500	
Accumulated depreciation at 1 April 20X2: – buildings		20,000
– plant and equipment		24,500
Inventory at 31 March 20X3	43,700	
Trade receivables	42,200	
Bank		6,800
Deferred tax (Note (ii))		6,200
Trade payables		35,100
Revenue		550,000
Cost of sales	411,500	
Distribution costs	21,500	
Administrative expenses	30,900	
Dividends paid	20,000	
Bank interest	700	
Current tax (Note (ii))		1,200
	725,000	725,000

The following notes are relevant.

(i) Non-current assets:

On 1 April 20X2, the directors of Atlas decided that the financial statements would show an improved position if the land and buildings were revalued to market value. At that date, an independent valuer valued the land at $12 million and the buildings at $35 million and these valuations were accepted by the directors. The remaining life of the buildings at that date was 14 years. Atlas does not make a transfer to retained earnings for excess depreciation. Ignore deferred tax on the revaluation surplus.

Plant and equipment is depreciated at 20% per annum using the reducing balance method and time apportioned as appropriate. All depreciation is charged to cost of sales, but none has yet been charged on any non-current asset for the year ended 31 March 20X3.

(ii) Atlas estimates that an income tax provision of $27.2 million is required for the year ended 31 March 20X3 and at that date the liability to deferred tax is $9.4 million. The movement on deferred tax should be taken to profit or loss. The balance on current tax in the trial balance represents the under/over provision of the tax liability for the year ended 31 March 20X2.

Required

(a) Prepare the statement of profit or loss and other comprehensive income for Atlas for the year ended 31 March 20X3.   **(8 marks)**

(b) Prepare the statement of financial position of Atlas as at 31 March 20X3.   **(10 marks)**

(c) Calculate basic earnings per share for the year ended 31 March 20X3.   **(2 marks)**

(20 marks)

32 On 1 October 20X2, Paradigm acquired 75% of Strata's equity shares by means of a share exchange of two new shares in Paradigm for every five acquired shares in Strata. In addition, Paradigm issued to the shareholders of Strata a $100 10% loan note for every 1,000 shares it acquired in Strata. Paradigm has not recorded any of the purchase consideration, although it does have other 10% loan notes already in issue.

The market value of Paradigm's shares at 1 October 20X2 was $2 each.

The summarised statements of financial position of the two companies at 31 March 20X3 are:

	Paradigm $'000	Strata $'000
ASSETS		
Non-current assets		
Property, plant and equipment	47,400	25,500
Financial asset: equity investments (Note (i))	7,500	3,200
	54,900	28,700
Current assets		
Inventory (Note (ii))	17,400	8,400
Trade receivables (Note (iii))	14,800	9,000
Bank	5,100	–
Total assets	92,200	46,100
EQUITY AND LIABILITIES		
Equity		
Equity shares of $1 each	40,000	20,000
Retained earnings/(losses) – at 1 April 20X2	19,200	(4,000)
– for year ended 31 March 20X3	7,400	8,000
	66,600	24,000
Non-current liabilities		
10% loan notes	8,000	–
Current liabilities		
Trade payables (Note (iii))	17,600	13,000
Bank overdraft	–	9,100
Total equity and liabilities	92,200	46,100

The following information is relevant.

(i) At the date of acquisition, Strata produced a draft statement of profit or loss which showed it had made a net loss after tax of $2 million at that date. Paradigm accepted this figure as the basis for calculating the pre- and post-acquisition split of Strata's profit for the year ended 31 March 20X3.

Also at the date of acquisition, Paradigm conducted a fair value exercise on Strata's net assets which were equal to their carrying amounts (including Strata's financial asset equity investments) with the exception of an item of plant which had a fair value of $3 million below its carrying amount. The plant had a remaining economic life of three years at 1 October 20X2.

Paradigm's policy is to value the non-controlling interest at fair value at the date of acquisition. For this purpose, a share price for Strata of $1.20 each is representative of the fair value of the shares held by the non-controlling interest.

(ii) Each month since acquisition, Paradigm's sales to Strata were consistently $4.6 million. Paradigm had marked these up by 15% on cost. Strata had one month's supply ($4.6 million) of these goods in inventory at 31 March 20X3. Paradigm's normal mark-up (to third party customers) is 40%.

(iii) Strata's current account balance with Paradigm at 31 March 20X3 was $2.8 million, which did not agree with Paradigm's equivalent receivable due to a payment of $900,000 made by Strata on 28 March 20X3, which was not received by Paradigm until 3 April 20X3.

(iv) The financial asset equity investments of Paradigm and Strata are carried at their fair values as at 1 April 20X2. As at 31 March 20X3, these had fair values of $7.1 million and $3.9 million respectively.

(v) There were no impairment losses within the group during the year ended 31 March 20X3

Required

Prepare the consolidated statement of financial position for Paradigm as at 31 March 20X3.

(20 marks)

Answers

**DO NOT TURN THIS PAGE UNTIL YOU HAVE
COMPLETED THE MOCK EXAM**

A plan of attack

If this were the real Financial Reporting exam and you had been told to turn over and begin, what would be going through your mind?

Perhaps you're having a panic. You've spent most of your study time on groups and interpretation of accounts (because that's what your tutor/BPP study Text told you to do), plus a selection of other topics, and you're really not sure that you know enough. So calm down. Spend the first few moments or so **looking at the paper,** and develop a **plan of attack.**

Looking through the paper:

The first section is 15 2-mark questions. These will cover all sections of the syllabus. Some you may find easy and some more difficult. Don't spend a lot of time on anything you really don't know. You are not penalised for wrong answers, so you should answer all of them. If all else fails – guess!

Section B has 15 2-mark questions in total arranged around three scenarios.

- Scenario 1 is on interpretation of financial statements.
- Scenario 2 is on borrowing costs
- Scenario 3 deals with non-current assets

Section C has two 20-mark questions

Question 1 is a single-company financial statements preparation question.

Question 2 is a consolidated statement of financial position.

All of these questions are compulsory.

This means that you do not have to waste time wondering which questions to answer.

Allocating your time

BPP's advice is always allocate your time **according to the marks for the question** in total and for the parts of the question. But **use common sense**. If you're confronted by a Section A question on a topic of which you know nothing, pick an answer and move on. Use the time to pick up marks elsewhere.

After the exam…Forget about it!

And don't worry if you found the paper difficult. More than likely other candidates will too. If this were the real thing you would need to **forget** the exam the minute you left the exam hall and **think about the next one**. Or, if it's the last one, **celebrate**!

SECTION A

1	B			$'000
		Return	(3,000 + 150 + 250)	3,400%
		Capital employed	(12,550 + 1,400 + 1,200 + 750)	15,900
				= 21.4%

2	D	Net profit margin × net asset turnover	

3	C		Shares '000
		80million × 2 / 1.84 × 3/12	21,739
		100million × 9/12	75,000
			96,739
		EPS = 31,200 / 96,739 = $0.323	

4	D	Equity	(9.75 + 2.8)	12.55
		Debt	(3.125 + 1.5 − 1.725 + .45)	3.35
		Gearing:	(3.35 / (3.35 + 12.55)) × 100 =	21%

10% ignores the finance leases
35% adds the loan note repayment instead of deducting it
28% incorporates both of these errors

5   B   The only amount to be included is loan interest of $500,000 ($10 million × 10% × 6/12). The transaction is a financing arrangement, not a sale, so there is no profit to be credited.

6   A   (i) does represent withdrawal from a separate geographical area, so qualifies to be classified as a discontinued operation. (ii) does not represent withdrawal from either a geographical area or a major line of business (as it has other hotels in Country B) so would not be treated as a discontinued operation.

7   A   Global harmonisation of accounting standards does not affect currencies, so exchange differences would still arise. The other options have all been identified as possible advantages.

8   C   This does not qualify as a discontinued operation, so A and B are incorrect, but a restructuring provision should be made. It is not a discontinued operation because it does not represent withdrawal from either a major line of business or a geographical area of operations.

9   C   Provisions cannot be made for future operating losses. The other options would all give rise to valid provisions.

10	C		$'000
		Depreciation to 1.10.20X2 (($2m / 20) × 6/12)	(50)
		Revaluation gain ($2.34m − $2.3m)	40
		Charge to profit or loss	(10)

Note that the surplus from $2m to $2.3m will go to other comprehensive income, not profit or loss.

11   D   Fair value less costs to sell

12   A   Relevance and faithful representation

13   B   Current cost. Historical cost is the original amount of the asset or liability. Realisable value is the amount that would be received to transfer the asset or the amount that would have to be paid to settle the liability. Present value is the discounted amount of the future cash flows that can be obtained from continuing to use an asset.

14	C		$
		Balance 1 January 20X1	50,000
		Depreciation (45,000 × 2/5)	(18,000)
		Balance 1 January 20X3	32,000
		Upgrade	15,000
			47,000
		Depreciation (42,000 / 5)	(8,400)
		Balance 1 January 20X4	38,600
		Proceeds	(7,000)
		Loss on disposal	31,600

15   C   This calls into question the inventory valuation at the year end. The other options describe events that have arisen after the year end and do not call into question conditions at the year end.

Section B

16   B   Current ratio = current assets/current liabilities = 133/103 = 1.29

17   C   Make a rights issue of ordinary shares

This would increase both cash and share capital, increasing current assets without incurring any additional liabilities.

Offering a settlement discount to customers would make cash received lower than receivables which would decrease the current ratio.

Making a bonus issue of shares would generate no cash at all and would not affect the current ratio.

Selling current asset investments would simply replace one current asset with another, at the same amount.

18   A   Acid test ratio = (current assets – inventories)/current liabilities = (133 – 96)/103 = 0.36

19   D   Proposal 1 – decrease ratio / Proposal 2 – increase ratio

Proposal 1 will cause the acid test ratio to fall because, although receivables will convert into cash more quickly, the amount of cash received will be less than the amount of the receivables. Current assets will fall without any change in current liabilities, so the acid test ratio will fall.

Proposal 2 will cause the acid test ratio to rise, by delaying the reduction in cash that would occur by paying suppliers. Since the acid test ratio is less than 1, anything that prevents an equal fall in current assets and current liabilities will boost the ratio.

20   C   Non-current asset turnover

A manufacturing company will have high non-current assets (factory, plant and machinery), so this ratio will measure how efficiently it is using its non-current assets to generate revenue.

The P/E ratio is a measure of market confidence in the future of the entity. Gearing relates to long-term solvency and the current ratio relates to liquidity.

21   D   An asset that takes a substantial period of time to get ready for use or sale

22   C   IAS 23 has no requirements in respect of the stage of completion of the asset.

23   A $625,000   (($10m 7.5%) × 10/12)

24   D

	%
10% × 50/80	6.25
8% × 30/80	3.0
	9.25

25   C   The investment proceeds were earned before construction began, so are not deducted from the borrowing costs which are being capitalised.

26   A

		$m
Land		85
Building	180 × 19/20	171
		256

27   D $35m

		$m
Existing plant	150 × 20%	30
New plant	50 × 10%	5
		35

28	B	There is no requirement to disclose the professional qualifications of the valuer.
29	C	

	$m
Balance 1.10.X8	270
Depreciation to 30.9.X9	(30)
	240
Impairment loss (β)	(140)
Recoverable amount	100

30   A   Higher of fair value less costs of disposal and value in use

Section C answers

31

Marking scheme

			Marks
(a)	Statement of profit or loss and OCI		
	Revenue	1	
	Cost of sales	2	
	Distribution costs	½	
	Administrative expenses	½	
	Finance costs	½	
	Income tax	2½	
	Other comprehensive income	1	
			8
(b)	Statement of financial position		
	Property, plant and equipment	3½	
	Inventory	½	
	Trade receivables	½	
	Retained earnings	2½	
	Deferred tax	1½	
	Trade payables	½	
	Current tax	½	
	Bank overdraft	½	
			10
(c)	Earnings per share		2
			20

(a) STATEMENT OF PROFIT OR LOSS AND OTHER COMPREHENSIVE INCOME FOR THE YEAR ENDED 31 MARCH 20X3

	$'000
Revenue	550,000
Cost of sales (W1)	(428,000)
Gross profit	122,000
Distribution costs	(21,500)
Administrative expenses	(30,900)
Finance costs	(700)
Profit before tax	68,900
Income tax expense ((27,200 – 1,200) + (9,400 – 6,200))	(29,200)
Profit for the year	39,700
Other comprehensive income:	
Gain on revaluation of property (W3)	7,000
Total comprehensive income for the year	46,700

(b)   STATEMENT OF FINANCIAL POSITION AS AT 31 MARCH 20X3

	$'000	$'000
ASSETS		
Non-current assets		
Property, plant and equipment (W2)		100,500
Current assets		
Inventory	43,700	
Trade receivables	42,200	
		85,900
Total assets		186,400
EQUITY AND LIABILITIES		
Equity		
Share capital		50,000
Share premium		20,000
Revaluation surplus		7,000
Retained earnings (11,200 + 39,700 – dividend 20,000)		30,900
		107,900
Non-current liabilities		
Deferred tax		9,400
Current liabilities		
Trade payables	35,100	
Tax payable	27,200	
Overdraft	6,800	
		69,100
		186,400

Workings

1   *Expenses*

	Cost of sales	Distribution costs	Administrative expenses
	$'000	$'000	$'000
Per TB	411,500	21,500	30,900
Depreciation (W2)	16,500	–	–
	428,000	21,500	30,900

2   *Property, plant and equipment*

	Land	Buildings	Plant	Total
	$'000	$'000	$'000	$'000
Cost	10,000	50,000	94,500	
Accumulated depreciation	–	(20,000)	(24,500)	
Balance 1 April 20X3	10,000	30,000	70,000	110,000
Revaluation surplus	2,000	5,000		7,000
Revalued amount	12,000	35,000		
Depreciation (35/14) (70 × 20%)	–	(2,500)	(14,000)	(16,500)
	12,000	32,500	56,000	100,500

(c)   EPS = 39,700/100,000 = $0.4

32

Text references. Chapter 9.

Top tips. There are two important issues in this question – Strata showed a pre-acquisition loss and had a negative fair value adjustment. The question was otherwise straightforward.

Easy marks. Five marks are allocated for the goodwill calculation and plenty of marks are available for standard consolidation issues.

Examination Team's comments. The question included a fair value adjustment for plant which was below its carrying amount – which many candidates treated as a surplus. Most candidates correctly calculated and accounted for the value of the share exchange and the NCI but there were some errors in calculating the number of loan notes issued. Some candidates incorrectly calculated post-acquisition profit as $6 million.

Marking scheme

		Marks
(a)	Statement of financial position	
	Property, plant and equipment	1½
	Goodwill	5
	Equity investments	1
	Inventory	1
	Trade receivables	1½
	Bank	1
	Equity shares	1½
	Share premium	½
	Retained earnings	3
	Non-controlling interest	1½
	10% loan notes	1
	Trade payables	1
	Bank overdraft	½
		20

(a)   CONSOLIDATED STATEMENT OF FINANCIAL POSITION AS AT 31 MARCH 20X3

	$'000	$'000
ASSETS		
Non-current assets		
Property, plant and equipment (47,400 + 25,500 – 2,500 (W6))		70,400
Goodwill (W1)		8,500
Financial asset: equity investments (7,100 + 3,900)		11,000
		89,900
Current assets		
Inventory (17,400 + 8,400 – 600 (W2))	25,200	
Receivables (14,800 + 9,000 – 900 (W3) – 2,800 interco)	20,100	
Cash (5,100 + 900 (W3))	6,000	
		51,300
Total assets		141,200
EQUITY AND LIABILITIES		
Equity attributable to owners of Paradigm		
Share capital (40,000 + 6,000 (W1))		46,000
Share premium (W1)		6,000
Retained earnings (W4)		34,000
		86,000
Non-controlling interest (W5)		8,800
		94,800
Non-current liabilities		
10% loan notes (8,000 + 1,500 (W1))		9,500
Current liabilities		
Trade payables (17,600 + 13,000 – 2,800 intercompany)	27,800	
Overdraft	9,100	
		36,900
Total equity and liabilities		141,200

Workings

1   *Goodwill*

	$'000	$'000
Consideration transferred:		
Shares (20m × 2/5 × 75% × $2)		12,000
Loan notes (15m × 100 / 1,000)		1,500
		13,500
Non-controlling interest (5m × $1.2)		6,000
		19,500
Net assets at acquisition;		
Share capital	20,000	
Retained earnings ((4,000) + (2,000))	(6,000)	
Fair value adjustment (W5)	(3,000)	
		(11,000)
Goodwill		8,500

2   *PURP*

Intercompany sales in inventory $4.6m
PURP = $4.6m x 15 / 115 = $600,000

3   *Intercompany cash in transit*

	$'000	$'000
Dr Cash	900	
Cr Receivables		900

4   *Retained earnings*

	Paradigm $'000	*Strata* $'000
Per draft	26,600	4,000
Add back pre-acquisition loss		6,000
		10,000
PURP (W2)	(600)	
Gain (loss) on equity investments*	(400)	700
Movement on fair value adjustment (W6)		500
		11,200
Group share of Strata – 75% × 11,200	8,400	
Group retained earnings	34,000	

*Loss on equity investments in Paradigm: (7,500 – 7,100)

5   *Non-controlling interest*

	$'000
Fair value at acquisition (W1)	6,000
Share of post –acquisition retained earnings (11,200 (W4) × 25%)	2,800
	8,800

6   *Movement on fair value adjustment*

	At acquisition $'000	*Movement* $'000	*At year end* $'000
FVA on plant (W1)	(3,000)	500	(2,500)

ACCA

Fundamentals Level

Paper F7

Financial Reporting

Mock Examination 2

Time allowed: 3 hours 15 minutes

This question paper is divided into three sections:

Section A – ALL 15 questions are compulsory and MUST be attempted

Section B – ALL 15 questions are compulsory and MUST be attempted

Section C – BOTH questions are compulsory and MUST be attempted

Do NOT open this question paper until instructed by the supervisor.

Do NOT record any of your answers on the question paper.

This question paper must not be removed from the examination hall.

Section A – ALL 15 questions are compulsory and MUST be attempted

1   Which TWO of the following are possible effects of rising prices upon financial statements?

☐   Understatement of capital employed
☐   Overstatement of capital employed
☐   Overstatement of profits
☐   Understatement of profits

(2 marks)

---

2   On 1 September 20X3 Laidlaw factored (sold) $2 million of trade receivables to Finease for an immediate payment of $1.8 million and further amounts depending on how quickly Finease collects the receivables. Finease will charge a monthly administration fee and interest on the outstanding balance and any receivables not collected after four months would be sold back to Laidlaw.

How should Laidlaw account for this factoring arrangement in its financial statements for the year ended 30 September 20X3?

☐   Derecognise the receivables and recognise a loss on disposal of $200,000
☐   Continue to recognise the receivables and treat the $1.8 million received as a loan
☐   Continue to recognise the receivables and treat the $1.8 million as deferred income
☐   Derecognise the receivables and make a provision for the loss of $200,000   **(2 marks)**

---

3   Which pair of ratios would provide the most useful information to a bank providing a long-term loan to a business?

☐   Asset turnover and ratio of expenses to sales
☐   Gearing and interest cover
☐   ROCE and gross profit margin
☐   Return on equity and EPS   **(2 marks)**

---

4   Penfold holds several properties under operating leases. If these were treated as finance leases how would that affect these ratios?

	ROCE	Gearing
☐	Decrease	Decrease
☐	Decrease	Increase
☐	Increase	Decrease
☐	Increase	Increase

(2 marks)

5   Raycroft operates a nuclear power station. The power station is due to be decommissioned on 31 December 20X8 but will be fully operational up to that date. It has been estimated that the cost of decommissioning the power station and cleaning up any environmental damage, as required by legislation, will be $60 million. Raycroft recognised a provision for the present value of this expenditure at 31 December 20X0. A suitable discount rate for evaluating costs of this nature is 12%, equivalent to a present value factor after eight years of 0.404. The decommissioning cost will be depreciated over eight years.

What is the total charge to profit or loss in respect of this provision for the year ended 31 December 20X1?

☐ $2,880,800
☐ $3,030,000
☐ $5,938,800
☐ $7,500,000   **(2 marks)**

---

6   On 1 December 20X4 Scaffold acquired 80% of the 3,000,000 issued ordinary shares of Plank. The consideration for each share acquired comprised a cash payment of $1.20 and two ordinary shares in Scaffold. The market value of a $1 ordinary share in Scaffold on 1 December 20X4 was $1.50, rising to $1.60 by the entity's year end on 31 December 20X4. Professional fees paid to Scaffold's external accountants and legal advisors in respect of the acquisition were $400,000.

At what amount would the investment in Plank be recorded in the entity financial statements of Scaffold for the year ended 31 December 20X4?

$ ☐   **(2 marks)**

---

7   Where the purchase price of an acquisition is less than the aggregate amount of the non-controlling interest plus fair value of net assets acquired, IFRS 3 requires that the value of the assets acquired and liabilities assumed be reassessed. If no change is made as a result of this reassessment, how should the difference be treated?

☐   Deduct from goodwill in the consolidated statement of financial position
☐   Recognise immediately as a gain in other comprehensive income
☐   Recognise in profit or loss over its useful life
☐   Recognise immediately as a gain in profit or loss   **(2 marks)**

---

8   Ravenscroft is closing one of its production facilities and satisfies the requirements for a restructuring provision. The facility has 250 employees. 50 will be retrained and deployed to other subsidiaries; the remainder will accept redundancy and be paid an average of $5,000 each. Plant has a carrying amount of $2.2 million but is only expected to sell for $500,000, incurring $50,000 of selling costs. The facility itself is expected to sell for a profit of $1.2 million.

What amount should be provided for restructuring?

$ ☐   **(2 marks)**

9   Which TWO of the following items would qualify for treatment as a change in accounting estimate according to IAS 8 *Accounting policies, changes in accounting estimates and errors*?

☐   Provision for obsolescence of inventory
☐   Correction necessitated by a material error
☐   A change of inventory valuation from FIFO to weighted average
☐   A change in the useful life of a non-current asset

(2 marks)

10   Pisces has an asset carried at $6.5 million in its statement of financial position at 31 December 20X2. The present value of the cash flows which the asset will generate for the rest of its useful life is $5.8 million. The current cost of an identical asset of the same age is $6.1 million. Pisces has received an offer of $6.2 million for the asset. The cost of dismantling the asset and transporting it to the customer would be $200,000.

At what amount should the asset be recognised in the statement of financial position at 31 December 20X2?

$ [   ]

(2 marks)

11   The components of the cost of a major item of equipment are given below:

	$
Purchase price	780,000
Import duties	117,000
VAT (refundable)	78,000
Site preparation	30,000
Installation	28,000
Testing	10,000
Initial losses before asset reaches planned performance	50,000
Discounted cost of dismantling and removal at end of useful life	40,000
	1,133,000

What amount should be recognised as the cost of the asset in accordance with IAS 16 *Property, plant and equipment*?

$ [   ]

(2 marks)

12   Which one of the following would be included in the cost of inventories of goods for resale in accordance with IAS 2 *Inventories*?

☐   Storage costs
☐   Administrative overheads
☐   Import duties
☐   Selling costs

(2 marks)

13 The following information relates to the position at 31 March 20X9 of a contract where performance obligations are satisfied over time.

	$
Contract price	900,000
At 31 March:	
Costs to date	720,000
Estimated costs to complete	480,000
Progress payments invoiced	400,000
Percentage complete	60%

What amount should appear as 'contract asset/liability' in respect of this contract in the statement of financial position as at 31 March 20X9?

☐ $220,000 contract liability

☐ $20,000 contract asset

☐ $180,000 contract liability

☐ $100,000 contract asset **(2 marks)**

---

14 On 1 January 20X3 Wincarnis purchased 30,000 $1 shares in a listed entity for $5 per share. Transaction costs were $2,000 and Wincarnis elected to recognise the shares at fair value through other comprehensive income. At the year end of 31 December 20X3 the shares were trading at $6.50.

At what amount will the shares be recognised in the statement of financial position of Wincarnis at 31 December 20X3?

$ ☐ **(2 marks)**

---

15 A company's statement of profit or loss showed a profit before tax of $1.8 million. After the end of the reporting period and before the financial statements were authorised for issue, the following events took place.

(i) The value of an investment held at the year end fell by $85,000.

(ii) A customer who owed $116,000 at the year end went bankrupt owing a total of $138,000.

(iii) Inventory valued at $161,000 in the statement of financial position was sold in year-end condition for $141,000.

(iv) Assets with a carrying amount at the year end of $240,000 were unexpectedly expropriated by the government.

What is the company's profit before tax after making the necessary adjustments for these events?

$ ☐ **(2 marks)**

Section B

The following scenario relates to questions 16-20

On 1 April 20X3, Polestar acquired 75% of the 12 million 50 cent equity shares of Southstar. Southstar had been experiencing difficult trading conditions and making significant losses. Its retained earnings at the acquisition date were $14.3 million. In allowing for Southstar's difficulties, Polestar made an immediate cash payment of only £1.50 per share. In addition, Polestar will pay a further amount in cash on 30 September 20X4 if Southstar returns to profitability by that date. The value of this contingent consideration at the date of acquisition was estimated to be $1.8 million, but at 30 September 20X3 in the light of continuing losses, its value was estimated at only $1.5 million. The contingent consideration has not been recorded by Polestar. Overall, the directors of Polestar expect the acquisition to be a bargain purchase leading to negative goodwill.

At the date of acquisition shares in Southstar had a listed market price of $1.20 each.

The statements of profit or loss of both companies are as follows.

STATEMENTS OF PROFIT OR LOSS FOR THE YEAR ENDED 30 SEPTEMBER 20X3

	Polestar	Southstar
	$'000	$'000
Revenue	110,000	66,000
Cost of sales	(88,000)	(67,200)
Gross profit (loss)	22,000	(1,200)
Distribution costs	(3,000)	(2,000)
Administrative expenses	(5,250)	(2,400)
Finance costs	(250)	–
Profit (loss) before tax	13,500	(5,600)
Income tax (expense)/relief	(3,500)	1,000
Profit (loss) for the year	10,000	(4,600)

The following information is relevant:

(i)   At the date of acquisition, the fair values of Southstar's assets were equal to their carrying amounts with the exception of a leased property. This had a fair value of $2 million above its carrying amount and a remaining lease term of ten years at that date. All depreciation is included in cost of sales.

(ii)   Polestar transferred raw materials at their cost of $4 million to Southstar in June 20X3. Southstar processed all of these materials incurring additional direct costs of $1.4 million and sold them back to Polestar in August 20X3 for $9 million. At 30 September 20X3 Polestar had $1.5 million of these goods still in inventory. There were no other intragroup sales.

(iii)   Polestar's policy is to value the non-controlling interest at fair value at the date of acquisition. For this purpose, Southstar's share price at that date can be deemed to be representative of the fair value of the shares held by the non-controlling interest.

(iv)   All items in the above statements of profit or loss are deemed to accrue evenly over the year unless otherwise indicated.

16 What was the fair value of Southstar's net assets at the acquisition date?

☐ $20 million

☐ $17.7 million

☐ $24.6 million

☐ $22.3 million

17 What is consolidated revenue for the year ended 30 September 20X3?

☐ $130 million

☐ $143 million

☐ $163 million

☐ $156 million

18 The estimated value of the contingent consideration has fallen from $1.8m to $1.5m. How should this be accounted for?

☐ DR Liability / CR Profit or loss

☐ DR Profit or loss / CR Liability

☐ DR Goodwill / CR Profit or loss

☐ DR Profit or loss / CR Goodwill

19 What is the amount of the adjustment to profit attributable to the non-controlling interest in respect of unrealised profit?

$ ☐

20 Polestar measures the non-controlling interest in Southstar at fair value. Which one of the following applies when non-controlling interest is measured at fair value?

☐ The non-controlling interest will be allocated their share of any negative goodwill

☐ The non-controlling interest will be allocated the whole of the pre-acquisition profits

☐ The non-controlling interest will be allocated their share of any goodwill impairment

☐ If the subsidiary's share price falls, the non-controlling interest will be adjusted

The following scenario relates to questions 21-25

Elite Leisure is a private limited liability company that operates a single cruise ship. The ship was acquired on 1 October 20W6 (ten years before 20X6). Details of the cost of the ship's components and their estimated useful lives are:

Component	Original cost ($ million)	Depreciation basis
Ship's fabric (hull, decks etc)	300	25 years straight–line
Cabins and entertainment area fittings	150	12 years straight–line
Propulsion system	100	Useful life of 40,000 hours

At 30 September 20X4 no further capital expenditure had been incurred on the ship.

In the year ended 30 September 20X4 the ship had experienced a high level of engine trouble which had cost the company considerable lost revenue and compensation costs. The measured expired life of the propulsion system at 30 September 20X4 was 30,000 hours. Due to the unreliability of the engines, a decision was taken in early October 20X4 to replace the whole of the propulsion system at a cost of $140 million. The expected life of the new propulsion system was 50,000 hours and in the year ended 30 September 20X5 the ship had used its engines for 5,000 hours.

At the same time as the propulsion system replacement, the company took the opportunity to do a limited upgrade to the cabin and entertainment facilities at a cost of $60 million and repaint the ship's fabric at a cost of $20 million. After the upgrade of the cabin and entertainment area fittings it was estimated that their remaining life was five years (from the date of the upgrade). For the purpose of calculating depreciation, all the work on the ship can be assumed to have been completed on 1 October 20X4. All residual values can be taken as nil.

21   At 30 September 20X4 the ship is 8 years old. What is the carrying amount of the ship at that date?

☐ $279m

☐ $275m

☐ $229m

☐ $254m

22   What is the amount of depreciation that should be charged in respect of the propulsion system for the year ended 30 September 20X5?

☐ $14m

☐ $39m

☐ $17.5m

☐ $16.5m

23   Apart from depreciation, what is the total charge to profit or loss for the year ended 30 September 20X5?

$ [   ]

24   Elite Leisure's ship has to have a safety check carried out every five years at a cost of $50,000 in order to be licensed to operate. How should this be accounted for?

☐   Set up a provision for the discounted present value and unwind over five years

☐   Accrue the cost of the check over five years until it takes place

☐   Charge $50,000 to profit or loss when incurred

☐   Capitalise the cost when incurred and amortise over five years

25   Elite Leisure is being sued for $250,000 by a passenger who slipped on one of the gangways and twisted an ankle. The company's lawyer estimates that there is a 55% chance that it will lose the case. Legal costs for Elite Leisure will be $40,000. What amount should Elite Leisure provide in respect of this case?

- [ ] $137,500
- [ ] $290,000
- [ ] $177,000
- [ ] $159,500

The following scenario relates to questions 26-30

Pinto is a publicly listed company. The following financial statements of Pinto are available:

STATEMENT OF PROFIT OR LOSS AND OTHER COMPREHENSIVE INCOME FOR YEAR ENDED 31 MARCH 20X8 (extract)

	$'000
Profit before tax	440
Income tax expense	(160)
Profit for the year	280
Other comprehensive income	
Gains on property revaluation	100
Total comprehensive income	380

STATEMENTS OF FINANCIAL POSITION AS AT

	31 March 20X8		31 March 20X7	
	$'000	$'000	$'000	$'000
Non-current assets (note (i))				
Property, plant and equipment		2,880		1,860
Investment property		420		400
		3,300		2,260
Current assets				
Inventory	1,210		810	
Trade receivables	480		540	
Income tax asset	nil		50	
Bank	10	1,700	nil	1,400
Total assets		5,000		3,660
Equity and liabilities				
Equity shares of 20 cents each (note (iii))		1,000		600
Share premium	600		nil	
Revaluation reserve	150		50	
Retained earnings	1,440	2,190	1,310	1,360
		3,190		1,960
Non-current liabilities				
6% loan notes (note (ii))	nil		400	
Deferred tax	50	50	30	430

Current liabilities

Trade payables	1,410		1,050	
Bank overdraft	nil		120	
Warranty provision (note (iv))	200		100	
Current tax payable	150	1,760	nil	1,270
Total equity and liabilities		5,000		3,660

The following supporting information is available:

(i)   An item of plant with a carrying amount of $240,000 was sold at a loss of $90,000 during the year. Depreciation of $280,000 was charged (to cost of sales) for property, plant and equipment in the year ended 31 March 20X8.

   Pinto uses the fair value model in IAS 40 *Investment property*. There were no purchases or sales of investment property during the year.

(ii)   A dividend of 3 cents per share was paid on 1 January 20X8.

(iii) $60,000 was included in Pinto's profit before tax for the year ended 31 March 20X8 in respect of income and gains on investment property.

You are preparing a statement of cash flows for Pinto for the year to 31 March 20X8.

26   What is the amount of tax that Pinto either received or paid during the year?

☐ $60,000 paid

☐ $60,000 received

☐ $10,000 paid

☐ $10,000 received

27   Pinto has spent $1,440,000 on purchase of plant. What is the net cash used in investing activities?

   $ ☐

28   What was the amount of the dividend paid on 1 January 20X8?

☐ $150,000

☐ $300,000

☐ $240,000

☐ $120,000

29   Under which classification(s) can dividends paid be shown in the statement of cash flows?

☐   Investing activities

☐   Financing activities

☐   Operating activities and investing activities

☐   Operating activities and financing activities

30   Which one of the following items will **not** be adjusted against Pinto's profit before tax in arriving at net cash from operating activities?

☐   The early redemption penalty

☐   The proceeds from sale of plant

☐   The increase in the warranty provision

☐   The investment income

BPP
LEARNING MEDIA

Section C questions

31

Shown below are the recently issued (summarised) financial statements of Harbin, a listed company, for the year ended 30 September 20X7, together with comparatives for 20X6 and extracts from the Chief Executive's report that accompanied their issue.

STATEMENT OF PROFIT OR LOSS

	20X7	20X6
	$'000	$'000
Revenue	250,000	180,000
Cost of sales	(200,000)	(150,000)
Gross profit	50,000	30,000
Operating expenses	(26,000)	(22,000)
Finance costs	(8,000)	(nil)
Profit before tax	16,000	8,000
Income tax expense (at 25%)	(4,000)	(2,000)
Profit for the year	12,000	6,000

STATEMENT OF FINANCIAL POSITION

	20X7	20X6
	$'000	$'000
Non-current assets		
Property, plant and equipment	210,000	90,000
Goodwill	10,000	nil
	220,000	90,000
Current assets		
Inventory	25,000	15,000
Trade receivables	13,000	8,000
Bank	nil	14,000
	38,000	37,000
Total assets	258,000	127,000
Equity and liabilities		
Equity shares of $1 each	100,000	100,000
Retained earnings	14,000	12,000
	114,000	112,000
Non-current liabilities		
8% loan notes	100,000	nil
Current liabilities		
Bank overdraft	17,000	nil
Trade payables	23,000	13,000
Current tax payable	4,000	2,000
	44,000	15,000
Total equity and liabilities	258,000	127,000

Extracts from the Chief Executive's report:

'Highlights of Harbin's performance for the year ended 30 September 20X7:

An increase in sales revenue of 39%

Gross profit margin up from 16.7% to 20%

A doubling of the profit for the period

In response to the improved position the Board paid a dividend of 10 cents per share in September 20X7 an increase of 25% on the previous year.'

You have also been provided with the following further information.

On 1 October 20X6 Harbin purchased the whole of the net assets of Fatima (previously a privately owned entity) for $100 million, financed by the issue of $100,000 8% loan notes. The contribution of the purchase to Harbin's results for the year ended 30 September 20X7 was:

	$'000
Revenue	70,000
Cost of sales	(40,000)
Gross profit	30,000
Operating expenses	(8,000)
Profit before tax	22,000

There were no disposals of non-current assets during the year.

The following ratios have been calculated for Harbin for the year ended 30 September.

	20X6
Return on year-end capital employed	7.1%
(profit before interest and tax over total assets less current liabilities)	
Net asset (equal to capital employed) turnover	1.6
Net profit (before tax) margin	4.4%
Current ratio	2.5
Closing inventory holding period (in days)	37
Trade receivables' collection period (in days)	16
Trade payables' payment period (based on cost of sales) (in days)	32
Gearing (debt over debt plus equity)	nil

Required

(a)   Calculate equivalent ratios for Harbin for 20X7   **(5 marks)**

(b)   Assess the financial performance and position of Harbin for the year ended 30 September 20X7 compared to the previous year. Your answer should refer to the information in the Chief Executive's report and the impact of the purchase of the net assets of Fatima.   **(15 marks)**

(Total = 20 marks)

32

The following trial balance relates to Moby as at 30 September 20X3.

	$'000	$'000
Revenue		227,800
Cost of sales	164,500	
Long-term contract (note (i))	4,000	
Distribution costs	13,500	
Administrative expenses	16,500	
Bank interest	900	
Dividend	2,000	
Lease rental paid on 30 September 20X3 (note (ii))	9,200	
Land ($12 million) and building ($48 million) at cost (note (ii))	60,000	
Owned plant and equipment at cost (note (ii))	65,700	
Leased plant at initial carrying amount (note (ii))	35,000	
Accumulated depreciation at 1 October 20X2:		
Building		10,000
Owned plant and equipment		17,700
Leased plant		7,000
Inventory at 30 September 20X3	26,600	
Trade receivables	38,500	
Bank		5,300
Insurance provision (note (iii))		150
Deferred tax (note (iv))		8,000

	$'000	$'000
Finance lease obligation at 1 October 20X2 (note (ii))		29,300
Trade payables		21,300
Current tax (note (iv))		1,050
Equity shares of 20 cents each		45,800
Share premium		3,200
Loan note (note (v))		40,000
Retained earnings at 1 October 20X2	–	19,800
	436,400	436,400

The following notes are relevant.

(i)   The balance on the long-term contract is made up of the following items.

Cost incurred to date $14 million
Value of invoices issued (work certified) $10 million

The contract commenced on 1 October 20X2 and is for a fixed price of $25 million. Performance obligations are satisfied over time. The costs to complete the contract at 30 September 20X3 are estimated at $6 million. Moby's policy is to recognise satisfaction of performance obligations (and therefore accrue profits) on such contracts based on a stage of completion given by the work certified as a percentage of the contract price.

(ii) Non-current assets:

Moby decided to revalue its land and buildings for the first time on 1 October 20X2. A qualified valuer determined the relevant revalued amounts to be $16 million for the land and $38.4 million for the building. The building's remaining life at the date of the revaluation was 16 years. This revaluation has not yet been reflected in the trial balance figures. Moby does not make a transfer from the revaluation surplus to retained earnings in respect of the realisation of the revaluation surplus. Deferred tax is applicable to the revaluation surplus at 25%.

The leased plant was acquired on 1 October 20X1 under a five-year finance lease which has an implicit interest rate of 10% per annum. The rentals are $9.2 million per annum payable on 30 September each year.

Owned plant and equipment is depreciated at 12.5% per annum using the reducing balance method.

No depreciation has yet been charged on any non-current asset for the year ended 30 September 20X3. All depreciation is charged to cost of sales.

(iii) On 1 October 20X2 Moby received renewal quote of $400,000 from the company's property insurer. The directors were surprised at how much it had increased and believed it would be less expensive for the company to 'self-insure'. Accordingly, they charged $400,000 to administrative expenses and credited the same amount to the insurance provision. During the year, the company incurred $250,000 of expenses relating to previously insured property damage which it has debited to the provision.

(iv) A provision for income tax for the year ended 30 September 20X3 of $3.4 million is required. The balance on current tax represents the under/over provision of the tax liability for the year ended 30 September 20X2. At 30 September 20X3 the tax base of Moby's net assets was $24 million less than their carrying amounts. This does not include the effect of the revaluation in Note 2 above. The income tax rate of Moby is 25%.

(v)   The $40 million loan note was issued at par on 1 October 20X2. No interest will be paid on the loan; however it will be redeemed on 30 September 20X5 for $53,240,000, which gives an effective finance cost of 10% per annum.

(vi) A share issue was made on 31 December 20X2 of 4 million shares for $1 per share. It was correctly accounted for.

Required

(a)   Prepare the statement of profit or loss and other comprehensive income for Moby for the year ended 30 September 20X3.   **(13 marks)**

(b)   Prepare the statement of changes in equity for Moby for the year ended 30 September 20X3.

(7 marks)

(Total = 20 marks)

Answers

DO NOT TURN THIS PAGE UNTIL YOU HAVE
COMPLETED THE MOCK EXAM

A plan of attack

Managing your nerves

As you turn the pages to start this mock exam a number of thoughts are likely to cross your mind. At best, examinations cause anxiety so it is important to stay focused on your task for the exam period! Developing an awareness of what is going on emotionally within you may help you manage your nerves. Remember, you are unlikely to banish the flow of adrenaline, but the key is to harness it to help you work steadily and quickly through your answers.

Working through this mock exam will help you develop the exam stamina you will need to keep going for three hours.

Managing your time

Planning and time management are two of the key skills which complement the technical knowledge you need to succeed. To keep yourself on time, do not be afraid to jot down your target completion times for each question, perhaps next to the title of the question on the paper. As all the questions are **compulsory**, you do not have to spend time wondering which question to answer!

Doing the exam

Actually doing the exam is a personal experience. There is not a single **right way**. As long as you submit complete answers to all questions after the three hours are up, then your approach obviously works.

Looking through the paper

Section A has 15 OTQs. This is the section of the paper where the examination team can test knowledge across the breadth of the syllabus. Make sure you read these questions carefully. The distractors are designed to present plausible, but incorrect, answers. Don't let them mislead you. If you really have no idea – guess. You may even be right.

Section B has 15 OTQs in total – questions 16-30. These are arranged as three scenarios with five questions each.
Scenario 1 is on consolidated financial statements.
Scenario 2 is on property, plant and equipment.
Scenario 3 is on the statement of cash flows.

Section C has two 20-mark questions.
Question 31 is on interpretation of financial statements
Question 32 is on preparation of single company financial statements

Allocating your time

BPP's advice is to always allocate your time **according to the marks for the question**. However, **use common sense**. If you're doing a question but haven't a clue how to do part (b), you might be better off re-allocating your time and getting more marks on another question, where you can add something you didn't have time for earlier on. Make sure you leave time to recheck the OTQs and make sure you have answered them all.

SECTION A

1   The correct answers are:
Understatement of capital employed
Overstatement of profits

When prices are rising, the historical cost of inventory will be less than the cost of replacing it, giving rise to an understatement of operating costs and overstatement of profits. Where non-current assets are held at cost, they may have fallen significantly below replacement cost, leading to an understatement of the value of capital employed.

2   The correct answer is:
Continue to recognise the receivables and treat the $1.8 million as deferred income
The receivables have been factored 'with recourse', so Laidlaw still bears the risks and rewards.

3   The correct answer is:
Gearing and interest cover

These will give the bank the most information regarding whether this client will be able to make repayments on a loan.

4   The correct answer is:

ROCE decrease / Gearing increase
Capital employed (assets) would increase, causing ROCE to decrease and debt (amounts due under finance leases) would increase, thereby increasing gearing.

5        $5,938,800

	$
Unwinding of discount (24,240,000* × 12%)	2,908,800
Depreciation (24,240,000/8)	3,030,000
	5,938,800

* 60 million × 0.404 = 24,240,000

6        $10,080,000

	$'000
Cash (80% × 3 million × $1.20)	2,880
Shares (80% × 3 million × 2 × $1.50)	7,200
	10,080

7   The correct answer is:
Recognise immediately as a gain in profit or loss
This is treated as negative goodwill arising from a bargain purchase and recognised as a gain in profit or loss.

8        $2,750,000

	$'000
Redundancy (200 × 5)	1,000
Plant impairment (2,200 − (500 − 50))	1,750
	2,750

Retraining costs are not included in a restructuring provision. The profit on sale of the facility cannot be recognised until realised.

9   The correct answers are:
Provision for obsolescence of inventory
A change in the useful life of a non-current asset

The provision for inventory obsolescence and a change in useful life are both arrived at using estimates. Correction of a material error and a change in inventory valuation will both be accounted for retrospectively.

10    $6 million

Fair value less costs of disposal ($6.2m – $0.2m)	$6 million
Value in use	$5.8 million
Recoverable amount (higher)	$6 million

11
    $1,005,000

	$'000
Purchase price	780
Import duty	117
Site preparation	30
Installation	28
Testing	10
Dismantling	40
	1,005

12   The correct answer is:

Import duties

The other expenses are included in distribution or administrative costs.

13    $20,000 contract asset

	$'000
Costs to date	720
Less loss (900 – (720 + 480))	(300)
	420
Less billings	(400)
Due from customer	20

14    $197,000

	$'000
30,000 × $6.50	195,000
Transaction costs	2,000
	197,000

Note that because the shares are held at fair value through other comprehensive income the transaction costs are added to fair value in the statement of financial position.

15    $1,664,000

	$'000
Unadjusted profit	1,800
Irrecoverable debt	(116)
Loss on sale of inventory	(20)
	1,664

Section B

16 $22.3 million

	$'000
Share capital	6,000
Retained earnings at 30.9.X3	14,300
Fair value adjustment on property	2,000
	22,300

17 $130 million

(110m + (66m × 6/12) – 13m intragroup)

18   The correct answer is:

DR Liability / CR Profit or loss

This fall has taken place since acquisition, so goodwill is not adjusted.

19 $150,000

Unrealised profit = 9m – 5.4m = 3.6m

Still in inventory = 3.6m × 1.5/9 = 600,000 × 25% = 150,000

20   The correct answer is:

The non-controlling interest will be allocated their share of any goodwill impairment.

The other options are incorrect.

21 $279m

	Cost $m	Depn period	Depn to date	Carrying amount
Ships fabric	300	8/25	(96)	204
Cabins etc	150	8/12	(100)	50
Propulsion	100	30/40 hrs	(75)	25
				279

22 $14m   (140m × 5,000/50,000)

23 $45m   (Repainting 20 + Loss on disposal 25)

24   The correct answer is:

Capitalise the cost when incurred and amortise over five years

25 $290,000

(250 + 40)   At 55% losing the case is 'probable' so must be provided for.

26 $60,000 received

	$
B/f current (asset)	(50,000)
B'f deferred tax	30,000
Charge for the year	160,000
Received (balance)	60,000
C/f (current + deferred)	200,000

27 $1,250,000

	$'000
Proceeds from sale of plant (240 – 90)	150
Purchase of plant (W)	(1,440)
Investment property income (60 – 20)	40
	1,250

28    $150,000

(1,310 (retained earnings) + 280 − 1,440) or (1,000 × 5 × 0.03)

29   The correct answer is:
Operating activities and financing activities

Dividends paid can be presented under operating activities or financing activities.

30   The correct answer is:
The proceeds from sale of plant

It is the profit on disposal of the plant that will be adjusted against profit before tax, not the proceeds of disposal.

Section C answers

31

<table>
<tr><td>Text references. Chapters 19 and 20.</td></tr>
</table>

Text references. Chapters 19 and 20.

Top tips. You have been given most of the ratios in this question. You can probably see that additional ratios are relevant here, to illustrate the effect of the purchase of Fatima. The examination Team frequently points out that to compare two ratios and say something went up or down is not analysis. You must look behind the numbers and make some suggestion regarding why this has happened.

Easy marks. You were told that the purchase of Fatima was significant, so you must allow for this in looking at the ratios and compute additional ratios as needed. If you did this, the ratios gave you plenty to analyse.

Examination Team's comments. Unfortunately, the performance assessment in this question was quite poor. Some candidates did not even point out obvious issues arising from the purchase of Fatima.

Marking scheme

	Marks
Ratios	8
Consideration of Chief Executive's report	3
Impact of purchase	6
Remaining issues -½ mark per valid point	3
	20

(a) **Ratios for 20X7**

	20X7
Return on year-end capital employed	11.2%
(profit before interest and tax over total assets less current liabilities)	
Net asset (equal to capital employed) turnover	1.17
Net profit (before tax) margin	6.4%
Current ratio	0.86:1
Closing inventory holding period (in days)	46
Trade receivables' collection period (in days)	19
Trade payables' payment period (based on cost of sales) (in days)	42
Gearing (debt over debt plus equity)	46.7%

(b) It is clear that the acquisition of Fatima has had a very positive impact on Harbin's results for the year ended 30 September 20X7. For this reason it is instructive to look at the 20X7 ratios which have been affected by the acquisition and see what they would have been without the addition of Fatima's results. The additional ratios are at the end of this report.

Profitability

It is immediately apparent that without the purchase of Fatima the Chief Executive's report would have looked very different. The increase in sales revenue of 39% would have disappeared. The sales revenue of Harbin is static. The increase in gross profit margin from 16.7% to 20% would have been a fall to 11.1%. The profit for the period would not have doubled. It would have gone from an $8m profit before tax in 20X6 to a $2m profit before tax in 20X7, assuming that the loan note interest would not have arisen. This would have given an ROCE of 2.05% for 20X7 rather than the 11.2% when Fatima is included. If we break ROCE down into net profit% and asset turnover, we can see that Fatima's results have increased the net profit% by almost six times, while having an adverse effect on the asset turnover due to the $100m funding through

208   Mock exam 2: answers

loan notes. There is some distortion in the 20X7 figures arising from interest charges which are not deducted in calculating ROCE but have been deducted in arriving at net profit.

Liquidity

While it has greatly enhanced Harbin's profitability, the purchase of Fatima has done little for liquidity, an aspect not touched on in the extract from the Chief Executive's report. Harbin borrowed $100m to pay for Fatima, so the purchase was not funded from working capital. However, it has paid $8m loan note interest, increased its inventory holding by $10m, invested in additional property, plant and equipment and paid a $10m dividend. In this way it has, despite the increased profit, converted a positive cash balance of $14m to an overdraft of $17m. The ratios show this very clearly. Harbin's current ratio has declined from 2.5:1 to 0.86:1 and its quick ratio (not shown above) has declined from 1.47:1 to 0.30:1, casting some doubt upon whether it will be able to continue to meet its commitments as they fall due.

The increase in the inventory holding period is worrying, as it suggests that Harbin may have inventory which is slow-moving, and the increase in the payables period by ten days suggests problems paying suppliers. Harbin has a $4m tax bill outstanding. If this is not paid on time it will incur interest, which will further weaken the cash position.

Gearing

The cost of acquiring Fatima is directly reflected in the gearing ratio, which has gone from nil in 20X6 to 46.7% in 20X7, with the issue of the loan notes. This will reduce profits available for distribution to shareholders in the future and if Harbin's cash position does not improve it may be forced to seek further loans. In the light of this, the increase of 25% in the dividend is hard to justify.

Appendix – ratios adjusted for purchase of Fatima

	With Fatima 20X7	Without Fatima 20X7
Return on year-end capital employed	11.2%	
24,000* – 22,000/ 114,000 – (22,000 – 5.500**)		2.05%
(profit before interest and tax over total assets less current liabilities)		
Net asset (equal to capital employed) turnover	1.17	
250,000 – 70,000 / 114,000 – (22,000 – 5,500)		1.85
Net profit (before tax) margin	6.4%	
24,000 – 22,000 / 250,000 – 70,000		1.1%

* Without the acquisition of Fatima the finance costs of $8,000 would not be incurred.

** $5,500 = 25% tax

32

Marking scheme

			Marks
(a)	Statement of profit or loss and other comprehensive income		
	Revenue	2	
	Cost of sales	3½	
	Distribution costs	½	
	Administrative expenses	1	
	Finance costs	2	
	Income tax expense	2	
	Gain on revaluation	1	
	Deferred tax on gain	1	
			13
(b)	Statement of changes in equity		
	Opening balances	1	
	Share issue	2	
	Dividend	1	
	Total comprehensive income	2	
	Closing balances	1	
			7
			20

(a) STATEMENT OF PROFIT OR LOSS AND OTHER COMPREHENSIVE INCOME FOR THE YEAR ENDED 30 SEPTEMBER 20X3

	$'000
Revenue (227,800 + 10,000 (W3))	237,800
Cost of sales (W1)	(187,900)
Gross profit	49,900
Distribution costs	(13,500)
Administrative expenses (W1)	(16,350)
Finance costs (900 + 4,000 (W5) + 2,930 (W6))	(7,830)
Profit before tax	12,220
Income tax expense (W4)	(350)
Profit for the year	11,870
Other comprehensive income:	
Gain on revaluation of land and buildings (W2)	4,400
Deferred tax on gain (W4)	(1,100)
Total other comprehensive income	3,300
Total comprehensive income for the year	15,170

(b) STATEMENT OF CHANGES IN EQUITY FOR THE YEAR ENDED 30 SEPTEMBER 20X3

	Share capital $'000	Share premium $'000	Retained earnings $'000	Revaluation surplus $'000	Total $'000
Balance at 1 October 20X2	45,000	–	19,800	–	64,800
Share issue	800	3,200			4,000
Dividend paid			(2,000)		(2,000)
Total comprehensive income	–	–	11,870	3,300	15,170
Balance at 30 September 20X3	45,800	3,200	29,670	3,300	81,970

Workings

1   *Expenses*

	Cost of sales $'000	Distribution costs $'000	Administrative expenses $'000
Per question	164,500	13,500	16,500
Contract (W3)	8,000		
Depreciation (W2) – building	2,400		
– owned plant	6,000		
– leased plant	7,000		
Insurance provision reversal			(150)
	187,900	13,500	16,350

2   *Property, plant and equipment*

	Land $'000	Building $'000	Plant $'000	Leased plant $'000
Cost 1.10.X2	12,000	48,000	65,700	35,000
Depreciation b/f		(10,000)	(17,700)	(7,000)
	12,000	38,000	48,000	28,000
Revaluation	4,000	400		
	16,000	38,400	48,000	28,000
Depreciation:				
Building (38,400 / 16)		(2,400)		
Plant (48,000 × 12.5%)			(6,000)	
Leased (35,000 / 5)				(7,000)

3　*Contract with performance obligations satisfied over time*

This contract is currently expected to make a profit of $5m.

	$'000
Revenue (work certified (10 / 25 = 40%)	10,000
Cost of sales ((14 + 6) × 40%)	(8,000)
Profit to date	2,000

4　*Income tax*

	$'000
Deferred tax balance:	
On taxable temporary difference (24m × 25%)	6,000
On revaluation (4,400 × 25%)	1,100
Liability at 30 September 20X3	7,100
Balance b/f at 1 October 20X2	8,000
Reduce balance by	900
Income tax charge:	
Provision for year	3,400
Prior year over-provision	(1,050)
Reduction in deferred tax balance	(900)
Deferred tax on revaluation debited to revaluation surplus	(1,100)
Charge for year	350

5　*Loan note*

	$'000
Proceeds	40,000
Interest 10%	4,000
Balance	44,000

6　*Leased plant*

	$'000
Cost 1.10.X1	35,000
Interest 10%	3,500
Instalment paid	(9,200)
Balance 30.9.X2	29,300
Interest 10%	2,930

ACCA

Fundamentals Level

Paper F7

Financial Reporting

Mock Examination 3 (Specimen Exam)

Time allowed: 3 hours 15 minutes

This question paper is divided into three sections:

Section A – ALL 15 questions are compulsory and MUST be attempted

Section B – ALL 15 questions are compulsory and MUST be attempted

Section C – BOTH questions are compulsory and MUST be attempted

Do NOT open this question paper until instructed by the supervisor.

Do NOT record any of your answers on the question paper.

This question paper must not be removed from the examination hall.

CANDIDATE ANSWER BOOKLET

SAMPLE PAGE ONLY

USE THIS PAGE TO RECORD ANSWERS TO MULTIPLE CHOICE QUESTIONS

- If your question paper has less than 60 questions, fill in the relevant answers only.

- Each multiple choice question has only one correct answer. Fill in one bubble only (A, B, C, or D) to indicate your choice of answer.

- The mark available for each question is indicated on your question paper. There is no penalty for incorrect answers or unanswered questions.

- No marks are awarded if you do not clearly indicate your final choice or if more than one bubble per question is filled in.

- To void a selected answer, place a cross (X) over the bubble.

HOW TO SHADE THE BUBBLES

EXAMPLE

Right mark   Wrong mark

To amend your selection place a cross over unwanted bubble

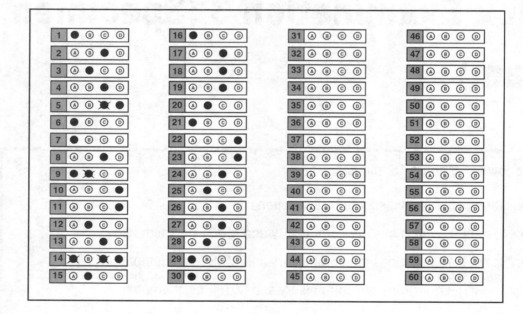

Section A – ALL 15 questions are compulsory and MUST be attempted

Each question is worth 2 marks.

1   Which of the following should be capitalised in the initial carrying amount of an item of plant?

(1)   Cost of transporting the plant to the factory
(2)   Cost of installing a new power supply required to operate the plant
(3)   Cost of a three-year plant maintenance agreement
(4)   Cost of a three-week training course for staff to operate the plant

A   (1) and (3)
B   (1) and (2)
C   (2) and (4)
D   (3) and (4)

---

2   When a parent is evaluating the assets of a potential subsidiary, certain intangible assets can be recognised separately from goodwill, even though they have not been recognised in the subsidiary's own statement of financial position.

Which of the following is an example of an intangible asset of the subsidiary which may be recognised separately from goodwill when preparing consolidated financial statements?

A   A new research project which the subsidiary has correctly expensed to profit or loss but the directors of the parent have reliably assessed to have a substantial fair value

B   A global advertising campaign which was concluded in the previous financial year and from which benefits are expected to flow in the future

C   A contingent asset of the subsidiary from which the parent believes a flow of future economic benefits is possible

D   A customer list which the directors are unable to value reliably

---

3   On 1 October 20X4, Flash Co acquired an item of plant under a five-year finance lease agreement. The plant had a cash purchase cost of $25m. The agreement had an implicit finance cost of 10% per annum and required an immediate deposit of $2m and annual rentals of $6m paid on 30 September each year for five years.

What is the current liability for the leased plant in Flash Co's statement of financial position as at 30 September 20X5?

A $19,300,000
B $4,070,000
C $5,000,000
D $3,850,000

4 Financial statements represent transactions in words and numbers. To be useful, financial information must represent faithfully these transactions in terms of how they are reported.

Which of the following accounting treatments would be an example of faithful representation?

A Charging the rental payments for an item of plant to the statement of profit or loss where the rental agreement meets the criteria for a finance lease

B Including a convertible loan note in equity on the basis that the holders are likely to choose the equity option on conversion

C Treating redeemable preference shares as part of equity in the statement of financial position

D Derecognising factored trade receivables sold without recourse to the seller

5 On 1 October 20X4, Kalatra Co commenced drilling for oil from an undersea oilfield. Kalatra Co is required to dismantle the drilling equipment at the end of its five-year licence. This has an estimated cost of $30m on 30 September 20X9. Kalatra Co's cost of capital is 8% per annum and $1 in five years' time has a present value of 68 cents.

What is the provision which Kalatra Co would report in its statement of financial position as at 30 September 20X5 in respect of its oil operations?

A $32,400,000
B $22,032,000
C $20,400,000
D $1,632,000

6 When a single entity makes purchases or sales in a foreign currency, it will be necessary to translate the transactions into its functional currency before the transactions can be included in its financial records.

In accordance with IAS 21 *The Effect of Changes in Foreign Currency Exchange Rates*, which of the following foreign currency exchange rates may be used to translate the foreign currency purchases and sales?

(1) The rate which existed on the day that the purchase or sale took place
(2) The rate which existed at the beginning of the accounting period
(3) An average rate for the year, provided there have been no significant fluctuations throughout the year
(4) The rate which existed at the end of the accounting period

A (2) and (4)
B (1) only
C (3) only
D (1) and (3)

7 On 1 October 20X4, Hoy Co had $2·5 million of equity share capital (shares of 50 cents each) in issue.

No new shares were issued during the year ended 30 September 20X5, but on that date there were outstanding share options which had a dilutive effect equivalent to issuing 1·2 million shares for no consideration.

Hoy's profit after tax for the year ended 30 September 20X5 was $1,550,000.

In accordance with IAS 33 *Earnings Per Share*, what is Hoy's diluted earnings per share for the year ended 30 September 20X5?

A $0.25
B $0.41
C $0.31
D $0.42

8   Fork Co owns an 80% investment in Spoon Co which it purchased several years ago. The goodwill on acquisition was valued at $1,674,000 and there has been no impairment of that goodwill since the date of acquisition.

On 30 September 20X4, Fork Co disposed of its entire investment in Spoon Co, details of which are as follows:

	$'000
Sales proceeds of Fork Co's entire investment in Spoon Co	5,580
Cost of Fork Co's entire investment in Spoon Co	3,720

Immediately before the disposal, the consolidated financial statements of Fork Co included the following amounts in respect of Spoon Co:

	$'000
Carrying amount of the net assets (excluding goodwill)	4,464
Carrying amount of the non-controlling interests	900

What is the profit/loss on disposal (before tax) which will be recorded in Fork Co's CONSOLIDATED statement of profit or loss for the year ended 30 September 20X4?

A $1,860,000 profit
B $2,016,000 profit
C $342,000 profit
D $558,000 loss

---

9   Consolidated financial statements are presented on the basis that the companies within the group are treated as if they are a single economic entity.

Which of the following are requirements of preparing consolidated financial statements?

(1)   All subsidiaries must adopt the accounting policies of the parent in their individual financial statements

(2)   Subsidiaries with activities which are substantially different to the activities of other members of the group should not be consolidated

(3)   All entity financial statements within a group should normally be prepared to the same accounting year end prior to consolidation

(4)   Unrealised profits within the group must be eliminated from the consolidated financial statements

A   (1) and (3)
B   (2) and (4)
C   (3) and (4)
D   (1) and (2)

---

10   A parent company sells goods to its 80% owned subsidiary during the financial year, some of which remains in inventory at the year end.

What is the adjustment required in the consolidated statement of financial position to eliminate any unrealised profit in inventory?

A	DEBIT	Group retained earnings
	CREDIT	Inventory

B	DEBIT	Group retained earnings
	DEBIT	Non-controlling interest
	CREDIT	Inventory

C	DEBIT	Inventory
	CREDIT	Group retained earnings

D	DEBIT	Inventory
	CREDIT	Group retained earnings
	CREDIT	Non-controlling interest

11   Caddy Co acquired 240,000 of Ambel Co's 800,000 equity shares for $6 per share on 1 October 20X4. Ambel Co's profit after tax for the year ended 30 September 20X5 was $400,000 and it paid an equity dividend on 20 September 20X5 of $150,000.

On the assumption that Ambel Co is an associate of Caddy Co, what would be the carrying amount of the investment in Ambel Co in the consolidated statement of financial position of Caddy Co as at 30 September 20X5?

A $1,560,000
B $1,395,000
C $1,515,000
D $1,690,000

12   Quartile Co is in the jewellery retail business which can be assumed to be highly seasonal. For the year ended 30 September 20X5, Quartile Co assessed its operating performance by comparing selected accounting ratios with those of its business sector average as provided by an agency. Assume that the business sector used by the agency is a meaningful representation of Quartile Co's business.

Which of the following circumstances may invalidate the comparison of Quartile Co's ratios with those of the sector average?

(1)   In the current year, Quartile Co has experienced significant rising costs for its purchases

(2)   The sector average figures are compiled from companies whose year ends are between 1 July 20X5 and 30 September 20X5

(3)   Quartile Co does not revalue its properties, but is aware that other entities in this sector do

(4)   During the year, Quartile Co discovered an error relating to the inventory count at 30 September 20X4. This error was correctly accounted for in the financial statements for the current year ended 30 September 20X5

A   (1) and (3)
B   (2) and (4)
C   (2) and (3)
D   (1) and (4)

13 Which of the following criticisms does NOT apply to historical cost financial statements during a period of rising prices?

    A   They are difficult to verify because transactions could have happened many years ago
    B   They contain mixed values; some items are at current values and some are at out of date values
    C   They understate assets and overstate profit
    D   They overstate gearing in the statement of financial position

14 The following information has been taken or calculated from Fowler's financial statements for the year ended 30 September 20X5:

Cash cycle at 30 September 20X5	70 days
Inventory turnover	six times
Year-end trade payables at 30 September 20X5	$230,000
Credit purchases for the year ended 30 September 20X5	$2 million
Cost of sales for the year ended 30 September 20X5	$1.8 million

What is Fowler's trade receivables collection period as at 30 September 20X5?

    A   106 days
    B   89 days
    C   56 days
    D   51 days

15 On 1 October 20X4, Pyramid Co acquired 80% of Square Co's 9 million equity shares. At the date of acquisition, Square Co had an item of plant which had a fair value of $3m in excess of its carrying amount. At the date of acquisition it had a useful life of five years. Pyramid Co's policy is to value non-controlling interests at fair value at the date of acquisition. For this purpose, Square Co's shares had a value of $3·50 each at that date. In the year ended 30 September 20X5, Square Co reported a profit of $8m.

At what amount should the non-controlling interests in Square Co be valued in the consolidated statement of financial position of the Pyramid group as at 30 September 20X5?

    A $26,680,000
    B $7,900,000
    C $7,780,000
    D $12,220,000

(30 marks)

Section B – ALL 15 questions are compulsory and MUST be attempted

Each question is worth 2 marks.

The following scenario relates to questions 16–20.

Telepath Co has a year end of 30 September and owns an item of plant which it uses to produce and package pharmaceuticals. The plant cost $750,000 on 1 October 20X0 and, at that date, had an estimated useful life of five years. A review of the plant on 1 April 20X3 concluded that the plant would last for a further three and a half years and that its fair value was $560,000.

Telepath Co adopts the policy of revaluing its non-current assets to their fair value but does not make an annual transfer from the revaluation surplus to retained earnings to represent the additional depreciation charged due to the revaluation.

On 30 September 20X3, Telepath Co was informed by a major customer that it would no longer be placing orders with Telepath Co. As a result, Telepath revised its estimates that net cash inflows earned from the plant for the next three years would be:

Year ended 30 September:	$
20X4	220,000
20X5	180,000
20X6	200,000

Telepath Co's cost of capital is 10% which results in the following discount factors:

Value of $1 at 30 September:	
20X4	0.91
20X5	0.83
20X6	0.75

Telepath Co also owns Rilda Co, a 100% subsidiary, which is treated as a cash generating unit. On 30 September 20X3, there was an impairment to Rilda's assets of $3,500,000. The carrying amount of the assets of Rilda Co immediately before the impairment were:

	$
Goodwill	2,000,000
Factory building	4,000,000
Plant	3,500,000
Receivables and cash (at recoverable amount)	2,500,000
	12,000,000

16 In accordance with IAS 36 *Impairment of assets*, which of the following explains the impairment of an asset and how to calculate its recoverable amount?

   A   An asset is impaired when the carrying amount exceeds its recoverable amount and the recoverable amount is the higher of its fair value less costs of disposal and its value in use

   B   An asset is impaired when the recoverable amount exceeds its carrying amount and the recoverable amount is the lower of its fair value less costs of disposal and its value in use

   C   An asset is impaired when the recoverable amount exceeds its carrying amount and the recoverable amount is the higher of its fair value less costs of disposal and its value in use

   D   An asset is impaired when the carrying amount exceeds its recoverable amount and the recoverable amount is the lower of its fair value less costs of disposal and its value in use

17 Prior to considering any impairment, what is the carrying amount of Telepath Co's plant and the balance on the revaluation surplus at 30 September 20X3?

	Plant carrying amount	Revaluation surplus
	$000	$000
A	480	nil
B	300	185
C	480	185
D	300	nil

18 What is the value in use of Telepath Co's plant as at 30 September 20X3?

A $600,000
B $450,000
C $499,600
D $nil

19 Which of the following are TRUE in accordance with IAS 36 *Impairment of Assets*?

(1) A cash generating unit is the smallest identifiable group of assets for which individual cash flows can be identified and measured

(2) When considering the impairment of a cash generating unit, the calculation of the carrying amount and the recoverable amount does not need to be based on exactly the same group of net assets

(3) When it is not possible to calculate the recoverable amount of a single asset, then that of its cash generating unit should be measured instead

A (1) only
B (2) and (3)
C (3) only
D (1) and (3)

20 What is the carrying amount of Rilda Co's plant at 30 September 20X3 after the impairment loss has been correctly allocated to its assets?

A $2,479,000
B $2,800,000
C $2,211,000
D $3,500,000

The following scenario relates to questions 21–25.

At a board meeting in June 20X3, Neutron Co's directors made the decision to close down one of its factories by 30 September 20X3 and market both the building and the plant for sale. The decision had been made public, was communicated to all affected parties and was fully implemented by 30 September 20X3.

The directors of Neutron Co have provided the following information relating to the closure:

Of the factory's 250 employees, 50 will be retrained and deployed to other subsidiaries within the Neutron group during the year ended 30 September 20X4 at a cost of $125,000. The remainder accepted redundancy at an average cost of $5,000 each.

The factory's plant had a carrying amount of $2.2 million, but is only expected to sell for $500,000, incurring $50,000 of selling costs. The factory itself is expected to sell for a profit of $1.2 million.

The company also rented a number of machines in the factory under operating leases which have an average of three years to run after 30 September 20X3. The present value of these future lease payments at 30 September 20X3 was $1 million, however, the lessor has stated that they will accept $850,000 if paid on 30 October 20X3 as a full settlement.

Penalty payments, due to the non-completion of supply contracts, are estimated to be $200,000, 50% of which is expected to be recovered from Neutron Co's insurers.

21 Which of the following must exist for an operation to be classified as a discontinued operation in accordance with IFRS 5 *Non-current Assets Held for Sale and Discontinued Operations*?

(1) The operation represents a separate major line of business or geographical area
(2) The operation is a subsidiary
(3) The operation has been sold or is held for sale
(4) The operation is considered not to be capable of making a future profit following a period of losses

A (2) and (4)
B (3) and (4)
C (1) and (3)
D (1) and (2)

22 IFRS 5 *Non-current Assets Held for Sale and Discontinued Operations* prescribes the recognition criteria for non-current assets held for sale. For an asset or a disposal group to be classified as held for sale, the sale must be highly probable.

Which of the following must apply for the sale to be considered highly probable?

(1) A buyer must have been located
(2) The asset must be marketed at a reasonable price
(3) Management must be committed to a plan to sell the asset
(4) The sale must be expected to take place within the next six months

A (2) and (3)
B (3) and (4)
C (1) and (4)
D (1) and (2)

23 What is the employee cost associated with the closure and sale of Neutron Co's factory which should be charged to profit or loss for the year ended 30 September 20X3?

A $125,000
B $1,250,000
C $1,125,000
D $1,000,000

24 What is the profit or loss on discontinued operations relating to property, plant and equipment for the year ended 30 September 20X3?

A $1.75 million loss
B $1.75 million profit
C $550,000 loss
D $550,000 profit

25 In respect of the operating leases and penalty payments, what provision is required in the statement of financial position of Neutron Co as at 30 September 20X3?

A $950,000
B $1,200,000
C $1,050,000
D $1,100,000

The following scenario relates to questions 26–30.

Speculate Co is preparing its financial statements for the year ended 30 September 20X3. The following issues are relevant:

1. **Financial assets**

    Shareholding A – a long-term investment in 10,000 of the equity shares of another company. These shares were acquired on 1 October 20X2 at a cost of $3·50 each. Transaction costs of 1% of the purchase price were incurred. On 30 September 20X3 the fair value of these shares is $4·50 each.

    Shareholding B – a short-term speculative investment in 2,000 of the equity shares of another company. These shares were acquired on 1 December 20X2 at a cost of $2·50 each. Transaction costs of 1% of the purchase price were incurred. On 30 September 20X3 the fair value of these shares is $3·00 each.

    Where possible, Speculate Co makes an irrevocable election for the fair value movements on financial assets to be reported in other comprehensive income.

2. **Taxation**

    The existing debit balance on the current tax account of $2·4m represents the over/under provision of the tax liability for the year ended 30 September 20X2. A provision of $28m is required for income tax for the year ended 30 September 20X3. The existing credit balance on the deferred tax account is $2·5m and the provision required at 30 September 20X3 is $4·4m.

3. **Revenue**

    On 1 October 20X2, Speculate Co sold one of its products for $10 million. As part of the sale agreement, Speculate Co is committed to the ongoing servicing of the product until 30 September 20X5 (i.e. three years after the sale). The sale value of this service has been included in the selling price of $10 million. The estimated cost to Speculate Co of the servicing is $600,000 per annum and Speculate Co's gross profit margin on this type of servicing is 25%. Ignore discounting.

26   Which of the following meet the definition of a financial asset in accordance with IFRS 9 *Financial Instruments*?

      (1)   An equity instrument of another entity
      (2)   A contract to exchange financial instruments with another entity under conditions which are potentially favourable
      (3)   A contract to exchange financial instruments with another entity under conditions which are potentially unfavourable
      (4)   Cash

      A   (1) and (2) only
      B   (1), (2) and (4)
      C   (1), (3) and (4)
      D   (4) only

27   In respect of the financial assets of Speculate Co, what amount will be included in other comprehensive income for the year ended 30 September 20X3?

      A $9,650
      B $10,650
      C $10,000
      D $nil

28 What is the total amount which will be charged to the statement of profit or loss for the year ended 30 September 20X3 in respect of taxation?

A $28,000,000
B $30,400,000
C $32,300,000
D $29,900,000

29 What is the amount of deferred income which Speculate Co should recognise in its statement of financial position as at 30 September 20X3 relating to the contract for the supply and servicing of products?

A $1.2 million
B $1.6 million
C $600,000
D $1.5 million

30 Which of the following are TRUE in respect of the income which Speculate Co has deferred at 30 September 20X3?

(1) The deferred income will be split evenly between the current and non-current liabilities in Speculate Co's statement of financial position as at 30 September 20X3

(2) The costs associated with the deferred income of Speculate Co should be recognised in the statement of profit or loss at the same time as the revenue is recognised

(3) The deferred income can only be recognised as revenue by Speculate Co when there is a signed written contract of service with its customer

(4) When recognising the revenue associated with the service contract of Speculate Co, the stage of its completion is irrelevant

A (1) and (2)
B (3) and (4)
C (2) and (3)
D (1) and (4)

(30 marks)

Section C – Both questions are compulsory and MUST be attempted

31   After preparing a draft statement of profit or loss for the year ended 30 September 20X5 and adding the current year's draft profit (before any adjustments required by notes (i) to (iii) below) to retained earnings, the summarised trial balance of Kandy Co as at 30 September 20X5 is:

	$'000	$'000
Equity shares of $1 each		20,000
Retained earnings as at 30 September 20X5		15,500
Proceeds of 6% loan note (note (i))		30,000
Investment properties at fair value (note (ii))	20,000	
Land ($5 million) and buildings – at cost (note (ii))	35,000	
Plant and equipment – at cost (note (ii))	58,500	
Accumulated depreciation at 1 October 20X4: buildings		20,000
plant and equipment		34,500
Current assets	68,700	
Current liabilities		43,400
Deferred tax (notes (ii) and (iii))		2,500
Interest paid (note (i))	1,800	
Current tax (note (iii))		1,100
Suspense account (note (ii))		17,000
	184,000	184,000

The following notes are relevant:

(i)   The loan note was issued on 1 October 20X4 and incurred issue costs of $1 million which were charged to profit or loss. Interest of $1.8 million ($30 million at 6%) was paid on 30 September 20X5. The loan is redeemable on 30 September 20X9 at a substantial premium which gives an effective interest rate of 9% per annum. No other repayments are due until 30 September 20X9.

(ii)   Non-current assets:

On 1 October 20X4, Kandy owned two investment properties. The first property had a carrying amount of $15 million and was sold on 1 December 20X4 for $17 million. The disposal proceeds have been credited to a suspense account in the trial balance above. On 31 December 20X4, the second property became owner occupied and so was transferred to land and buildings at its fair value of $6 million. Its remaining useful life on 31 December 20X4 was considered to be 20 years. Ignore any deferred tax implications of this fair value.

The price of property has increased significantly in recent years and so the directors decided to revalue the land and buildings. The directors accepted the report of an independent surveyor who, on 1 October 20X4, valued the land at $8 million and the buildings at $39 million on that date. This revaluation specifically excludes the transferred investment property described above. The remaining life of these buildings at 1 October 20X4 was 15 years. Kandy does not make an annual transfer to retained profits to reflect the realisation of the revaluation gain; however, the revaluation will give rise to a deferred tax liability. The income tax rate applicable to Kandy is 20%.

Plant and equipment is depreciated at 12½% per annum using the reducing balance method.

No depreciation has yet been charged on any non-current asset for the year ended 30 September 20X5.

(iii) A provision of $2.4 million is required for income tax on the profit for the year to 30 September 20X5. The balance on current tax in the trial balance is the under/over provision of tax for the previous year. In addition to the temporary differences relating to the information in note (ii), Kandy has further taxable temporary differences of $10 million as at 30 September 20X5.

Required

(a) Prepare a schedule of adjustments required to the retained earnings of Kandy Co as at 30 September 20X5 as a result of the information in notes (i) to (iii) above.

(b) Prepare the statement of financial position of Kandy Co as at 30 September 20X5.

Note: The notes to the statement of financial position are not required.

(c) Prepare the extracts from Kandy Co's statement of cash flows for operating and investing activities for the year ended 30 September 20X5 which relate to property, plant and equipment.

The following mark allocation is provided as guidance for this question:
(a) 8 marks
(b) 9 marks
(c) 3 marks

(20 marks)

32   The summarised consolidated financial statements for the year ended 30 September 20X5 (and the comparative figures) for the Tangier group are shown below.

Consolidated statements of profit or loss for the year ended 30 September:

	20X5	20X4
	$m	$m
Revenue	2,700	1,820
Cost of sales	(1,890)	(1,092)
Gross profit	810	728
Administrative expense	(345)	(200)
Distribution costs	(230)	(130)
Finance costs	(40)	(5)
Profit before taxation	195	393
Income tax expense	(60)	(113)
Profit for the year	135	280

Consolidated statements of financial position as at 30 September:

	20X5	20X5	20X4	20X4
	$m	$m	$m	$m
Non-current assets				
Property, plant and equipment		680		310
Intangible asset: manufacturing licences		300		100
Goodwill		230		200
		1,210		610
Current assets				
Inventory	200		110	
Trade receivables	195		75	
Bank	nil	395	120	305
Total assets		1,605		915
Equity and liabilities				
Equity shares of $1 each		330		250
Other components of equity		100		nil
Retained earnings		375		295
		805		545
Non-current liabilities				
5% secured loan notes	100		100	
10% secured loan notes	300	400	nil	100
Current liabilities				
Bank overdraft	110		nil	
Trade payables	210		160	
Current tax payable	80	400	110	270
Total equity and liabilities		1,605		915

At 1 October 20X4, the Tangier group consisted of the parent, Tangier Co, and two wholly owned subsidiaries which had been owned for many years. On 1 January 20X5, Tangier Co purchased a third 100% owned investment in a subsidiary called Raremetal Co. The consideration paid for Raremetal Co was a combination of cash and shares. The cash payment was partly funded by the issue of 10% loan notes. On 1 January 20X5, Tangier Co also won a tender for a new contract to supply aircraft engines which Tangier Co manufactures under a recently acquired long-term licence. Raremetal Co was purchased with a view to securing the supply of specialised materials used in the manufacture of these engines. The bidding process had been very competitive and Tangier Co had to increase its manufacturing capacity to fulfil the contract.

Required

(a) Comment on how the new contract and the purchase of Raremetal Co may have affected the comparability of the consolidated financial statements of Tangier Co for the years ended 30 September 20X4 and 20X5.

(b) Calculate appropriate ratios and comment on Tangier Co's profitability and gearing. Your analysis should identify instances where the new contract and the purchase of Raremetal Co have limited the usefulness of the ratios and your analysis.

Note: Your ratios should be based on the consolidated financial statements provided and you should not attempt to adjust for the effects of the new contract or the consolidation. Working capital and liquidity ratios are not required.

(c) Explain what further information you might require to make your analysis more meaningful.

The following mark allocation is provided as guidance for this question:

(a) 5 marks
(b) 12 marks (up to 5 marks for the ratio calculations)
(c) 3 marks

(20 marks)

Answers

A plan of attack

What's the worst thing you could be doing right now if this was the actual exam paper? Sharpening your pencil? Wondering how to celebrate the end of the exam in just over three-hours' time? Panicking, flapping and generally getting in a right old state?

Well, they're all pretty bad, so turn back to the paper and let's sort out a **plan of attack**!

First things first

You have three hours and fifteen minutes for this exam. This paper is the examination team's specimen paper, so it is the best indication of what you will see in your exam. Read it carefully.

The F7 paper has 15 2-mark questions in Section A, 15 2-mark questions in Section B and two long-form questions in Section C. All questions are compulsory. Therefore, you do not have to spend time working out which questions to answer.

It's a good idea to just start with the Section A questions. Once you have them done, you will feel more relaxed. Leave any that you are unsure of and come back to them later but don't leave any unanswered.

Section B: Questions 16-20 are on non-current assets. Questions 21-25 are on discontinued operations. Questions 26-30 cover three issues – financial assets, taxation and revenue. For each of these section B questions make sure you read the scenario carefully.

Question 31 requires you to adjust retained earnings and prepare a statement of financial position and some cash flow extracts. There is nothing difficult here but you need to work methodically.

Question 32 is an interpretation question. Remember you do not get marks for simply saying that a ratio went up or down. It is your job to look at why this happened..

You've got spare time at the end of the exam.....?

If you have allocated your time properly then you **shouldn't have time on your hands** at the end of the exam and you should start by checking the Section A questions to make sure you have left none unanswered. But if you find yourself with five or ten minutes to spare, check over your work to make sure that there are no silly arithmetical errors.

Forget about it!

And don't worry if you found the paper difficult. More than likely other candidates will too. If this were the real thing you would need to **forget** the exam the minute you leave the exam hall and **think about the next one**. Or, if it's the last one, **celebrate**!

Section A

1   B   Only the transportation and the power supply can be included. The maintenance agreement and the training course are profit or loss items.

2   A   The research project only as the customer list cannot be reliably valued. The advertising campaign cannot be capitalised and contingent assets are not recognised.

3   B

     25,000 – 2,000 = 23,000 + 2,300 (10% int) – 6,000 (pmt) = 19,300
     19,300 + 1,930 (10% int) – 6,000 (pmt) = 15,230
     Current liability = 19,300 – 15,230 = $4,070

4   D   Trade receivables factored without recourse are no longer an asset of the seller. The other options are incorrect.

5   B

     Dismantling provision at 1 October 20X4 is $20.4 million (30,000 × 0.68) discounted

     This will increase by an 8% finance cost by 30 September 20X5 = $22,032,000

6   D   The rate at the transaction date or the average rate.

7   A

     (1,550/(2,500 × 2 + 1,200)) = $0.25

8   C

	$000
Sales proceeds	5,580
Net assets at disposal	4,464
Goodwill at disposal	1,674
Less: carrying value of NCI	(900) (5,238)
	342

9   C   Adjustments will be made on consolidation for different accounting policies. Subsidiaries with dissimilar activities are still consolidated.

10   A   As the sale is made by the parent there is no charge against non-controlling interest.

11   C

	$'000
Cost (240,000 × $6)	1,440
Share of associate's profit (400 × 240/800)	120
Less dividend received (150 × 240/800)	(45)
	1,515

12   C   Rising costs will have affected all of the business sector and the inventory adjustment will have been corrected in the prior year, so no actual effect in 20X5.

13   A   They are easy to verify because there will be a record of the transaction.

14   D

     Inventory turnover is 61 days (365/6).
     Trade payables period is 42 days (230,000 × 365/2 million).
     Therefore, receivables collection period is 51 days (70 – 61 + 42).

15   C

	$000
FV NCI at 1 October 14 (9000 × 20% × $3·50)	6,300
Post-acquisition profit (8000 – (3000/5)) = 7,400 at 20%	1,480
	7,780

Section B

16   A

17   C

Annual depreciation prior to the revaluation is $150,000 (750/5). At the date of revaluation (1 April 20X3), the carrying amount is $375,000 (750–(150 × 2.5 yrs)). Revalued to $560,000 with a remaining life of 3.5 years results in a depreciation charge of $160,000 per annum which means $80,000 for six months. The carrying amount at 30 September 20X3 is therefore $480,000 (560 – 80).

Alternative calculation: $560,000 – ($560,000/3.5 × 6/12) = $480,000.

The revaluation surplus has a balance of $185,000 (560,000 – 375,000).

18   C

	Cash flow $'000	Discount factor at 10%	Present value $'000
Year ended: 30 September 20X4	220	0.91	200.2
30 September 20X5	180	0.83	149.4
30 September 20X6	200	0.75	150.0
			499.6

19   D   The assets of the CGU must remain the same when calculating impairment.

20   B

	Carrying amount before $'000	Impairment loss $'000	Carrying amount after $'000
Goodwill	2,000	2,000	Nil
Property	4,000	800	3,200
Plant	3,500	700	2,800
Cash and receivables	2,500	Nil	2,500
	12,000	3,500	8,500

21   C   The operation does not have to be a subsidiary. Future profit forecasts are not relevant.

22   A   A buyer does not need to have been specifically located and the sale must be expected to take place within the next 12 months.

23   D

200 employees at $5,000 = $1,000,000 redundancy costs. The retraining costs are a future cost.

24   A

Impairment loss on plant is $1,750,000 (2,200,000 – (500,000 – 50,000)).

25   C

Onerous contract $850,000 + penalty payments $200,000 = $1,050,000. The possible insurance receipt should be ignored as there is no certainty that it would be received and it would not be netted off against the provision anyway.

26   B   A contract to exchange financial instruments under potentially unfavourable conditions would be a financial liability.

27   A

Shareholding A is not held for trading as an election made – FVTOCI.

Shareholding B is held for trading and so FVTPL (transaction costs are not included in carrying amount).

Cost of shareholding A is 10,000 × $3.50 × 1.01 = $35,350.

FV at 30 September 20X3 10,000 × $4.50 = $45,000.

Gain = 45,000 – 35,350 = $9,650.

28   C

	$'000
DT provision required at 30 September 20X3	4,400
DT Provision at 1 October 20X2	(2,500)
	1,900
Write off of the overprovision for the year ended 30 September 20X2	2,400
Income tax for the year ended 30 September 20X3	28,000
Charge for the year ended 30 September 20X3	32,300

29   B

At 30 September 20X3 there are two more years of servicing work, thus $1.6 million ((600,000 × 2) × 100/75) must be treated as deferred income.

30   A   A written service contract is not needed, but the stage of completion is important in recognising revenue.

Section C

31

		Marks
(a)	**Schedule of retained earnings as at 30 September 20X4**	
	Retained earnings per trial balance	½
	Issue costs	1
	Loan finance costs	1
	Gains on investment properties	1
	Depreciation charges	3
	Income tax expense	1½
		8
(b)	**Statement of financial position**	
	Property, plant and equipment	2
	Current assets	½
	Equity shares	½
	Revaluation surplus	2
	Deferred tax	1
	6% loan note	1½
	Current liabilities (per trial balance)	½
	Current tax payable	1
		9
(c)	**Extracts from the statement of cash flows**	
	Cash flows from operating activities:	
	Add back depreciation	1
	Less gain on revaluation of investment property	½
	Less gain on disposal of investment property	½
	Cash flows from investing activities:	
	Investment property disposal proceeds	1
		3
		20

(a)   **Schedule of retained earnings of Kandy as at 30 September 20X5**

	$'000
Retained earnings per trial balance	15,500
Adjustments re:	
Note (i)	
Add back issue costs of loan note (W1)	1,000
Loan finance costs (29,000 × 9% (W1)	(2,610)
Note (ii)	
Gain on disposal of investment property (17,000 – 15,000)	2,000
Gain on revaluation of investment property prior to transfer (6,000 – 5,000)	1,000
Depreciation of buildings (W2)	(2,825)
Depreciation of plant and equipment (W2)	(3,000)
Note (iii)	
Income tax expense (W3)	(800)
Adjusted retained earnings	10,265

(b)   STATEMENT OF FINANCIAL POSITION AS AT 30 SEPTEMBER 20X5

	$'000	$'000
Assets		
Non-current assets		
Property, plant and equipment (50,175 + 21,000 (W2))		71,175
Current assets (per trial balance)		68,700
Total assets		139,875
Equity and liabilities		
Equity		
Equity shares of $1 each		20,000
Revaluation surplus (32,000 – 6,400 (W2) and (W3))	25,600	
Retained earnings (from (a))	10,265	35,865
		55,865
Non-current liabilities		
Deferred tax (W3)	8,400	
6% loan note (W1)	29,810	38,210
Current liabilities		
Per trial balance	43,400	
Current tax payable	2,400	45,800
Total equity and liabilities		139,875

Workings (monetary figures in brackets in $'000)

1   *Loan note*

The issue costs should be deducted from the proceeds of the loan note and not charged as an expense. The finance cost of the loan note, at the effective rate of 9% applied to the carrying amount of the loan note of $29 million (30,000 – 1,000), is $2,610,000. The interest actually paid is $1·8 million. The difference between these amounts of $810,000 (2,610 – 1,800) is added to the carrying amount of the loan note to give $29,810,000 (29,000 + 810) for inclusion as a non-current liability in the statement of financial position.

2   *Non-current assets*
Land and buildings
The gain on revaluation and carrying amount of the land and buildings will be:

	$'000
Carrying amount at 1 October 20X4 (35,000 – 20,000)	15,000
Revaluation at that date (8,000 + 39,000)	47,000
Gain on revaluation	32,000

Buildings depreciation for the year ended 30 September 20X5:	
Land and buildings existing at 1 October 20X4 (39,000/15 years)	2,600
Transferred investment property (6,000/20 x 9/12)	225
	2,825
Carrying amount at 30 September 20X5 (47,000 + 6,000 – 2,825)	50,175

Plant and equipment	
Carrying amount at 1 October 20X4 (58,500 – 34,500)	24,000
Depreciation for year ended 30 September 20X5 (12½% reducing balance)	(3,000)
Carrying amount at 30 September 20X5	21,000

3   *Taxation*

Income tax expense:	$'000
Provision for year ended 30 September 20X5	2,400
Less over provision in previous year	(1,100)
Deferred tax (see below)	(500)
	800

	$'000
Deferred tax	
Provision required at 30 September 20X5 ((10,000 + 32,000) × 20%)	8,400
Provision at 1 October 20X4	(2,500)
Movement in provision	5,900
Charge to revaluation of land and buildings (32,000 × 20%)	(6,400)
Balance – credit to profit or loss	(500)

(c)

	$'000
Cash flows from operating activities:	
Add back depreciation	5,825
Deduct gain on revaluation of investment property	(1,000)
Deduct gain on disposal of investment property	(2,000)
Cash flows from investing activities:	
Investment property disposal proceeds	17,000

32

Marking scheme

		Marks
(a)	Analysis of results	
	A like for like comparison taking account of the consolidation and the contract	5
(b)	Up to 5 marks for ratio calculations	5
	Profitability	4½
	Gearing and interest cover	2½
		12
(c)	Additional information	
	Any three of the six suggestions provided	3
		20

(a) Note: References to '20X5' are in respect of the year ended 30 September 20X5 and '20X4' refers to the year ended 30 September 20X4.

The key matter to note is that the ratios for 20X4 and 20X5 will not be directly comparable because two significant events, the acquisition of Raremetal Co and securing the new contract, have occurred between these dates. This means that the underlying financial statements are not directly comparable. For example, the 20X4 statement of profit or loss (SOPL) will not include the results of Raremetal Co or the effect of the new contract. However, the 20X5 SOPL will contain nine months of the results of Raremetal Co (although intra-group transactions will have been eliminated) and nine months of the effects of the new contract (which may have resulted in either a net profit or loss). Likewise, the 20X4 statement of financial position does not contain any of Raremetal Co's assets and liabilities, whereas that of 20X5 contains all of the net assets of Raremetal Co and the cost of the new licence. This does not mean that comparisons between the two years are not worthwhile, just that they need to be treated with caution. For some ratios, it may be necessary to exclude all of the subsidiaries from the analysis and use the single entity financial statements of Tangier Co as a basis for comparison with the performance of previous years. Similarly, it may still be possible to compare some of the ratios of the Tangier group with those of other groups in the same sector although not all groups will have experienced similar acquisitions.

Assuming there has been no impairment of goodwill, the investment in Raremetal Co has resulted in additional goodwill of $30 million which means that the investment has cost more than the carrying amount of Raremetal Co's net assets. Although there is no indication of the precise cost, it is known to have been achieved by a combination of a share exchange (hence the $180 million new issue of shares) and a cash element (funded from the proceeds of the loan issue and the decrease in the bank balance). Any intra-group sales have been eliminated on consolidation and it is not possible to determine in which individual company any profit on these intra-group sales will be reported; it is therefore difficult to measure any benefits of the investment. Indeed, the benefit of the investment might not be a financial one but merely to secure the supply of raw materials. It would be useful to establish the cost of the investment and the profit (if any) contributed by Raremetal Co so that an assessment of the benefit of the investment might be made.

(b)

Relevant ratios:	20X5	20X4
Gross profit margin % (810/2,700 × 100)	30.0%	40.0%
Operating profit margin (235/2,700 × 100)	8.7%	21.9%
ROCE (235/(805 + 400))	19.5%	61.7%
Non-current asset turnover (2,700/1,210)	2.23 times	2.98 times
Debt/equity (400/805)	49.7%	18.3%
Interest cover (235/40)	5.9 times	79.6 times

All of the issues identified in part (a) make a comparison of ratios difficult and, if more information was available, then some adjustments may be required. For example, if it is established that the investment is not generating any benefits, then it might be argued that the inclusion of the goodwill in the ROCE and non-current asset turnover is unjustified (it may be impaired and should be written off). Goodwill has not been excluded from any of the following ratios.

The increase in revenues of 48.4% (880/1,820 × 100) in 20X5 will be partly due to the consolidation of Raremetal Co and the revenues associated with the new contract. Yet, despite these increased revenues, the company has suffered a dramatic fall in its profitability. This has been caused by a combination of a falling gross profit margin (from 40% in 20X4 to only 30% in 20X5) and markedly higher operating overheads (operating profit margin has fallen from 21·9% in 20X4 to 8.7% in 20X5). Again, it is important to note that some of these costs will be attributable to the consolidation of Raremetal Co and some to the new contract. It could be speculated that the 73% increase in administrative expenses may be due to one-off costs associated with the tendering process (consultancy fees, etc) and the acquisition of Raremetal Co and the 77% increase in higher distribution costs could be due to additional freight/packing/insurance cost of the engines, delivery distances may also be longer (even to foreign countries) (although some of the increase in distribution costs may also be due to consolidation).

This is all reflected in the ROCE falling from an impressive 61.7% in 20X4 to only 19.5% in 20X5 (though even this figure is respectable). The fall in the ROCE is attributable to a dramatic fall in profit margin at operating level (from 21.9% in 20X4 to only 8.7% in 20X5) which has been compounded by a reduction in the non-current asset turnover, with only $2·23 being generated from every $1 invested in non-current assets in 20X5 (from $2.98 in 20X4).

The information in the question points strongly to the possibility (even probability) that the new contract may be responsible for much of the deterioration in Tangier Co's operating performance. For example, it is likely that the new contract may account for some of the increased revenue; however, the bidding process was 'very competitive' which may imply that Tangier Co had to cut its prices (and therefore its profit margin) in order to win the contract.

The costs of fulfilling the contract have also been heavy: investment in property, plant and equipment has increased by $370 million (at carrying amount), representing an increase of 61% (no doubt some of this increase will be due to the acquisition of Raremetal Co). The increase in licence costs to manufacture the new engines has cost $200 million plus any amortisation and there is also the additional goodwill of $30 million.

An eight-fold increase in finance cost caused by the increased borrowing at double the interest rate of the borrowing in 20X4 and (presumably) some overdraft interest has led to the dramatic fall in the company's interest cover (from 79.6 in 20X4 to only 5.9 in 20X5). The finance cost of the new $300 million 10% loan notes to partly fund the investment in Raremetal Co and other non-current assets has also increased debt/equity (one form of gearing measure) from 18.3% in 20X4 to 49.7% in 20X5 despite also issuing $180 million in new equity shares. At this level, particularly in view of its large increase from 20X4, it may give debt holders (and others) cause for concern as there is increased risk for all Tangier Co's lenders. If it could be demonstrated that the overdraft could not be cleared for some time, this would be an argument for including it in the calculation of debt/equity, making the 20X5 gearing level even worse. It is also apparent from the movement in the retained earnings that Tangier Co paid a dividend during 20X5 of $55 million (295,000 + 135,000 – 375,000) which may be a questionable policy when the company is raising additional finance through borrowings and contributes substantially to Tangier Co's overdraft.

Overall, the acquisition of Raremetal Co to secure supplies appears to have been an expensive strategy, perhaps a less expensive one might have been to enter into a long-term supply contract with Raremetal Co.

(c)   Further information which would be useful to obtain would therefore include:

(i)   The cost of the investment in Raremetal Co, the carrying amount of the assets acquired and whether Tangier Co has carried out a goodwill impairment test as required under IFRS.

(ii)   The benefits generated from the investment; for example, Raremetal Co's individual financial statements and details of sales to external customers (not all of these benefits will be measurable in financial terms).

(iii)   The above two pieces of information would demonstrate whether the investment in Raremetal Co had been worthwhile.

(iv)   The amount of intra-group sales made during the year and those expected to be made in the short to medium term.

(v)   The pricing strategy agreed with Raremetal Co so that the effects on the profits reported in the individual financial statements of Raremetal Co and Tangier Co can be more readily determined.

(vi)   More information is needed to establish if the new contract has been detrimental to Tangier Co's performance. The contract was won sometime between 1 October 20X4 and 1 January 20X5 and there is no information of when production/sales started, but clearly there has not been a full year's revenue from the contract. Also there is no information on the length or total value of the contract.

Review Form – Paper F7 Financial Reporting (02/16)

Name: _____   Address: _____

_____

_____

How have you used this Kit?
(Tick one box only)

☐ On its own (book only)

☐ On a BPP in-centre course_____

☐ On a BPP online course

☐ On a course with another college

☐ Other_____

Why did you decide to purchase this Kit?
(Tick one box only)

☐ Have used the complimentary Study Text

☐ Have used other BPP products in the past

☐ Recommendation by friend/colleague

☐ Recommendation by a lecturer at college

☐ Saw advertising

☐ Other_____

During the past six months do you recall seeing/receiving any of the following?
(Tick as many boxes as are relevant)

☐ Our advertisement in *Student Accountant*

☐ Our advertisement in *Pass*

☐ Our advertisement in *PQ*

☐ Our brochure with a letter through the post

☐ Our website www.bpp.com

Which (if any) aspects of our advertising do you find useful?
(Tick as many boxes as are relevant)

☐ Prices and publication dates of new editions

☐ Information on product content

☐ Facility to order books

☐ None of the above

Which BPP products have you used?

| Study Text | ☐ | Passcards | ☐ | Other | ☐ |
| Kit | ☑ | i-Pass | ☐ | | |

Your ratings, comments and suggestions would be appreciated on the following areas.

	Very useful	Useful	Not useful
Passing F7			
Questions			
Top Tips etc in answers			
Content and structure of answers			
Mock exam answers			

	Excellent ☐	Good ☐	Adequate ☐	Poor ☐
Overall opinion of this Practice & Revision Kit				

Do you intend to continue using BPP products?   Yes ☐   No ☐

The BPP author of this edition can be emailed at: accaqueries@bpp.com

Please return this form to: Head of ACCA & FIA Programmes, BPP Learning Media Ltd, FREEPOST, London, W12 8AA

Review Form (continued)

TELL US WHAT YOU THINK

Please note any further comments and suggestions/errors below.